D0984689

THE PRICE OF PEACE

Also by Lawrence Freedman
Atlas of Global Strategy
The Evolution of Nuclear Strategy
Britain and Nuclear Weapons
US Intelligence and the Soviet Strategic Threat

THE PRICE OF PEACE

Living with the Nuclear Dilemma

Lawrence Freedman

A New Republic Book
Henry Holt and Company
New York

Published in the United States by
Henry Holt and Company, Inc., 521 Fifth Avenue,
New York, New York 10175.

Published simultaneously in Canada.

Originally published in Great Britain by Waterstone & Company Limited.

Library of Congress Cataloging-in-Publication Data

Freedman, Lawrence.
  The price of peace.
  A collection of essays.
  Includes bibliographies and index.
  1. Nuclear disarmament.   2. Nuclear arms control.
3. Peace. I. Title.
JX1974. 7. F726 1986   327.1'74   86—7541
ISBN 0-8050-0041-0

First American Edition

Printed in Great Britain

10 9 8 7 6 5 4 3 2 1

ISBN 0-8050-0041-0

For Judith, Sam and Ruth

Contents

Acknowledgments

The author and publishers wish to thank the following who have kindly given permission for the use of copyright material: The Royal Institute of International Affairs for permission to publish "Indignation, Influence and Strategic Studies" from **International Affairs** (Summer 1984) and "The Atlantic Crisis" from **International Affairs** (Summer 1982); **Bulletin of the Atomic Scientists** for permission to publish "Disarmament and the Future of Europe"; **Foreign Policy** for permission to publish "The Fading Myth of Flexible Response"; Centre for Strategic & International Studies for permission to publish "Limited War, Unlimited Protest" from **The Nuclear Freeze Debate** ed. Paul Cole and William J. Taylor (Westview) and "The Four Stages of Arms Control" from **NATO: The Next Generation** (Westview); The Royal United Services Institute for Defence Studies for permission to publish "Flexible Response and the Concept of Escalation" prepared for the Nuneham Park Conference, and to appear in *RUSI & Brassey's Defence Yearbook* 1986; Frances Pinter Ltd. for permission to publish "Negotiations on Nuclear Forces in Europe 1969–83" from **The European Missile Crisis** ed. Hans Henrik Holm & Nikelaj Petersen; Frank Cass & Co. Ltd. for permission to publish "Europe and the Anti-Ballistic Missile Revival" from **Anti-Ballistic Missile Defence in the 1980s** ed. Ian Bellany & Coit D. Blacker; and The International Institute for Strategic Studies for permission to publish "The Strategic Defence Initiative — "Star Wars" from **Adelphi Paper No. 199.**

Acronyms

ABM	Anti-ballistic missile
ACDA	Arms Control and Disarmament Agency
ASAT	Anti-satellite weapon
ATBM	Anti-tactical ballistic missile
CND	Campaign for Nuclear Disarmament
ECU	European unit of account
EEC	European Economic Community
ERW	Enhanced radiation weapon
FBS	Forward-based system (US nuclear weapons in Europe)
GATT	General Agreement on Tariffs and Trade
GLCM	Ground-launched cruise missile
GNP	Gross National Product
ICBM	Intercontinental ballistic missile
INF	Intermediate nuclear forces
IRBM	Intermediate-range ballistic missile
LRTNF	Long-range theatre nuclear forces
MAD	Mutual assured destruction
MBFR	Mutual and Balanced Force Reduction talks
MC 14/3	NATO Defence Strategy Document, 1967
MIRV	Multiple independently-targetable re-entry vehicle
MX	Missile Experimental
NATO	North Atlantic Treaty Organisation
NIC	Newly industrialising country
NPG	Nuclear Planning Group
NSC	National Security Council
OECD	Organisation for Economic Co-operation and Development
OPEC	Organisation of Petroleum-exporting Countries
SALT	Strategic Arms Limitation Talks

SDI	Stategic Defence Initiative
SEATO	Southeast Asia Treaty Organisation
SLBM	Submarine-launched ballistic missile
START	Strategic Arms Reduction Talks
TNF	Theatre nuclear force

Foreword

Nuclear war would be an incomparable catastrophe. That much is agreed by nearly all the proponents of unilateral disarmament, pure deterrence, countervailing strategy and warfighting capability. That judgement has caused some scholars and some policy advocates to turn to a detailed analysis of warhead comparsions and of carefully planned escalation ladders, with clear rules agreed on both sides. But it would be unrealistic to expect a nuclear war to be fought like the campaigns of the 15th and 16th century Italian condottieri — and even those activities entailed a great deal of what is now called collateral damage. Other scholars, and millions of demonstrators, have seemed to urge unilateral disarmament, or at least paralysis, as the appropriate solution to the immense destructiveness of nuclear weapons in the hands of two superpowers with profoundly differing world views and conflicting national interests. American — and, so far, Western European — policy-makers have concluded that they cannot adopt either approach, and so have sought a set of diplomatic policies and a supporting military strategy based on deterrence that includes the threat of nuclear retaliation. This remains US policy despite the vision of a strategic defence that would protect populations and make the world as safe as if nuclear weapons were only a tale of science fiction. Deterrence by the threat of nuclear retaliation has been denounced by substantial segments of academic, religious, political, and even occasionally military opinion, on the basis of its flaws and limitations as a military strategy, its immorality as a human position, and its ineffectiveness as a political approach and the universal concern that it cannot be counted on to work indefinitely. But it has remained the policy, largely because the deterrence by the threat of nuclear retaliation is not only a policy or a strategy but a fact of life. But deterrence of what? And nuclear retaliation against what targets? How do the political factors, international and domestic, influence the operation of deterrence? How would they operate in a crisis that could lead to nuclear war, a crisis in which the actions of political leaders would determine whether or not nuclear war was avoided, if begun whether and how it might be terminated and could determine the political future of the countries involved in the crisis even if it did not lead to nuclear war? How does the US-Soviet political conflict, without which the nuclear dilemma would have quite different dimensions (in the limit, those which are exhibited by the US-China relationship, or that between the UK and France) interact with nuclear strategy?

These are the sorts of questions that Professor Lawrence Freedman explores in his book ''The Price of Peace: Living with the Nuclear Dilemma.'' He brings to the subject a sympathy for the left-liberal view of the nature of mankind and of society, but rejects the commitment to emotion as the proper determinant of policy that so often accompanies that view. He endorses the process of analysis that characterises so much of the response to the nuclear dilemma exhibited by the professional strategists. He properly insists, however, that in the absence of an understanding of the political context, both domestic and interallied, such analysis is of limited help both to the scholar's understanding and to the political leader's decisions.

Certainly the nuclear dilemma has sharpened in recent years. We have seen former Secretaries of State and Defence of the US proclaim to be unreliable the commitment they stoutly upheld in office, that the US would use nuclear weapons as necessary to prevent the success of a Soviet conventional invasion of Western Europe. And we have seen a convergence from left and right of attacks on deterrence by the threat of retaliation, using similar moral grounds. But many in both camps of critics have been forced to return in some measure to support of that same policy of deterrence. The left, by charging that the Strategic Defense Initiative (SDI) or various new offensive systems undermine deterrence, implicitly endorses deterrence. The right, by claiming that the SDI enhances deterrence, abandons or at least plays down for the time being the argument that SDI will transcend and replace it. But SDI, by offering the vision, however unreal, of a US and perhaps a USSR safe from nuclear attack or from retaliation through nuclear attack, sharpens another aspect of the dilemma. What happens to countries other than the superpowers (themselves not in a position, despite the claims of some extreme proponents of a maritime strategy, to attack each others homelands effectively with conventional weapons) if the superpowers become immune to nuclear attack? Understandably, US and European public attitudes as to the desirability of such a situation differ, and this in turn conditions the attitudes of political leaders on the two sides of the Atlantic toward SDI.

First-rate scholars of public affairs tend to have fewer prescriptions than they have analyses. Second-rates ones tend to have many prescriptions, practically all of them unworkable. Professor Freedman belongs in the first category. But he does have some specific suggestions: eliminating battlefield nuclear weapons and strengthening conventional capabilities. Both make sense. My own experience is that both are more difficult for European than for American policymakers to adopt. Various military-political arguments will be advanced against these changes. Doesn't dropping battlefield nuclear weapons cause a gap in the powder train of potential escalation that acts as a deterrent? My own view is that with the deployment of modernised US intermediate range nuclear forces, Soviet concerns about the likelihood of escalation to nuclear war will persist, while dropping battlefield nuclear weapons would reduce the chance of unintended escalation. Strengthening conventional forces will raise fears of increasing the chances of conventional war by raising the nuclear threshold. But I judge that nuclear deterrence operates through Soviet concerns about escalation to nuclear war. A protracted and effective conventional resistance would seem to offer a non-nuclear deterrent of its own and also an expectation of a US nuclear response if that conventional resistance should fail after a lengthy and high-intensity conventional conflict — a greater expectation than that of a US nuclear response after a successful three-day drive to the Channel.

The real barrier in the way of an increasing conventional capability — and to a lesser extent, to abandonment of battlefield nuclear weapons — comes from domestic political considerations (the balance between social welfare and defence expenditures, now in the ratio of about 6:1 in Western Europe) and lagging economic growth in Western Europe. Given the total population and economic output of the Western European countries, it would be possible in principle, even in the face of slow growth and with little if any modification in the ratio cited, for Western Europe to mount a conventional defence which the Soviets would have little confidence in breaching for a period of months. But it would take a military and political organisation of Western Europe that would go far further in the direction of unity than can be expected in the forseeable future. The discomforts entailed in achieving that sort of unity would be far more immediate and probable than the threat of nuclear war, however much more horrifying an actual nuclear war would be. Given that choice, political leaders will opt to continue to live with the nuclear dilemma.

An even more far reaching and fundamental question exists about US-Soviet relations. Even if one judges that nuclear deterrence has worked for decades in the face of the possession of thousands of nuclear weapons by each of two profoundly adversarial powers, one may doubt that the situation can go on forever without some use of nuclear weapons unless the nature of the US-Soviet relationship can be made less adversarial as time goes by. In other words, how do the two scorpions get out of the bottle? But this, and the question of European unity, are subjects for at least two other books. Professor Freedman has faced the world as it is, and faced it squarely.

Dr Harold Brown is Distinguished Visiting Professor of National Security Affairs at The John Hopkins Foreign Policy Institute. He was US Secretary of Defence from 1977–81 and Delegate to the Strategic Arms Limitation Talks from 1969–77.

Introduction

I was born in 1948. Unlike my parents and grandparents I have not had to cope with the perils and uncertainty of world war. My fortunate generation has been allowed to grow up in relative peace. Of course many of this generation joined the services and in some cases have found themelves in combat. But by the time that I reached my teens conscription had been abandoned and so there was no need for me to prepare for combat. I have not been required to fight for my country nor make any sacrifice at all and so I have enjoyed to the full the benefits of peace.

So for my generation the price of peace in a material sense has been cheap. Yet it may be that there is a terrible price still to be paid. Our peace has been gained at least in part by the sobering prospect of the destructiveness that would in all probability follow its collapse. Should the fear of nuclear war fail to deter its initiation then the resulting catastrophe would dwarf anything experienced by previous generations. Furthermore, while nuclear deterrence may be a relatively efficient means of preventing war, the sort of peace that results is unsatisfactory in that a policy of deterrence reinforces as much as helps overcome international hostility. Deterrence, and the alliance system upon which it rests, is inherently inflexible. It is therefore, difficult to move to a peace that is more durable and safe, one that might bring nations together rather than divide them from each other.

But nuclear weapons, and the scientific understandings and technologies that make them possible, cannot be readily eliminated. Nor is it the case that the divisions in the world are simply the product of alliances and armaments. Awareness of both these limitations discourages attempts to change to current system. It cannot be guaranteed that anything better will emerge to take its place; more seriously a miscalculation could be disastrous. This is the basis of the nuclear dilemma: how to gain the benefits derived from the fear of nuclear war by way of cautious and responsible international behaviour while at the same time reducing the risks of that fear being justified.

For the last fifteen years a good part of my working life has been bound up with this dilemma. While I have avoided a direct involvement in war I have earned my living studying it. As a result I have both a keen awareness of the benefits of our current peace and the risk of disaster upon which this peace apparently depends but cannot exclude. This collection of Essays represents an attempt to come to terms with the nuclear dilemma. The approach is academic, which might be found strange and even distasteful by some. My justification for this approach is found in the second part of this introduction. The first part puts the nuclear dilemma firmly in a political context, for these issues of war and peace cannot be treated solely as matters of principle or abstract theorising.

The Three Levels of Nuclear Politics

For a number of months the situation in Poland has been deteriorating steadily. Persistent economic problems and the growing boldness of Solidarity have shaken the Polish government. In Moscow there have been signs of restlessness at the inability of the Poles to put their house in order. Western intelligence has picked up signs of active preparation for a large-scale military intervention.

Throughout the crisis, the members of NATO have done their best to act as if this really was an internal matter for the Soviet bloc. Nevertheless, the Soviet Politburo and its few remaining allies in Poland have felt obliged to blame the West for attempting to promote an anti-communist uprising: they cannot allow that their problems are of their own making. The crisis develops as Polish soldiers refuse to fire to disperse food rioters. They have no such inhibitions in taking on Soviet troops sent in to restore socialist order. Control of airports and the main centres of communication are insufficient to quell the rebellion. In their frustration the Soviet leaders step up accusations against the West; there is even evidence in the activities of emigré organisations in West German to support them. In response, and as part of a diversionary effort to whip up some anti-German feeling in Poland as a unifying force, counter-pressure is applied by inhibiting access to West Berlin.

Within NATO there are active debates over how to respond. On the diplomatic front it is agreed that there should neither be any overt attempt to interfere in Poland nor concessions to Soviet demands on Berlin. There are greater divisions on the proper military response. All Warsaw Pact forces are on high alert. This is clearly related to the Polish situation; yet might not the Soviet leaders be tempted to turn these forces against the West in a desperate attempt to restore unity in the Warsaw Pact by provoking a crisis over supposed West German provocations, irredentism and aggression? This might argue for a corresponding increase in NATO's combat readiness, but might not that appear as if the alliance was seeking to exploit the Pact's moment of weakness and so validate Moscow's claims?

The position becomes even more difficult when it comes to nuclear weapons. In Washington the American President is advised to increase the alert status of the US strategic arsenal and to move nuclear submarines out of port. But how should he respond if the Russians do likewise? Simply raise the alert another notch? Moreover, a clamour is building up in the country to limit any nuclear commitments and if possible to avoid any involvement at all. In Europe the same debate is underway. Some feel it vital to warn the Soviet Union as clearly as possible of the awful consequences of any aggression against the West. Others are desperate to avoid mentioning the possibility of nuclear war, fearing that this will provoke the East into pre-emptive action. The President is convinced of the need to stand firm, yet he too is fearful of the consequences should the current crisis get out of hand. Perhaps, he thinks, this is the time to talk to his Soviet counterpart over the ''hot line'' . . .

Here we have, in an intense form, all the elements of nuclear politics. At one level, haunting any crisis diplomacy, is the prospect of a deliberate decision to initiate nuclear war. There is little to guide us if we try to surmise the manner in which such decisions might be taken, and the extent to which they could be said to be truly under political control. For any given scenario it is impossible to predict with confidence that the relevant political and military leaders will be cautious or bold. We cannot even be sure who will have to take the relevant decisions. In any crisis over Poland, for example, Sweden might soon find itself involved — perhaps elements of the Polish Navy will mutiny and attempt to escape to Swedish ports; perhaps in a mobilisation of the Soviet Navy its submarines will decide to pass through Swedish waters (they have been there many times before!). This would not be the first time that a great war started with a decision of a neutral to resist encroachments on its territory.

Fortunately such dilemmas have not been forced upon the leaders of any of the major powers, although in the crises over Cuba and Berlin in the early 1960s they got close enough. It remains difficult to anticipate either the form in which the critical decisions on nuclear war and peace might appear or the manner of their resolution. Nevertheless, the possibility of taking such decisions, and speculation over which way they might go, exercises a considerable influence on international politics at all times — not only when there is a crisis.

The second level of nuclear politics concerns the influence of nuclear weapons on the management of international relations. To what extent can drawing attention to the consequences of their use and the risks of setting in motion a train of events which could lead to such a catastrophe introduce a healthy degree of caution into East-West relations? How specific is it necessary to be about how and when, if at all, these weapons will be used to engender this caution? Are there means by which the costs and risks of managing international relations in this way could be reduced through negotiations either to hold down the nuclear arsenals or to alleviate the antagonism which makes their eventual use a serious possibility?

We can answer these questions with varying degrees of

confidence but there are no certainties. Because the stakes are so high, this uncertainty has encouraged a persistent debate in the West on the appropriate role for nuclear weapons in managing relations with the East. The character of this debate is governed by the fact that it takes place within an Alliance in which the interests at stake are by no means uniform.

The Atlantic Alliance developed in the late 1940s out of a fear in Western Europe of the overbearing power of the Soviet Union. It was believed that the only means of preventing the Soviet Union from further extending its sphere of influence was to draw the United States firmly into European politics. Initially it was American economic power that was considered most important in stabilising post-war Europe, but after a time it came to be assumed that it was American nuclear power that was critical in preserving this stability. This came to be known as "extended deterrence", in that the United States had committed itself to deterring attack not just against its own territory but also on that of its allies, by the threat of nuclear retaliation.

With the growth of the Soviet Union's own capacity for retaliation this threat increasingly took on suicidal overtones for the United States. Yet the commitment had been made. The West European states, most of which were non-nuclear, lacked obvious or acceptable alternatives to dependence on the United States. They did not have convincing responses either to the conventional or the nuclear power of the Soviet Union. Even though dependence on the United States has often been extremely uncomfortable and irksome, West European governments have preferred it to being forced to cope on their own with the full might of the Soviet state.

The effort to sustain extended deterrence has determined nuclear strategy over the past few decades. The tensions generated by this effort, and its interaction with the overall development of East-West relations, have given Alliance debates a peculiar intensity. Peculiar because while much of the discussion revolves around wholly hypothetical contingencies and raises questions to which there can be no definite answers, it exercises an important impact on everyday international politics.

Debate on this matter amongst those involved in making policy, or with an interest in security affairs, has been constant. Only occasionally does it reach down into the third level of nuclear politics: the domestic level. As a result strategic studies often proceed as if the countries involved lack any national debate on these issues. Their fundamental interests can therefore be defined on a more-or-less constant basis. It is common practice to discuss Alliance debates in terms of ''the West Europeans'' or ''the Americans'' (which does not always appear to include Canadians!). For much of the time this is a convenient and not too harmful shorthand, of which there are a disconcerting number of examples in the following pages. However it can clearly be misleading, not only in gliding over the important variations in policies among the nations of Western Europe, but also in neglecting the fierce national debates that often do rage over security policy. If the policies of individual nations appear to be reasonably consistent that is frequently because one view has tended to prevail in the national debates. It does not necessarily follow that this view will continue to prevail in the future.

Neglecting the domestic dimension of security policy leads to a forgetfulness of the extent to which the people taking the critical decisions also spend much of their time worrying about the level of taxation, competing demands on public expenditure, promoting their personal and party images, getting re-elected and so on. As a result, policy options which might be perfectly reasonable within some narrow security framework turn out to be wholly unrealistic in terms of the actual freedom of manoeuvre available to those responsible for taking the decisions. More seriously, erroneous judgements may be made concerning the ability of societies to cope with the strain of a major East-West crisis, especially one in which nuclear threats play a prominent role.

During the 1980s it became impossible to ignore the domestic level. The first stirrings of a renewed public interest in Europe in nuclear matters were felt in 1977–8 over the neutron bomb (or enhanced radiation weapon as NATO preferred to call it). It was the December 1979 decision of NATO to introduce cruise and Pershing missiles into Europe, coupled with the growing East-West tension (high-lighted later the same month by the Soviet invasion of Afghanistan), that stimulated a protest movement which soon forced nuclear issues towards the top of the political agenda first throughout Europe and then in the United States.

When this movement is judged in terms of its ability to effect changes in policy its record is not impressive. In particular it failed to stop the introduction of the new NATO missiles, the first of which arrived at the end of 1983. By and large the political parties of the Right have prospered over this period, rather than those on the Left more sympathetic-ally inclined to the ideals of the anti-nuclear movement. In another sense, however, the movement has performed a valuable service. Into a tired and somewhat exclusive dis-cussion came people who felt strongly about the issues, were prepared to ask hard questions, were left unsatisfied by glib formulas and tempted by unorthodox solutions. In contrast to the increasingly relaxed view of those who were confident that the nuclear menace was under control, the protesters were stimulated by the belief that the danger was real and immediate.

Those who had been involved in the mainstream debate were in no position to be scornful or patronising towards the intrusion of the protesters. They could hardly boast an unbroken line of achievement. Few who engaged the pro-test groups in serious discussion could say that their views were not sharpened or altered in any way through the experience. My interest in the debate stemmed not only from the fact that for a while my curious specialism was in demand but because I was well aware that if it had not been for a decade's immersion in strategic studies all my sympathies would have been with the protesters. As this gave a certain edge to my work it might be useful to describe the development of my involvement with nuclear weapons.

From Activist to Strategist

The first book that I read on the nuclear issue was **The Disarmers**[1], Christopher Driver's history of the first wave of the Campaign for Nuclear Disarmament in the late 1950s and early 1960s. It persuaded me of the justice of CND's case and I became rather regretful that I had missed all the excitement. Particularly moving was Driver's description of A J P Taylor's dramatic speech at the Campaign's launch at the Central Hall, Westminster, in 1958. After outlining the effects of an H-bomb explosion, the destruction, the uncontrollable fires, the lethal fallout, he paced about in silence before inquiring "Is there anyone here who would want to do this to another human being?" — a complete hush — "Then, why are we making the damned thing?" — thunderous applause. I am not sure whether I was more impressed by the sentiment or the reported effects of its delivery. I attempted — wholly unsuccessfully — to reproduce this effect when proposing a unilateralist resolution in a school debate.

By the time I arrived at Manchester University in 1967, enthused by the student radicalism of the period, nuclear weapons were not high on the political agenda. Those that might once have devoted their campaigning energies to CND were not protesting the use of conventional weapons in Vietnam. However, if my education on nuclear matters was now halted there was compensation in an intensive introduction to the problems of strategic thinking. At the time the student movement, which I joined with great hope and enthusiasm, took itself incredibly seriously as an agent of radical social change. With the evidence of the anti-Vietnam War movement and the May 1968 events in Paris none of this at the time appeared to be as fanciful as with hindsight it now seems.

This all gave a somewhat sharper edge to my own studies in sociology (inevitably!) and political science. The question of the means by which a society might undergo a radical transformation seemed to me to be a wholly practical problem deserving a thorough investigation.

By the late 1960s the sort of idealism that had inspired

CND and the civil rights movement in the United States — captured by the concept of non-violent action — was now being dismissed as naive and terribly bourgeois. It had been overtaken by a much more tough-minded and sometimes violent approach.

If the moral pressure of non-violence was unlikely to provide a route to a new society, were the more violent routes likely to be any more successful? Under cover of an undergraduate essay I examined the theories of two of the folk-heroes of the student Left — Che Guevara and Regis Debray — who had recently failed spectacularly in a guerrilla campaign in Bolivia, leaving the former dead and the latter imprisoned. It soon became apparent that they had exaggerated the intrinsic appeal of their political message and the ease with which the military authority of the state might be undermined. Moreover, in their techniques and essentially patronising approach there was no promise of a markedly better society. Would the methods required to overturn the status quo ensure that the replacement was as brutal and hierarchical?

All this left me somewhat disillusioned but also fascinated by strategic thinking in its broadest sense. Strategy itself is a supremely practical activity, concerned with how to achieve objectives in an often uncertain and complex environment in the face of a calculating and resourceful opponent. The particular challenge in strategic thinking derives from the competitive element — the need to make decisions on the basis of the anticipated decisions of an opponent. The key feature of military strategy is that the relevant decisions involve the manipulation of instruments of violence, but the problems of competitive decision-making or of relating ends to means are found in most human activities. The strategic thought of groups and individuals involved in any sort of conflict often betrays much of their understanding of human nature, their grasp of social and political dynamics, their sense of ethical conduct as well as their skill in deploying the resources that they have at their disposal. As such it touches the essence of political as well as military life.

The most effective strategic thinking requires a degree of

detachment. Self-delusion or under-estimation of the other side are frequent sources of defeat. I soon discovered that detachment is not a prized quality among radical political groups who tend to put a lot of stress on commitment and distrust attempts to see how things might look to the other side. Even more suspect is the recognition of how much decent objectives are often in contradiction and that political life involves awkward choices.

The continual intrusion of reality moderated my political enthusiasm, much to the irritation of my colleagues at the time. I became more respectful of the good sense of those who realised that there was more to life than perpetual political agitation, and saw the value of representative democracy and the established constitutional processes. A greater interest developed in the substance of policy, although initially my concern was much more with the problems of inner cities than with international relations.

A course in the politics of science and technology taught by Professor Roger Williams at Manchester had stimulated an interest both in the arms race and the role of experts in policy-making. When I went to York and later Oxford to pursue graduate work, I gravitated towards an examination of the US nuclear debate where scientists were playing prominent roles as supporters as well as opponents of ballistic missile defences. (This served as a dry run for the current arguments over President Reagan's Strategic Defence Initiative).

The more involved I became in this study the more interested I became in the strategic issues themselves and not just the character of the policy debate. Under the influence of my Oxford supervisor, Professor Michael Howard, I found myself moving into the rather vague area of strategic studies. Here was an important — indeed vital — area with all the relevance to policy one could want. It was also strikingly under-populated. This was a time of US-Soviet détente and remarkably little public interest in nuclear issues. For many of my generation, the study of military matters was less than wholesome unless confined to the preparation of indictments of the military-industrial complex.

For most of the 1970s it was therefore possible to develop an expertise in the intricacies of the nuclear balance and arms control negotiations without worrying about the implications and without responding to any active political concern. Discussion in Britain was confined to the policy élite; otherwise one looked to the large and thriving US strategic studies community as a source of ideas and information. The only serious debates on nuclear policy were in the United States. In the backlash against détente, many American strategists were arguing that the strategic balance was becoming increasingly unstable, largely to the advantage of the Soviet Union. My own, more sanguine, view kept me safely on the liberal side of the argument.

When the second wave CND eventually arrived with as much fervour as its predecessor, and considerably more sophistication, my initial response was to assume that I could be employed most usefully in the great debate by trying to ensure that it was well-informed. This turned out not to be good enough. It was necessary to think through the fundamental issues of nuclear deterrence and European security. It soon became apparent that however liberal I might be when compared with American hawks, I was quite reactionary when compared with European doves. I found it strange that the protesters shared many of the assumptions of the American hawks concerning the state of nuclear deterrence and the impact of new technologies and doctrines (indeed many of their anxieties were a response to the statements made by the hawks). Having resisted such assumptions when displayed on one part of the political spectrum I felt unable to accept them when they appeared elsewhere.

Another difficulty was that the rather detached approach to these matters I developed during a decade of study appeared to many in the disarmament movement as objectionable as the substance of my arguments. There were three complaints concerning this detachment. First, one has no right to talk and write about nuclear weapons without experiencing and constantly exhibiting an acute sense of discomfort and revulsion. A matter-of-fact style is simply inappropriate to something so horrific. Second, the professed academic objectivity was in fact an illusion since exponents of academic strategic studies operate within a conceptual framework which takes for granted the state system and the traditional exercise of military power. Third, an academic pose was just a handy means of avoiding a stand on the most vital issues of the day. An examination of each of these complaints in turn might help explain my approach.

Emotion and Reason

It is understandable that those who feel strongly about the dangers of nuclear deterrence are appalled by those who are prepared to indulge in a detailed and jargon-ridden analysis of alternative nuclear strategies, without apparent regard for the enormity of what is at stake; or to discuss the relative capabilities of nuclear weapons in the same style as a consumer association's report on the merits of different types of lawnmowers. Nuclear weapons are the ultimate immorality, an utter obscenity and we should have nothing to do with them. This is a straightforward matter of morality; a refusal to compromise in any way with wickedness. The difficulties arise once one tries to move beyond this revulsion to treating the avoidance of nuclear war as a practical problem.

To illustrate these difficulties let us consider the following point made in a letter to **New Society**:

> More crucial perhaps than the division between hawks and doves is a division between those who feel with their whole being that a nuclear war is the final human horror, and those who do not realise, or who not want to realise, this and who are ready to *relativise* it, to discuss pros and cons, to count warheads and launchers. [2]

Needless to say I was the target of this letter and came into the second category. The author appears to suggest that there is a higher truth in this debate with which mere factual truth should not be allowed to interfere. (The letter was prompted by an article I had written with a colleague, criticising a tendentious television documentary which had sought to demonstrate how mendacious governments were in handling nuclear issues but which was in fact riddled with errors of its own.) A more substantial concern raised by the letter is that in discussing the pros and cons of a whole range of issues connected with nuclear weapons but not directly related to the fundamental question of their abolition or preservation, one is unwittingly rendering them tolerable by making them a familiar part of everyday life.

A lot of effort has gone into demonstrating that nuclear war would indeed be "the final human horror". Some have explored, carefully and precisely, the consequences of nuclear war for our societies and indeed our planet and tried to calculate how much could survive even after a furious nuclear exchange. It might be shown that more might survive with a modicum of contingency planning. Yet few would deny that even quite limited nuclear use would result in a catastrophe beyond human experience. It appears to be felt by some in the anti-nuclear movement that nuclear war might be rendered tolerable should our leaders come to believe that the catastrophe would be less than total and that human civilisation might stagger on thereafter. It does not require much consideration of the effects of even a small number of nuclear explosions to realise that this is not the sort of thing that even the most robust industrial society could readily take in its stride, even if some sort of eventual recovery were possible.

The statistics of nuclear destruction are difficult to comprehend and after a point become almost meaningless. One can draw neat, concentric circles from a city landmark and remark on the numbers of human beings within each ring likely to be fried, blown apart, irradiated and so on and then demonstrate the effects of the great winds and firestorms. What our imaginations can barely cope with is the accumulation of individual tragedies implied by the speculative statistics: the debris and the carnage; the pitiful survivors with their screams, their pain, their loneliness, their fear.

That we are dealing with the capacity to unleash this sort of horror is a starting point for almost everything written on nuclear weapons. It is as critical to the construction of theories of nuclear deterrence as it is to campaigns for nuclear disarmament. It is not being forgotten just because a count of warheads is not methodically converted into images of Hiroshima. It is not necessary to turn a description of nuclear disaster into a sort of incantation as if that is the be-all and end-all of the debate. An enormous amount of effort, from pamphlets to television dramas, has been expended in reminding us of the awfulness of nuclear war, just in case it had slipped the mind of politicians or even of the public at large. This effort may have had diminishing returns. Apart from the fact that the effect can be numbing and encourage fatalism rather than action, it does not move the debate along. It is irrefutable that nuclear war would be a disaster but it is also obvious and there is no evidence that the great bulk of the population, let alone their political leaders, have ever thought otherwise.

A patient with a terrible affliction would be unimpressed by a consultant who could only offer graphic images of the disease in its terminal stages. He would soon seek a second opinion. It would then become even more irritating if all those consulted sought only to establish blame for the disease and still failed to discuss treatment. At some point the question of treatment has to be addressed and it is necessary to move beyond the description of the horror of it all.

Those convinced of the folly of current policies and anxious to get them changed need to identify what it is about current policies that they find unacceptable, what are the possible alternatives and how the desired change in direction might be brought about. The answers to these questions are by no means self-evident. Those seeking answers are obliged to engage in forms of strategic reasoning.

Strategies for Peace?

The analysis might start on familiar ground. Is the problem the very existence of nuclear weapons? In which case the only solution is their elimination. Very simple; but what if we are uncertain that their total elimination can be achieved! Very few in the anti-nuclear movement would argue that general and complete nuclear disarmament is on the political agenda, or have thought through the difficulties of ensuring that the prohibitions on nuclear arms were fully implemented and observed. On examination of the movement's literature what appears to be at stake is "another spiral in the arms race" or "more overkill" or "destabilising first strike weapons". Of course it can be argued that these are merely the most immediate manifestations of a deeper problem. They require urgent action: the elimination of all nuclear weapons must inevitably take longer. Meanwhile, judgements have to be made about the consequences of the weapons that are left after the most objectionable or superfluous have been dismantled. These judgements become more pressing if the weapons that are left are mainly to be found on the territory of another, not wholly friendly, country. What then makes most sense: a world in which the nuclear danger is clear and unambiguous or one where there may be less weapons or even less destructive weapons around but there is also great uncertainty which might tempt the reckless and advantage the unscrupulous?

So the debate in practice is not whether one is for or against nuclear weapons (let alone for or against nuclear war) but over alternative policies for the nuclear age. Much of the debate is not even about the pros and cons of nuclear deterrence. No serious campaign has been mounted against the idea that some nuclear weapons might well deter an unprovoked nuclear attack. The campaign against the introduction of US cruise and Pershing missiles into Western Europe has been phrased in terms which suggest a shameful departure from the comfortable norms of mutual assured destruction. A variety of charges have been made against these weapons: that they are for dangerous first strike against military targets rather than the relatively tolerable second strike against cities; that they threaten a dangerous departure from a stable nuclear balance; or that they threaten arms control.

It might be argued that the problem is not so much an arms race but the sort of political antagonism that creates a climate in which new weapons can be justified and the two sides can really contemplate doing such awful things to each other. The anti-nuclear movement after all commonly describes itself as the peace movement. Is it meant by peace the conditions under which nations can coexist peacefully without divesting themselves of either the trappings of sovereignty or substantial armed forces through the methods of old-fashioned statecraft? Or do we aim for a longer-term transformation of international society, with the barriers that divide nations being broken down and warfare as an institution abandoned?

If the latter, then national action is unlikely to be sufficient. It is necessary to work hard on behalf of organisations such as the United Nations which offer some hope of an alternative approach or with like-minded groups in other countries. Those with doubts about the prospects for major reform might argue for individual nations' withdrawal from the international system. In this case unilateralism involves not only unconditional disarmament designed to persuade others to take reciprocal measures but also a request to be written out of the strategic script.

What attitude should then be adopted to those actions taken by the governing élites which are designed to improve relations? For those who can see beyond short-term improvements in relations and cosmetic measures of arms control to an international system in which crisis is endemic, a whole campaign cannot be called off because of a summit meeting and a successful treaty negotiation. For those scornful of politicians that stockpile vast numbers of weapons and then brandish them in diplomacy, an agreement reached by such men can only be treated with derision and suspicion. And once one comes to see the behaviour of governments as being solely motivated by a desire to maintain their position and power politics as usual then, however concessionary they might appear on the surface, there is no choice but to reject them and all their works. This rejection soon takes in the state apparatus which sustains the élite. From there it is a short step to the argument that the bomb will remain a threat and that there can be no real peace unless something is done about ''capitalism'' or "imperialism", which are the root causes of the trouble, and so on.

If one is arguing for a major change in policy, against the wishes of the ruling élite, then questions of political strategy have to be confronted. Should one use the approved mechanisms of political influence, with all the tedium and frustration involved, or try to shake up the establishment by more dramatic, and possibly illegal, forms of action which can exploit the enthusiasm and energies of large numbers of supporters? The need to gain mass support might argue for a more moderate presentation of the issues and respectable forms of action. The supposed imperviousness of the state to radical demands may argue for attempts to circumvent the power structure.

These questions take one into the analysis of the nature of political power in the modern world and the organisation of the international system. My concern here is not to provide the answers but only to stress the unavoidability of the questions once one has decided that "something must be done" about nuclear weapons.

If it is argued that campaigns are justified on the grounds that something especially dangerous is happening in the nuclear area or in East-West relations, then it is necessary to be sure that the trends in nuclear strategy and international relations have been read accurately. Whatever the emotional factors that might make a person tend to one side of the argument rather than the other, requirements for analysis and interpretation continually intrude. Statements used to justify the rejection of cruise missiles — such as "they will make the verification of arms control impossible" or "they are part of an American plan for limited nuclear war" — need to be supported with evidence.

To contrast cold-blooded strategic reasoning with the moral impulses of the campaigner is therefore to set up a false dichotomy. Strategic reasoning does not need to be amoral and insensitive to the human implications of what is under discussion. It just needs to respect the principles of logic and evidence. An anti-nuclear campaign may get started on the basis of an emotional reaction to the prospective horrors of nuclear war but it is not going to get very far unless it engages in some strategic reasoning of its own and also pays respect to those principles.

The Conceptual Framework

It would seem that when the campaigns move beyond the emotions to the intellect the conceptual frameworks in use are borrowed directly from the mainstream theorists of the 1960s, who were seeking to describe and retain a situation in which two antagonistic nuclear powers could coexist without blowing each other up. Even those searching for an alternative framework cannot avoid the questions which have preoccupied the mainstream theorists or the choice between alternative force structures and strategies.

The same might be said for attempts to challenge nuclear strategy by questioning the ''realist'' perspective which is said to inform its understanding of the international system. According to this perspective the most important characteristic of the international system is that it is, and will remain, made up of sovereign states. As there is no effective world government, each state must depend on its own resources for its security and so, if need be, must prepare for conflict. The fortunes of the institution of war and the institution of the state are closely linked. The ability to organise and exercise military power is one of the defining features of a state. In addition it is the state itself that is normally at issue in war: being enlarged, divided, merged or simply put under new management.

This sort of realism is criticised for being so bound up with the world as it is conventionally seen to be that it makes no allowances for the world as it could be. Because it views the world through the perspective of the nation state, it fails to recognise the dire consequences of actions undertaken in the name of national security for the international system as a whole.

The difficulty is that the state is not simply an intellectual construction which might be replaced with something more wholesome, but the major form in which communities beyond a certain size are organised. With decolonisation the numbers of states have grown, not diminished. In withstanding the vicissitudes of supra-nationalism and interdependence the institution has proved to be resilient. So long as the state remains the basic organising unit for the international community we ignore its preoccupations at our peril.

This is why it is necessary to take seriously the terms in which governments frame, and act upon, their security problems. This does not mean that a state-oriented approach by itself is sufficient. In the search for understanding there is no inevitable conflict between approaches based on national security and those based on the needs of the international community or those concerned with the condition of individual human beings. Recognising the legitimacy of the security concerns of states is one thing; identifying with them is another. A state-centred perspective provides a way of organising the debate on security policy: it does not force us to adopt one position in this debate.

An illustration of this point comes with the work of Jonathan Schell, one of the leading theorists of the antinuclear movement in the United States. In 1982 Schell wrote a best seller — **The Fate of the Earth** — in which he argued that the only answer to the prospect of nuclear destruction was a "political revolution" leading towards world government:

> We must lay down our arms, relinquish sovereignty, and found a political system for the peaceful settlement of international disputes.

Two years later he was no longer a revolutionary. In **The Abolition** he still argued for nuclear disarmament but had now abandoned world government, because of the unlimited delegation of power this must involve, was attracted by the idea of freezing the international status quo and even saw merit in deterrence. Now he sought:

> An agreement freezing the world's boundaries in place and abolishing nuclear arms while keeping deterrence in force by retaining the ability to rebuild them.

When reviewing **The Abolition**[3] I was struck by Schell's interest in scientific modes of thought and so attempted to explain his change of view through an adaptation of a famous equation.

The equation is $E = MC^2$ where E is the energy released in a collision (war) between states (the basic elements of political matter), M is the military power at the states' disposal, and C is the speed at which the collision takes place. According to this equation, the problem for the international community of states is that collisions between the "heavier" elements, with nuclear levels of M at their disposal, are likely to destroy the international community as a whole.

In **The Fate of the Earth**, Schell was essentially arguing that it would be difficult to reduce M to less dangerous levels until one had reduced C to zero. That is, because states move at their own pace and in their own preferred direction (the condition of sovereignty) and are very bad at co-ordinating their movements, it is only by removing this capacity for independent movement that the risk of collision can be avoided.

But once Schell recognised that the attempt to fuse all these elements together into a world government will produce a highly undesirable result, he was forced to return to the equation for an alternative approach. If we cannot keep E down by eliminating C then something must be done about M. Disarmament has traditionally focused on this problem — getting M down to as low a level as possible, preferably zero. But, the theorists of deterrence point out, we are stuck with high levels of M because nuclear weapons cannot be disinvented and even if the level were much reduced a collision would still be catastrophic. That is the bad news. The good news is that because they are self-directing and understand fully the relationship between E and M, the relevant heavy states respond by staying still and thus avoid collision. Schell acknowledges that the deterrence theorists may be right. The institution of war has been "fatally undermined".

Unfortunately, the system may not still be wholly stable despite the self-evident futility of a deliberate collision. States may believe that they can move without collision and miscalculate. Even a glancing blow might result in a catastrophe. Schell's idea is to remove the danger of miscalculation through the abolition of nuclear weapons while securing deterrence by underlining the fact that in a conflict these weapons may be rebuilt. The system that he designs to achieve this is of such complexity that it is hard to be confident that it will be any more stable than the one he seeks to replace; and like all radical solutions in this area there are tremendous problems with the transition from one system to the other. However the purpose of this digression has not been to evaluate Schell's work but to illustrate the extent to which divergent views can be accommodated within a state-centred model of the international system.

The Role of the Academic

Lastly, let us turn to the third of the complaints against academic detachment: that it is an excuse for passivity and a failure to take action against an objectionable and dangerous state of affairs. There is no reason why those who wish to study issues of war and peace in universities should feel obliged to offer any special justification. War is an important phenomenon, showing up mankind in some of its extreme moods and offering fascinating insights into the human condition. It tells us a great deal about the dilemmas of international affairs and it helps explain critical aspects of our history. Its intrinsic interest means that the study of war and strategy really requires no more elaborate defence than any other academic endeavour.

However, those academics working in this area have hardly been shrinking violets when it comes to public debate. This is an area where there is often both a hope and an expectation that the fruits of scholarship can be brought to bear on policy. For many exponents strategic studies do not so much involve the study of the strategies of others as the study of alternative strategies for government. Even those not angling for government contracts, recognise that there is something strange about working in an area of great public interest and failing to join in the argument.

The academic does not necessarily have to become an advocate in order to perform a useful role. I suggested earlier that the nuclear debate is not only driven by emotion and intellect but also by conflicting views on a series of issues concerning the implications of particular weapons, the state of the strategic balance and the nature of international affairs. The academic, able to draw on specialist knowledge and familiar with the relevant material which is often extremely technical and complex, should be able to help. The issues can be addressed using conventions of analysis and interpretation: checking sources, looking for corroboration, correcting biases and so on.

There are, however, limits to this academic approach. When it comes to some of the more critical questions there can be no definitive answers. The most scrupulous scholars often disagree for this is an area where much of the relevant information is unknown or unknowable or subject to dispute, and a large part of the argument revolves around speculation and conjecture. When they reach their judgements their answers reflect broader perceptions and perspectives.

The academic specialist might, therefore, attempt to keep the debate informed and the advocates honest but the interventions cannot be decisive because with many issues there can be no firm conclusions. Beyond that there is no particular reason why the academic's broader political and moral judgements should be deemed more authoritative than those of a politician, soldier or ordinary citizen.

This does not stop many engaging in the debate or offering policy advice in the belief that their views ought to be deemed more authoritative because of their great knowledge and learning and freedom from bias. Unfortunately I do not believe that the notion of the student of strategy as a source of reliable and independent policy advice, untainted by political distortions, is tenable. There is an inevitable conflict between engaging in strategic studies to improve policy and as a form of scholarship. Those who seek to offer specialist advice in politically sensitive areas may well find themselves compromised as they seek to ensure that their message gets over loud and clear, or simply that anyone is listening. If the intention is to serve some actor in the political arena — whether a policy-maker, a campaigner or an opposition politician — then it is necessary to address their immediate concerns, which are often short-term and narrow and distorted by their overall political circumstances. To the academic these concerns may seem eccentric and quite inappropriate but if he tries to impose his own priorities the client may soon lose interest.

The professional problems associated with being an adjunct to any political group are manageable so long as the role is marginal or the group is marginal. Once on centre stage the adviser will become associated with a package of policies, prescriptions and rationalisations. On being forced to defend this package in a highly-charged debate there may be a tendency towards rigidity and a reluctance to acknowledge evidence that is inconvenient. So engagement has its costs. Such a heated policy debate may make one feel terribly useful and even stimulate earnest scholarship but it is no supporter of detachment and objectivity.

Furthermore, a highly-charged debate encourages polarisation and dogmatism and can easily degenerate into point-scoring and polemics. This can be frustrating for those who want to contribute without toeing a party line. It also creates an impression of a far more limited range of choice on the issues than is in fact the case, as exemplified by the ease with which many people accept that the real choice is "red or dead".

There is a dilemma here. Debate on defence issues either seems to be among a select few who understand the systems and the jargon but who rarely challenge each others' underlying assumptions, or it is broadly based but dependent upon mass demonstrations and the resulting simplifications and confrontations. One cannot expect to get people to march behind banners proclaiming "yes, but" and "no, however" and "it is all very difficult".

Part of the role of academics may be to attempt to keep such a debate in perspective but it is also to try to keep the issues alive when the protest movements run out of steam and the nuclear question ceases to be so politically prominent. Widespread apathy and fatalism is no more atttractive because too much is then left unchallenged. At times of complacency, as much as at times of obsession, the academic may be well placed to extend the range of options under political consideration. In this sense the most valuable contributions are likely to be radical, not in the sense of occupying a particular point on the political spectrum but in broadening the debate. It may still be that the most valuable contributions are those that are truly academic, in that they move beyond the short-term needs of policy but advance the general understanding of modern conflict, or bring to bear a perspective that puts current problems firmly in their historical, political and social context.

Academic detachment need not mean insisting on agnosticism on critical issues; it should involve being ready to criticise and contradict those with whom one is basically in sympathy; recognising the merit of particular arguments put forward by those with whom one is generally out of step; and exploring lines of analysis and prescription that have no obvious political constituency. I tend to agree with the late Professor Hedley Bull: "Inquiry has its own morality, and is necessarily subversive of political institutions and movements of all kinds, good as well as bad".[4]

So the Essays in this volume represent an attempt to contribute to the nuclear debate of recent years without simply serving as an advocate for one side in the political argument. Some of the pitfalls are discussed in the first article which should also serve to provide a more general background to the rest of the book.

It is followed by a piece written in an effort to set down my position vis-à-vis the anti-nuclear movement and to engage some of its leaders in debate. The rest of the Essays consist of attempts to relate the substance of the nuclear issue to the political context in which it was being discussed, and to examine critically the main solutions proposed: reform of strategic doctrine; arms control and disarmament; President Reagan's Strategic Defence Initiative.

Apart from the Essay on the Strategic Defence Initiative, which has been simplified and updated for this volume, the others appear here as first published. I have allowed myself a few slight stylistic changes and corrections which should have been made at proof stage last time round. But judgements that now seem dubious and a number of inconsistencies have been left. There is inevitably a degree of overlap though I trust not an excessive amount.

Notes

1. Christopher Driver, **The Disarmers**, (London: Hodder & Stoughton, 1964).
2. H. Koning, **New Society**, 31 March 1983.
3. Jonathan Schell, **The Abolition** (New York; Knopf, 1984). The review appeared in **New Republic** (11 June 1984).
4. Hedley Bull, **The Anarchical Society** (London: Macmillan, 1977), p. xv.

1 Indignation, Influence and Strategic Studies

My inaugural lecture as Professor of War Studies at King's College provided an opportunity to explore the extent to which strategic studies can serve as a dispassionate policy science. An analysis of the role of professional strategists in the nuclear debates of the past three decades provides grounds for scepticism.

In his Inaugural Lecture in the Chair of Military Studies at King's College in January 1927, Sir Frederick Maurice developed his case for equipping "the young men who come to our great universities with the ambition to take part in public life" with the means of studying war:

> No one has ever suggested that epidemic disease or pauperism or any other such evil could be abolished or reduced without an examination of the causes, or application of the remedies by experts, and the education of public opinion. Only in regard to one of the greatest social evils of all—war—have these processes been but very partially applied.

Thirty-seven years later, in his Inaugural Lecture in the Chair of War Studies, Professor Michael Howard found the situation much the same:

> Pronouncements about military power and disarmament are still made by public figures of apparent intelligence and considerable authority with a naive dogmatism of a kind such as one finds in virtually no other area of social studies or public affairs.

Almost two decades on there is no doubting the growth of academic activity in this area. To what extent this has been fed into policy, let alone how far there has been a commensurate improvement in policy itself, is debatable. It may be that any meeting between the worlds of scholarship and of policy is doomed to be awkward and unsatisfactory. To the hard-pressed official, much academic advice inevitably appears as discursive, unfocused and innocent of political realities. The academic, for his part, may well feel that the issues of war and peace can only be properly illuminated by taking the widest possible historical and social perspective. Such an approach contributes most to a policy debate by broadening it, which is why it may not always be well received in government. But the academics cannot be expected to sacrifice content in order to cultivate influence.

It is often argued, however, that there does exist a compelling example of how matters might be organised differently. In the United States remarkably close ties have developed between the strategic studies community and policy-makers. Differences between the two political and administrative systems make this an inappropriate model for Britain; it is at any rate a product of particular historical circumstances. Moreover, the US experience suggests that such an intimate relationship is hardly an unmixed blessing, and may not have done either academic study or public policy as much good as is often supposed. The relevance of the American experience is that it has shaped to a remarkable extent the development of both the theory and the practice of contemporary strategy, and not just in the United States. The consequences are evident in the current debate raging in the West on nuclear weapons. Indeed, this debate has created as much of a crisis for strategic studies as it has done for Western policy.

The crisis affects the self-image of strategic studies, forged and bolstered through years of influence, as a dispassionate policy science. The role of strategic studies, according to this point of view, is not so much to broaden the policy debate as to keep it focused. The issues of war and peace are naturally vulnerable to the influence of strong passions, to displays of indignation. In the nuclear age, with so much at stake, to allow such passions to reign unchecked is extraordinarily dangerous. Strategic studies must therefore serve as an alternative source of policy to fear, rage and instinct. The specialists must keep their emotions in check and provide policy-makers with a full range of options, some possibly quite unpleasant, so that choices can be made on the basis of the best possible information and a complete appreciation of the full implications of any course of action. This article is concerned to explain how this view of strategic studies took root, the consequences of its application and the reasons why it may now be untenable.

It has long been expected of strategic studies that they will be tailored to meet the direct needs of policy-makers. The great postwar expansion of the subject was a response to the novel and awesome challenges of the nuclear age, as the pursuit of national security became a far more demanding and hazardous exercise than ever before. Academics were not, by and large, drawn to the subject as disinterested seekers after truth. They were impelled by the thought that here their labours might be put to good use—and perhaps also a sneaking suspicion that if war was now too important to be left to the generals, and even to the politicians, it might just about be safe with the professors.

Development of Strategic Studies

Contemporary strategic studies developed in the 1950s in the United States as part of the reaction to the Eisenhower administration's policy of "massive retaliation". This policy appeared to threaten nuclear hostilities in response to quite modest provocations. Once the Soviet Union acquired an equivalent capacity to deliver nuclear weapons, for the United States to implement a strategy of "massive retaliation" would be suicidal and so to threaten it would be incredible. The resultant combination of illogicality and recklessness was almost designed to incite academics, who, spurred on by public concern over the immediate state of the arms race, as well as over its ultimate logic, moved into the hitherto underpopulated area of strategic studies. They began to examine in detail the contradictions of the Eisenhower administration's policy while exploring a whole range of alternative policies that might restore credibility to deterrence by means of anything from technological fixes to artful tactics.

Few problems could be as perplexing as that of how real political and military muscle could be extracted from a nuclear arsenal that was in the process of being neutralised by the main adversary. It was a problem that was not only the most pressing facing the nation, and indeed all mankind, but which also involved a close association with some of the more dramatic areas of technological advance. Nuclear strategy was to be played for the highest of stakes, at the frontiers of knowledge, with the most fantastic and awesome of instruments and at an unusually demanding intellectual level. The demands of the nuclear age on defence policy were so unique that not even the experience of warfare or responsibility for the weaponry ensured any useful insights. Indeed, any assumption of continuity from the pre-nuclear age might lead to disastrous misjudgements. Even in military affairs, brawn had to give way to brain.

Contemporary strategic studies was based on this exhilarating prospect, and from the start it took the form of the mobilisation of civilian intellectual resources to serve the higher goals of national security policy. The effort was organised through specially constituted "think tanks", the most notorious of which was the Rand Corporation. Here fine and committed minds could be brought together. The large issues could be addressed without the hindrances of academic life such as students, committees, the rigid confines of the established disciplines and the need to spend time with people with quite different interests and concerns to one's own! Through the think tanks, access to classified information and the channels of communication to the government apparatus could be readily arranged. Soon these new strategists were losing contact with the wider academic community, drawing on information that their former colleagues could not share to write reports that they could not read. The work had to be presented in such a way as to impress itself on busy officials rather than earn plaudits in scholarly journals.

By the beginning of the 1960s members of the American strategic studies community were already making a distinct contribution—as both critics and consultants—to American policy. With the start of the Kennedy administration in 1961 they achieved a greater influence. Strategic studies became not just a special sort of discipline, but also a route to high office. Kennedy's Secretary of Defence, Robert McNamara, sought to fight prejudice and self-interest in the Pentagon with ruthless logic. He saw the new academic strategists as the source of this logic. The generals and admirals, protecting their service traditions and interests, and the businessmen and lawyers, doing their stints of public service, were displaced. In came earnest young men, sporting doctorates instead of campaign medals and club ties. Instead of playing the old routines of budgetary fudging and political fixing, they wielded new fangled tools of analysis, normally involving quantification. This revolution was accompanied by cries of rapture from other academics in the fields of business administration and political science, who saw in it a model by which all policy-making might be put on a rational technocratic basis.

By the end of the decade these same students of administration and politics were less sure. They were wondering at the revelation that policy output could still be usefully understood as the product of a bargaining process between competing interests rather than as the application of refined methodology. It transpired that McNamara's opponents, working on the principle of "if you can't beat 'em, join 'em", had realised that his major innovation had been to change the rules of the old game. To play by these rules merely required the acquisition of civilian strategists of a congenial disposition who understood the new jargon, could manipulate the new techniques and could trade statistics with the best.

One net result of the policy-making revolution was to generate a requirement for every point of view to be supported by some impressive-sounding strategic analysis. Another lasting result, of which more below, was that the conceptual framework within which the security debate took place had been narrowed and recast according to the requirements of the new strategic studies.

What I have been describing has been largely an American experience. Elsewhere the political culture or the organisation of the bureaucracy militated against such a development, and somewhat broader and less focused forms of strategic studies evolved. Nevertheless, the influence of the American community has hardly been confined to Washington. It has succeeded in shaping the way that most Western governments view their security problems, especially where nuclear weapons are concerned. Furthermore, it is through the American experience that the scope and character of contemporary strategic studies was defined. It came to be seen as policy science, preoccupied with reformulating some of the most fundamental and complex issues of our time into sets of technical propositions. This, it was hoped, would provide an invaluable aid to those responsible for managing the unusually dangerous international system.

This role for strategic studies has long been questioned. As its exponents became more prominent in policy-making they came under criticism for the narrowness of their vision and their over-reliance on sophisticated techniques. This particular line of criticism was highlighted by the association of many of the stars of the strategic studies community with the Vietnam disaster. Now, the criticism is of helping to promote the arms race.

A recurrent theme has been the charge that influence has been cultivated by suppressing the indignation that ought to form part of any human being's reaction to the nuclear age. The guilty strategists treat nuclear weapons as normal and acceptable instruments of power politics. They tolerate an international structure underpinned by a capacity for mutual assured destruction. They describe this awful state of affairs and devise plans to work within it using sanitised language and concepts that obscure the horrendous implications of what is going on. The incapacity for indignation has become a professional distortion, and because of the influence of the nuclear strategists this distortion is transmitted to the political system as a whole.

This indictment was developed as soon as nuclear strategy

looked like becoming respectable. It has been revived with
renewed vigour in recent years as part of the general
challenge being mounted in the West to the artefacts of the
nuclear age. The familiarity of the indictment has resulted in
a well-rehearsed defence. It is agreed that strategic studies
does present itself as an attempt at dispassionate analysis.
However, it is a argued that this attempt is wholly to be
welcomed because any alternative approach would be much
more dangerous. The emotions that could soon be brought
to bear on policy might not only be an understandable
revulsion at weapons of terror and genocide, but also the
most crude and aggressive forms of jingoism. Those who
provided the early resistance to the rise of nuclear strategic
studies were hawks much more than doves. They were
appalled at the suggestions that the adversary might be
something other than brutish, capable of rational calculation, and with whom there might be in some areas a coincidence of interests. Popular indignation has swept nations to
war in the past. A movement from another direction that
might restrain governments from acting firmly in pursuit of
national interests is merely the other side of the same coin.
A set of casualty figures can produce one cry demanding
that the madness stop at once before more young men fall;
another that the military effort be redoubled to ensure that
the deaths were not in vain and would be avenged.

Strategy is about the pursuit of political ends with military
means in the international environment. It requires judgements as to when to hold back and when to go forward; it
involves a realistic appreciation of the relative power of
oneself and an adversary, and of the likely respective skill in
wielding this power. Such assessments need to be made
with care, they are best made without the intrusion of
excessive bravado, anger or fear.

In the nuclear age fear might seem the only honest
reaction. But, the new strategists warned, that could give an
unscrupulous power capable of manipulating this fear a
dangerous advantage. As the margins of safety contracted
the need was for more, not less, dispassionate analysis; a
continuing and most careful calculation of the balance of
risks. When two hostile, nuclear-armed camps confronted

each other, so the argument went on, the balance of terror could be tilted by the prospect of terror making a deeper impression on one side than on the other. Part of the analytical effort, therefore, must be to keep the risk of terror in perspective and to examine thoroughly all means of alleviating the terror should it occur. If policy came to be overwhelmed by a revulsion and horror at nuclear weapons then the United States could be placed at a strategic disadvantage. If discussion of civil defence was abjured because it was repellent to address the details of the holocaust, then not only might an important source of advantage be lost but the nation would be ill-prepared should there be, by some mischance, a disastrous strategic failure. If discussion of alternative nuclear strategies was resisted, because contemplating the use of just one of these things was abhorrent, then should deterrence fail governments might find themselves drawn into massive genocidal attacks because that was the only way that the system had been programmed. So the defence was not just that indignation interfered with the effective study of strategy; it was a positive handicap. It was necessary, in the words of Herman Kahn that became almost a motto for the new strategy, to "think the unthinkable".

A Clinical Approach

The particular circumstances of the nuclear age thus encouraged an unusually clinical approach to strategic studies. Because of the aspirations to the status of policy science and the nature of the clientele, work was expected to be rigorous and analytical and to betray few strong feelings. The powerful emotions brought forth by the prospect of nuclear war seemed to make this approach even more necessary. Otherwise, these emotions might overwhelm all thought, and in the resultant paralysis nations would soon become victims rather than masters of events. Victory could well go to an enemy whose political structure made him far more able to suppress indignation. The new strategists insisted that it was necessary to look carefully at nuclear battle plans, not because it was thought likely that they would ever be needed, but because the quality of peace-time deterrence depended largely on a convincing answer to the question of what was to be done if deterrence failed.

There are a number of familiar complaints about this clinical approach: that it is wrong to serve governments in their most dubious pursuits; that it is foolish to rely on abstract models and quantitative techniques, so misleading in their apparent precision; that the scientific affectations exclude moral values; that in thinking about the ''unthinkable'' the strategists render it thinkable for everyone else. Accusations of this sort are often misplaced, overstated or unfair; they were dealt with effectively some time ago by Hedley Bull.[1] Nuclear strategy is a legitimate area for study, and it is of such importance that one dare not preclude any particular methodology; and the fruits of any study should be available to governments. It is, however, worth asking whether the cumulative effect of decades of clinical, policy-orientated analysis has been to encourage a systematic distortion in our understanding of the basic problems of military power and international order; whether there is now some kind of institutionalised bias in the strategic studies community which makes it difficult to appreciate many of the key factors that shape and temper conflict in the modern world. In particular, this community has taken a proprietary interest in the theory and practice of nuclear deterrence. Is this a subject susceptible to a clinical approach?

It is necessary to go back to the formative years of the 1950s, when strategic studies was already displaying an inclination towards sophisticated techniques, towards the calculable factors of hardware and force levels in preference to the less calculable factors of history and culture. But these factors were qualified by a political context that was so unsettled that it could not be ignored. When Dulles made nuclear deterrence the centrepiece of US security policy in the first half of the 1950s he was acting in the traditional manner of a diplomat, seeking to employ available military power with particular problems—such as Korea and Indo-China — very much in mind. Even the elaboration of the

more complex and abstruse theories of the Kennedy administration was tuned to the crises over Berlin and Cuba. (It is
of note that, in both cases, the immediate logic of the crises
severely qualified and overrode the internal logic of the
long-term strategy.) Thereafter, as the Soviet military build-
up swept away the traces of superiority, American policy-
makers found that the detail of the strategic balance was of
only marginal relevance to the conduct of diplomacy and
even of war. The loss of nuclear superiority may have contributed to America's troubles, but, as it could not be
retrieved, it had to be replaced by something more appropriate to the new situation.

If nuclear deterrence was no longer so closely tied to
immediate crisis management, it was still very much a part
of protecting the United States itself from nuclear attacks
and of sustaining the network of alliance commitments that
had been taken on in easier times. These commitments
meant that the United States had to be prepared to use
nuclear weapons in response to a conventional attack on a
third party. This might have seemed plausible enough when
the United States enjoyed a comfortable margin of
superiority; it required much more of an act of faith to take
it seriously once it was realised that there was no obvious
route to victory in a nuclear war. Getting in with a first strike
could not disarm the enemy of all his means of retaliation
and so was likely to lead to the devastation of American
territory. With the passing of superiority, then, the
American nuclear guarantee became patently less credible;
yet, so long as there was some risk that the Americans might
do what they said they would do, deterrence could hold.
Among the allies no clearly preferable or generally available
alternatives to the guarantee emerged, so they stuck with it
as an act of faith. For their part, American governments
were unprepared to set in motion the international upheavals likely to follow on withdrawal from the nuclear
commitments.

In this way the political environment in which the early
theories of nuclear deterrence had been forged was frozen.
The people of Europe adjusted to the postwar arrangements
and organised their life accordingly; these arrangements

were sanctified by international agreements, so that they were no longer questioned as part of the diplomatic routine but only at the margins of political rhetoric. Despite all this, the essential security problem was assumed to be the same. How could the Soviet Union be prevented from exploiting some local turbulence and launching a full-blooded invasion to establish dominion over the continent? The fact that it became progressively more difficult to imagine the circumstances in which this might come to pass could be taken as a testament to the success of the original policy. But the success of containment and deterrence could only be partial. The problem had been held in check, not eliminated. Remove the military pillar and the whole edifice of security might crumble. In the Kremlin, a similar assessment was made, Soviet forces provided garrisons for the Eastern Europe satellites and were viewed by their masters as a necessary deterrent to NATO.

So the two blocs became frozen in the postures that they had adopted in the 1950s, destined to glower at each other forever with fists raised like two petrified victims of Vesuvius. Neither dared lower its guard because it could not be sure that the other would remain motionless if it did. Outside of this ossified structure in Europe, profound changes were under way. New states were created through decolonisation; new forms of power based on oil and economic strength emerged; new political groupings and new regional powers came to the fore; and the Soviet Union achieved strategic parity. This last fact at least might have been expected to qualify the American nuclear guarantee to Western Europe, but that guarantee was now fixed in place as part of the ossified European structure and could not be easily challenged. Whether it was really the case that the whole structure depended on this guarantee may have been doubtful. There was certainly little inclination to find out.

As the strategic studies community addressed the dilemma of attempting to extend deterrence in circumstances of nuclear parity, they discovered just how rigid NATO had become. All the major options for resolving the dilemma were ruled out of order. A drive to retrieve superiority by developing a true first strike capability was ruled out not only because it was technically extremely difficult, maybe impossible, but because the very effort was unsettling. The American government was unwilling to embark on the endless arms race that might ensue. Also, it was nervous about the development of the sort of delicate relationship that might turn a limited superpower skirmish anywhere in the globe into a massive nuclear exchange. Later on, the West Europeans argued against any visible drive for strategic superiority as being provocative and liable to interfere with the arms control and political dialogue that they saw as a parallel source of stability to that of military strength.

The removal of the dependence on the threat to use nuclear weapons first was unacceptable to NATO governments unwilling to fund the forces required to support full conventional deterrence, and worried that the effort would serve as an excuse for the Americans to remove all nuclear protection. Even the more efficient use of existing conventional resources was frustrated because of the demands of the national defence industries, and the need to demonstrate to West Germany a commitment to the defence of every inch of its territory, so that space could not be traded for time. On the other hand, the virtually automatic early use of nuclear weapons against invading enemy forces also could not be permitted because the Europeans were understandably nervous lest their continent be turned into a nuclear battlefield. The acquisition of nuclear weapons by West Germany, in many ways the simplest answer to the problems of the central front, alarmed all those in East and West with vivid memories of past offensives launched from Germany.

Thus it was not that the strategic studies community operated in a political vacuum: rather, the constraints of the political context of an established alliance forced them to seek answers to the basic dilemma in politically non-controversial areas. One key question was rarely asked directly. The politicians found it easier to live without a satisfactory solution to the dilemma of an incredible nuclear guarantee, than to contemplate the upheaval necessitated by following one of the possible solutions. Was this, in itself, a piece of evidence of considerable importance?

To give flavour to their analyses, the strategists would devise a scenario, usually some conjunction of otherwise unrelated events that together would provide an explosive mixture. Increasingly it was found that analysis that tried to plot the course of a conflict was, to quote the jargon, ''scenario-dependent''. Yet few seemed to have realised that they might be illustrating a point of strategic significance when it turned out that most of their scenarios were far-fetched and even preposterous. Furthermore, analyses of future wars played only a small part in the shaping of strategic policy. Much more important were the immediate requirements of alliance. American nuclear forces in Europe were viewed as symbols of a commitment to the continent, rather than as a means of bringing certain Warsaw Pact targets into range. The procedures that governed their release were designed to serve as a reassurance against recklessness, though the delays inherent in those procedures diminished their likely value in battle. NATO policy became designed to spread the risks and responsibilities of alliance and to accommodate a variety of distinct national requirements. Such schemes as the Multilateral Force could only be understood as complicated political statements: certainly not as serious preparations for conflict.

Even in the fundamental area of the strategic balance the requirements of peacetime overrode those of wartime. US Secretary of Defence Robert McNamara began the 1960s with changes in US targeting policy and force planning designed to give the American President a variety of nuclear options in war. He soon concluded that this attempt was creating unrealistic — and unhealthy — expectations, and argued instead for recognising the virtues of a stable strategic balance, calming the arms race and creating few incentives to pre-empt in a crisis. It was McNamara who set in motion the strategic arms control process by which the superpowers sought to consolidate this stability. The process went off in unexpected directions, but it still cast nuclear weapons in essentially political roles as counters in a self-serving negotiation or as as an index of power and status.

Impact of Technology

As a result of all this, by the mid-1960s the theory of deterrence was no longer being developed and informed by the experience of severe international crisis. The political factors that shaped it were related to the maintenance of Alliance solidarity and the sustenance of an emerging super-power détente. Where, then, did this leave the clinical strategists? By this time most of the interesting things about nuclear stratgegy had been said and the key concepts had been developed. The enormous creativity of the earlier years had been spent or frustrated by political constraints. The attempt to apply the techniques of strategic studies to the Vietnam war hardly did anything for their reputation; indeed, the unpopularity of the war soon rubbed off on all those associated with the military establishment. Strategic studies had never appeared particularly wholesome; it was now considered downright sinister. The environment was one in which speculation as to the conduct of nuclear war was considered neither necessary nor illuminating. It was presumed that the inevitable conclusion of such a war would be utter and complete devastation. When the ''unthinkable'' of all-out nuclear war had strayed into the realm of possibility then there had been good reason to give it thought. With a durable balance of terror now firmly in place that requirement had diminished.

The only question mark against the general sense of a comfortable strategic stability was the disruptive impact of technology. Might not some dramatic new development — as spectacular and as far-reaching in its implications as radar, the atom-bomb, the thermo-nuclear bomb and the ICBM had been in their day — suddenly transform the situation? For example, if a truly watertight defensive system could be devised, would that not create a decisive strategic advantage? This effort might fail itself but nevertheless stimulate counter-measures, provoke an arms race and undermine the political understanding between the super-powers.

The same urge towards precision which had led Robert McNamara and his associates to set exacting standards for nuclear war-fighting early in the 1960s led this group to set equally exacting standards for a stable nuclear balance later on in the decade. A level of unacceptable damage to the Soviet Union was set; US forces had to be able to inflict such damage even after absorbing a surprise first-strike. So long as destruction could be assured it was believed that deterrence was operating. It would do no harm, and even some good, if the Soviet Union could confidently judge its forces satisfactory by the same standard.

By this method the military aspect of a wider political stand-off was put in a typically systematic form. However, McNamara's approach failed to relate the strategic stalemate to the wider context. Deterrence involves a complex and inter-related set of factors—political, economic and organisational as well as military—that serve to introduce a healthy measure of caution and circumspection into the risk calculus of the major powers. The focus on the state of the strategic balance meant that deterrence came to be seen instead as a function of a particular relationship of military forces. In principle it could break down should anything happen to disturb that military balance.

With vast and diverse reserves of offensive nuclear power available to both sides there was no reason to believe that the balance was at all delicate. That was McNamara's basic message. But in his methodology and his pronouncements he had accepted that this balance could not be taken for granted and that it might be vulnerable to technological change. Given the expectation created during two decades of the arms race, with one dramatic breakthrough following another, it would probably have been politically difficult to adopt any alternative assumptions, even though the overall balance was becoming far less sensitive to such break-throughs. Technology was now considered the greatest threat to deterrence. It became the business of the strategic studies community — and it turned out to be good business — to monitor technological innovation for its likely impact on the strategic balance. Thus technology replaced academic imagination and political experience as the source of fresh ideas and insight in the study of strategy. The mysteries of research and development, the impact of scientific enthusiasms, the industrial interests involved and the 10-year gap between the conception of a new system and its birth all contrived to give the process of innovation in weapon design and production a quite independent character, apparently well removed from deliberate political choice. The mechanistic treatment of the strategic balance, the concentration on technological innovation and the neglect of political context accentuated the worst features of strategic studies. Without political criteria by which to assess the "decisiveness" of some new development, there was no way to distinguish a serious instability from a trivial disparity in force levels.

If McNamara's permissive criteria had been sustained then there would have been no problem. The balance of terror remained remarkably indelicate. But as the number of nuclear warheads and their individual accuracies increased, imaginations began to play with all sorts of offensive tactics that might secure a winning advantage despite the apparent stalemate. If it was the case that the state of the strategic balance was the fundamental factor governing the relations between the United States and the Soviet Union, and if it was possible to discern some trend making possible some tactic that might just create a real advantage, then the United States could be in trouble. Such an advantage could only make itself felt in war. Following this line of thought led soon to a questioning of whether nuclear war was really inconceivable or whether, at least, it was prudent to act on that assumption.

The American pledge to use nuclear weapons first on behalf of its allies in the event of war was presented as the essential underpinning of European security. If the advertised result of the implementation of this pledge was going to be mutual assured destruction, then this had obvious implications for its quality. We have seen how this credibility problem was tolerated out of a sense of the overall stability of the European security system and the feeling that even if the US guarantee was little more than a gigantic bluff, this was not the sort of bluff that any prudent Soviet leader was going to be inclined to call. But impose a strict logic on this problem and a deterrent threat that is palpably incredible seems bound to fail. Without the necessary capabilities and doctrine to back up the nuclear guarantee, the allies would have to act on the assumption that the United States was unreliable and make other arrangements. Add to that fear a sense that new technologies were creating sources of strategic advantage that the Soviet Union might be better placed to exploit, and the policy of deterrence was close to failure—unless corrective measures were taken early on.

The Road to Rearmament

Events in the 1970s conspired to give this approach to strategy far more authority than it deserved. An apparently relentless Soviet military build-up; the discovery of aspects of Soviet doctrine at variance with the prevailing American view on the non-usability of nuclear power; the disappointment with the meagre results of détente; a series of irritating Soviet excursions into Third World trouble-spots—all this created an impression that the Soviet Union was seeking to free itself from any constraints imposed upon it by American nuclear strength. Confidence in the robustness of the established framework declined. The ''unthinkable'' moved back into the realm of possibility.

That the Soviet Union had been emboldened by the clear loss of American nuclear superiority may have been the case. That it was being tempted to push its luck out of a belief in favourable trends within the strategic balance was far more questionable. Explanations for the troubles of the 1970s would have been better sought in the processes of change in the Third World, and the relative Soviet and American abilities to cope with these changes. The ascendant right wing in American politics, however, assigned the blame for the troubles and frustrations of the decade to unfavourable and dangerous trends in the strategic balance. Perhaps this was because such a simple explanation permitted a simple solution — rearmament.

Perhaps it was the prominence of arms control as the centre-piece of détente which drew attention to these strategic trends. The strategic arms limitation talks were based on those presumptions of assured destruction that were becoming increasingly discredited. At any rate, the challenge to the East-West policies of the Johnson, Nixon, Ford and Carter years reached a crescendo with the opposition to the 1979 Strategic Arms Limitation Talks — SALT II — treaty.

The impact of all this on the strategic studies community was profound. The community itself had expanded and in its character and its output reflected the concern with technology and the details of arms control. As the issues of nuclear strategy moved to the centre of the political stage, so did the number of government agencies, congressional offices and pressure groups interested and involved — and they all wanted the appropriate expertise on their staff. The security debate was being conducted using the terminology and concepts of clinical strategic studies and the participants wanted to be properly briefed. The profession was now of undoubted influence. Its products still consisted of abstract, speculative theorising about unlikely contingencies, bolstered by technical details and force comparisons. Yet while its products retained their clinical appearance they were now politically loaded. Moreover, many of those involved, particularly those of a hawkish disposition, knew exactly what they were doing. If their analyses were right then the past years had involved monumental folly. Appalled by those of their fraternity who had enjoyed the greatest influence over policy during the 1970s despite clinging to the imagery of a stable balance, and frustrated by their own lack of influence, these professional strategists put themselves to the fore of a political movement. The strategists, having lost their professional detachment, were now moved by a sense of indignation.

It did not seem to matter that the strategic analyses now wielded as potent political weapons were often quite dubious. They depended on questionable assumptions about the reliability and performance of unproven new tech-nologies, about the implementation of subtle and ingenious tactics in the most fraught military environment imaginable, and about the attitudes and behaviour of national leaders in the most extreme circumstances. In the willingness to explain and predict great and disastrous international events on the basis of tenuous logic, the effect was reminiscent of Stephen Potter's advice on Gamesmanship in chess. Potter advises White to make three moves at random, then to resign. White then establishes his psychological superiority by explaining to his bewildered opponent how a brilliant checkmate by Black was inevitable in 20 or so further moves, thereby leaving White little choice but resignation. It is made clear to Black that he has only gained victory because his opponent understands the game far better than he.[2] Similarly, at times it seemed as if the strategists were arguing that a virtual American surrender and the collapse of alliances were inevitable on recognition of the full implications of trends in the strategic balance that, thus far, they alone had been able to discern.

When the strategists of this persuasion rose to positions of influence in the Reagan administration, they had the opportunity to put their theories into practice. This is not the place to examine their experience. Suffice it to say that they discovered as many domestic and external political constraints as their predecessors of an earlier generation. NATO allies were as nervous as ever about disturbing the security structures of Europe. These remained in their frozen state, slightly modified only in the political and economic spheres. For domestic and alliance consumption it was still necessary to enter into arms control negotiations at least with the appearance of good faith. The early statements of strategic intent had to be qualified because they generated more alarm than reassurance.

Indeed, the influence of clinical strategic studies has been evident as much in the protest movements opposed to the new American policies as in the policies themselves. The critics have not reasserted a more relaxed, less frenetic view of the strategic balance or argued the danger of a fixation with technology, or the nonsense of exaggerated interpretations of scenarios for a future war. Instead, in their fascination with the aftermath of a nuclear war they have encouraged the view that deterrence is about to fail, and, in their focus on the arms race as the likely cause of this disaster, that a striving for strategic advantage, rather than real political differences, is to blame for the current international malaise. Their literature is replete with the language and concepts of strategic studies. They also argue for a new foreign policy in terms of adjustments to force levels.

In the 1970s the strategists became populists; in the 1980s the populists became strategists. It is not clear which of these developments was the least helpful. The combination of the two has resulted in a wholly artifical crisis of deterrence. It has become accepted in everyday comment, from both ends of the political spectrum, and much in between, that the future of our civilisation is dependent on a particular configuration of forces. The only real differences are over just what that configuration should be. It is not that the structure of forces or shifts in the balance are unimportant; in certain circumstances they would be extremely important, but we are nowhere near such circumstances. They are part of the story, but not the whole story. It is the political context that will produce the pressures for war, and it is the nature of these pressures—and its consequences for the cohesion of alliances and the determination of individual nations—that will shape the course of any war. Whatever else one can predict, it is certain that the political environment on Day One of some future war will bear only scant resemblance to that of today.

It is, in fact, a paradox to which I have been attempting to draw attention that the apolitical character of so many contemporary strategic studies is partly a product of a static political environment. With so much, at least in Europe, so fixed and firmly in place, study of the environment generated few fresh insights. The preference for the familiar and understood, the unwillingness to tamper with the delicate political and doctrinal compromises of years ago, now fortified by institutionalisation and inertia, the difficulty of getting a large group of nations to agree together on any dramatic change in policy, provided an unpromising backdrop for anyone interested in strategic innovation. As a result of the ossification of the European security structure, military preparations became steeped in a political symbolism designed to hold the Alliance together. This imposed constraints on military policy that were first found irritating and then simply not understood. Strategic studies found it easier to neglect the current political environment and think instead of a future military environment. There was little left for the strategists but to project current policy and inventories forward and to speculate on the impact of new technologies. As this could only be done with a detailed knowledge of the relevant hardware and sophisticated analytical methods, the view of strategic studies as something highly technical was reinforced.

However, the image of a detailed and dispassionate policy science, following the analysis to wherever it led, was soon dispelled. To operate in such a way required the comfortable framework of a political consensus, within which there was sufficient leeway to take account of the more interesting and useful contributions of the strategic studies community. Equally, if the analysis kept on leading to the conclusions that the balance of terror was remarkably stable, and that it could tolerate quite striking variations in force levels, then there was no need to get excited and the political masters could be left alone to use the analysis as they saw fit. Once the political consensus was undermined then the strategists were forced to make overt political judgements. If, then, by imposing one's own political judgements on the strategic analysis the balance seemed to be under threat, then of course it mattered. Because many strategists felt that only they really understood these issues, they felt obliged to draw attention to these dangers, and as the political system failed to respond they became indignant and began to campaign. When even modest proposals faced formidable political obstacles it was tempting to use strategic analysis to generate a sufficient sense of crisis and urgency to get politicans to agree to change.

Those who understood the analysis but disagreed with the conclusions, largely because they imposed alternative political judgements, then began to campaign in opposition. But they campaigned against the strategic analysis, arguing against one set of prescriptions on how to respond to the failure of deterrence with their own set, without asking the prior question of whether deterrence was really close to failure. A debate which really should have been about these alternative political judgements, concerning such matters as the relative risk-taking propensities of the Soviet Union and the United States and the real extent of their conflicts of interest in the various world trouble-spots, got bogged down in arguments over force structures and the conduct of total war.

I have argued that the difficulty in developing convincing scenarios for the outbreak of World War Three was not a professional failure but a strategic fact of some significance. Equally, the extent to which contemplation of World War Three produces widespread public indignation is also a strategic fact of some significance. If all this fuss has occurred in what are, despite the admittedly harsh international climate, hardly crisis conditions, what would be the state of opinion in a real crisis and how might that affect available strategies? The idea that strategic studies could serve as a counter-influence to public passions in the formation of security policy has therefore fallen on two counts. First, those with sufficiently strong feelings cannot be deflated merely by reciting to them the conclusions of experts. Secondly, the experts have shown themselves to be as susceptible to strong feelings as everyone else. The strategists, or at least forms of strategic analysis, have appeared on the expert wings of broad political movements rather than as independent servants of policy. In this way, strategic studies have served as a source of indignation as well as of influence.

The conclusion I would draw from this experience is that strategic studies must reintegrate politics into its analytical framework. If the analysis is serious then politics is unavoidable. Where this is not recognised the political judgements involved will be crude and dogmatic. The subject will be vulnerable to the charge of promoting a particular point of view under the cover of spurious expertise. Strategic studies based on political understanding as much as on technical competence may not appear so obviously as a source of specialist advice to policy-makers. But it might be able to make a more constructive contribution to public debate, and the advice that was sought would be more useful.

Notes

1. Hedley Bull ''Strategic studies and its critics'', **World Politics** July 1968, No. 4, pp. 593–605.
2. Stephen Potter, **The Theory of Gamesmanship** (London: Hart-Davis, 1947), pp. 93–5.

(First published in **International Affairs**, London, Summer 1984).

2 Disarmament and the Future of Europe

When the European Nuclear Disarmament (END) campaign was launched in 1980 I wrote a critique for the University of Sussex Armaments and Disarmament Information Unit newsletter which led to a spirited exchange with one of the campaign's leaders, Mary Kaldor. This is a consolidated statement of my critique prepared for the American **Bulletin of Atomic Scientists.** *Ms Kaldor's response appears in the same issue — December 1981.*

In the late 1950s there began a discernible shift among some of those who opposed the growing role of nuclear weapons in the strategies of the major powers. Instead of continuing to call for complete and immediate disarmament, they began to switch their attention to shoring up the emerging structure of mutual deterrence. It was a switch many were unable to make, for it implied that nuclear weapons were with us to stay.

This is the origin of the split between the ''arms controllers'', preoccupied with stability in the balance of terror and high nuclear thresholds, and the ''disarmers'', disgusted with the whole concept of deterrence, and assuming that the only way to avoid disaster is to remove the instruments of disaster.

In time, the cause of disarmament came to appear more hopeless and the world did seem to learn to live with the bomb. Arms control became the dominant liberal position. To discourage mistaken notions about nuclear weapons, their terroristic, genocidal features were stressed. Any clouding of this image by allowing nuclear weapons to acquire the features of more traditional military instruments was sternly discouraged.

Recently there has been a change. With the deterioration

in the international situation and the limited yield from years of arms control negotiations, there is a resurgence of hostility in Europe to anything (or anyone) that appears to accept the current position of nuclear weapons in international affairs. And there is a desire for immediate disarmament. These sentiments are manifested in such movements as the campaign for European Nuclear Disarmament. My criticisms of this movement derive not so much from outright opposition but out of concern that there has been insufficient thought given to the full implications of what is being proposed.

Any policy that seeks to influence the quantity, quality and distribution of nuclear weapons contains enormous risks. We may have stumbled on the "best of all possible nuclear worlds" in that we have turned the fear of holocaust into a source of stability. To argue for no policy other than the maintenance of the balance of terror into perpetuity, however, cannot be supported by either history or common sense.

Equally, those who argue for radical change must recognise that the process of transformation from a nuclear to a non-nuclear world, even if it were within our grasp, would carry its own dangers. It would unsettle an international order based on the restraint and circumspection induced by the existence of weapons of enormous destructive power.

This is not simply to warn that restraint by the West may be seen in the East more as an opportunity than as an example, though I do believe that this is a more serious possibility than many disarmers would have us believe. It is also to argue that our nuclear world must be handled with care. Unexploded bombs need to be approached and dismantled with caution and respect, with full regard for the environment, lest the attempt to render them safe cause an explosion. Florence Nightingale observed that the first requirement of a hospital was that it would not spread disease. Similarly, a first requirement of disarmament is that it should not cause war. Simple-minded schemes for disarmament might be cures more dangerous than the disease.

One feature of the current debate is that the anti-nuclear

groups have been animated mainly by objections to particular weapons — notably the neutron bomb and the cruise missile. Extra weapons have always been criticised for their "overkill" capacity, but this is largely rhetorical. It is essentially an argument against waste, since surplus capacity makes little difference either way: so long as there is "kill" why worry about "overkill"? Indeed if the calculations of risk become easier it could be suggested that the situation would be more delicate.

Three features of the new weapons are criticised as possibly undesirable: they contribute to a first-strike capability (or at least fears thereof); they suggest the possibility of a limited nuclear war; and they lower the nuclear threshold. If one accepts, as I do, a straightforward concept of mutual deterrence, then these criticisms are disturbing. However, the new weapons do not, by and large, deserve these criticisms.

The Pershing II could attack some Soviet missiles with slight warning, but as there are only to be 108 of them they are not going to make much dent in 1,400 Soviet ICBMs, even if they were designed to attack such targets — which they are not. Some of the wilder US strategists seem to believe in the possibility of first strikes, but with the variety and number of offensive systems, especially submarine-launched missiles, there is no serious possibility of a successful first strike.

Cruise missiles, with their remarkably slow speed and vulnerability to air defences, are patently unsuitable for first strikes. However, like Pershing IIs, they are designed to attack targets in the Soviet Union. The Soviet Union has made it perfectly clear that once weapons start exploding on its territory a war will not be limited. The whole point of long-range theatre nuclear forces is that they make it more, not less, likely that a nuclear war starting in the middle of Europe will spread to the superpowers. The theatre nuclear weapons that might justify the charge of risking a limited nuclear war are the short-range, battlefield nuclear weapons which have been around a long time.

The real danger of the battlefield nuclear weapons is that they do lower the nuclear threshold. In the event of conflict, conventional forces might provide a sufficient obstacle to aggression, and allow an opportunity for diplomatic activity that might prevent recourse to nuclear weapons. The "nuclear threshold" is the point where the choice is between accepting defeat and escalating to nuclear weapons.

Battlefield nuclear weapons are supposed to make first nuclear use easier by having conventional military forces as targets. The difficulty has always been the unpalatable consequences for the population being defended, and the risk of escalation. The neutron weapon was intended to circumvent these problems, but it was never plausible that a weapon which emphasised the most nuclear of effects — radiation — could avoid being seen as a step beyond the fateful threshold.

While we could well do without battlefield nuclear weapons, this would be insufficient in itself to avoid reaching the nuclear threshold. The best way to do this is to improve conventional forces. When conventional forces are obsolescent and poorly maintained, and only unambiguously ghastly nuclear weapons are tolerated, then limited conventional fighting could become a holocaust with frightening speed.

The strengthening of conventional forces is one of the more obvious ways to reduce the threat of nuclear war, but this approach has two drawbacks. First, it is expensive. Those who are anxious to pare down the defence budget should recognise that, as the only substantial savings can be made in conventional forces, the consequence is to increase dependence on a nuclear stategy. Second, a conventional war in the middle of Europe might well be almost as nasty for those in and around the battlefield as a nuclear war. Furthermore, if the risks of the war turning nuclear have been reduced to a minimum, war itself might seem in some way "safer." This could be described as lowering the "war threshold."

This position was argued in the 1960s by Europeans against the then American preference for conventional as opposed to nuclear strategies. The implication was that the United States was trying to renege on its responsibilities by removing nuclear protection from Western Europe, leaving it to face an enemy with overwhelming advantages in conventional forces. It was for this reason that Europeans insisted on continuing with local deployment of American theatre nuclear weapons, as a link between Europe's defence and American strategic nuclear strength.

One would never guess from the current campaign against cruise missiles that it was European governments that took the initiative in asking the United States to strengthen its theatre nuclear forces. It is currently assumed that these are an imposition, the result of American hegemony. Europeans who welcome their presence, we are told, have been put up to it by Washington, or have been duped by NATO propaganda; and NATO, as we all know, is an American instrument.

Before cruise missiles and theories of limited war, existing nuclear capabilities made life dangerous enough. The fundamental nuclear relationship has not altered significantly and is unlikely to do so in the foreseeable future. If we have any reason to feel more nervous now it is not because of new arms races but because of political friction. In the first instance we can serve best the cause of peace by addressing the political issue rather than allowing ourselves to be diverted by rhetorical exaggerations, from both hawks and doves, on the state of the military balance.

Choice of Evils

At this point we come to the political aspects of the problem — the challenge mounted by groups such as END to the whole panoply of security arrangements, including the alliances that have developed over the past 35 years. It is not my claim that nuclear alliances are so inevitably benign that they should be established wherever possible to suppress conflict. But in the specific circumstances of postwar Europe they have had a stabilising effect. A balance of terror requires that the two sides be relatively stable as well as possess equivalent terror. In disorderly conditions it is difficult to create a stable alliance, which is why the Baghdad

Pact was a failure and the Southeast Asia Treaty Organisation (SEATO) fell apart. In Europe, the East-West divide is clear, with distinct political and economic systems on either side. The existence of nuclear weapons, warning at each stage in the Cold War against attempts to alter the shape of the boundary lines by military means, helped to consolidate the division.

Our choices are living with the current arrangements, to the extent that they can endure; preparing for a much more fluid set of relationships without the constraints and discipline of the alliances; or else a mixture of these with continuing Soviet control over the East and disarray in the West.

I have yet to be convinced that the alternatives are better or safer. Those who argue for the withering away of the blocs seem to assume that a close, co-operative Europe will emerge, with the peoples of the continent recognising their common humanity, stripped of nationalistic blinkers. But just the opposite might happen — a resurgence of traditional squabbles, rivalries and enmities. Look at what happened when the influence of the blocs waned in Southern Europe: Yugoslavia and Bulgaria argued about Macedonia; Greece and Turkey prepared to fight over Cyprus and the resources in the Aegean. After the alliances disappear do we expect Germany to be reunited? What will the Dutch and Poles, not to mention the Russians and French, say about *that*? For some reason, disarmers believe that arms create conflict and to remove them is to introduce harmony. Those on the Left, active in the disarmament movements, seem to find international conflict far less real and comprehensible than they do domestic struggle. Classes, but not nations, have things worth fighting about. This illusion has been sadly and recurrently shattered through the century, from the collapse of the Second International in 1914 to the failure to straddle the religious divide in Northern Ireland.

There is a tendency to argue that the two superpowers, and their respective alliances, even if superficially different, must share the blame for the current situation. Maybe they should, but this does not mean that they share an equal capacity for dissolution. The Warsaw Pact is a much tighter organisation, firmly under Soviet control and underpinned by a series of bilateral treaties that would remain even if the formal organisation were dissolved. It would be unthinkable for American forces to be used to keep, say, Holland in NATO, but it is equally unthinkable that Soviet forces would not be used to prevent a Polish defection. Most fundamental of all is the fact that the Soviet Union is a regional power by virtue of geography while the United States is one only by virtue of alliance.

This is why the slogan of a nuclear-free zone, "from Portugal to Poland", is so frivolous and pernicious. These matters are too serious for objectives to be decided upon because of alliterative effect. Apart from neglecting Scandinavia, it avoids the critical question of the Soviets. It is like talking of a "zone of peace" in Africa, "from Mauritania to Mozambique", carefully overlooking South Africa. At least the old Gaullist slogan, "from the Atlantic to the Urals", was clear on Soviet geography.

The issue is not whether Western Europe can drive out the superpowers but whether we are prepared to co-exist with the Soviet Union with the help of the United States, or take our chances by ourselves. It is wishful thinking to believe that it is only NATO and its missiles that keep the Warsaw Pact intact. If we are a threat to the Soviet Union, it is more likely because our societies are proof that there are more attractive forms of social, economic and political organisations than those imposed on the East.

The END strategy appears to be to foment sufficient protest and outrage in both East and West to undermine the alliance system. And while the various national movements may not operate in the same manner or at the same pace, at least they will all operate in the same direction. Among the Warsaw Pact nations, however, protest cannot be interpreted as a desire to go it alone. When the Poles and Czechs have, in the past, tried to extend their freedoms they have been desperate to demonstrate that they wished to remain loyal members of the Pact. We know that in spite of these protests, the infectious spread of liberal notions or the denial of the leading role of the Party have been sufficient to stimulate Soviet intervention.

Nuclear disarmament may be valuable for its own sake, but it would be unwise to kid ourselves that all the Good Things we want — peace, democracy, equality, justice, prosperity — come in one package deal. Political life, and this includes disarmament efforts, gets its quality from dealing with areas where our values and interests are in contradiction.

Few single events are more likely to stimulate World War III than a successful revolt against the Warsaw Pact, and those who glibly encourage this in an attempt to prove that they are not pro-Soviet ought to ponder the consequences of their slogans being taken up. Fortunately, East European dissidents have been steadily pointing out the unrealism of the attempt to link disarmament with the democratisation of their countries, and how END, if it does anything, only gives succour to their oppressors.

The geographic position of the Soviet Union is also relevant to the notion of a nuclear-free zone in Europe. What its proponents overlook is that a nuclear-free zone is not a nuclear-safe zone. The concept does no justice to the range, mobility and versatility of modern weapons; the super-powers could still turn Europe into a nuclear battlefield by firing missiles from Nevada and Siberia. In fact, many of the Soviet SS-20 missiles targeted on Europe are based in the Asian part of the USSR and many of those based in Europe are targeted on the United States.

Reducing Superpower Competition

Whatever the political drawbacks and risks, the current alliance system in Europe is worth preserving. The strain of adapting to the oil crisis, the persistent tensions in the Middle East and the economic recession, among other problems, make it unwise to load upon our societies the trauma of the breakup of a political order which has provided a remarkable degree of peace and security over the past three decades. In these circumstances the main priority is to find ways of decelerating the current trend toward superpower competition. It is essential not to slide back into non-communication. Most worrying at the moment is the tendency to intervene in the Third World, where dangers lie precisely in the lack of clear boundaries and predictable allies such as exist in Europe.

There is a dilemma here, because the current system cannot last forever. We live in an old house. Those who wish to put it on stronger foundations may, in the process, bring it down around them; and it may just fall on those who content themselves with patching up the cracks.

The fundamental problem is political rather than military. We cannot make the world safe until we address the sources of conflict between the major powers, and this involves ideology as much as weaponry. There are useful possibilities with arms control but it would be misleading to offer them as a way out of the predicament.

The END appeal will not make a significant difference to the disposition of Soviet nuclear forces in Europe, and if there is substantial weakening of the West's position (particularly a loosening of the Alliance) then not only will multilateral disarmament be harder to negotiate but the Soviet position in Europe will be palpably stronger.

Despite END'S attempt to wish it away from the politics of Europe, the Soviet Union will be the predominant power. Unlike the END people, I do not see the two alliances as equally unpleasant. I am more partisan. My side, despite its faults, is the one of liberal democracy, free expression, mixed economies and agricultural surpluses. The other side, despite its achievements, is the one of single parties, censorship, command economies and agricultural shortages. I want my side to be able to resist pressure from the other.

This is not a matter of evil men in the Kremlin waiting to grab more territory at the first opportunity, but of everyday international politics. The Soviet leaders are inclined to bullying and bluster, relying on military power as their main instrument of persuasion. As they try to solve their own pressing problems, I do not want to risk their feeling able continually to demand economic and political concesssions from us.

This is not simply to advocate arming ourselves while waiting for something better to turn up. We need new thinking on defence because, apart from anything else, we cannot afford the current military posture. We should engage the other side in as constructive a dialogue as possible. And we should find ways to reduce the over-bearing role of nuclear weapons in international politics. But let us understand that in a continent full of proud nations with diverse interests, divided into two distinct political and economic systems, a haphazard series of gestures is not going to make life any safer or the future more promising.

(First published in **The Bulletin of the Atomic Scientists**, Chicago, December 1981)

3 The Fading Myth of Flexible Response

From the start the nuclear debate raised important questions about the quality of NATO'S doctrine of flexible response, especially its reliance on the threat to use nuclear weapons first. In this Essay the political and strategic costs of this reliance are examined, along with some tentative reforms such as the removal of battlefield nuclear weapons and a greater stress on conventional deterrence.

> I wonder if we could contrive ... some magnificent myth that would in itself carry conviction to our whole community. — Plato, **Republic**

Whether a strategic doctrine is acceptable to the people for whom it has been developed is as important in an alliance of democratic societies as the doctrine's ability to impress the enemy. This factor is important not only because of the twist the capacity to unleash nuclear destruction gives to arguments about government accountability and the problems of getting a coalition of nations to agree on how best to manage their collective defence. Democracy is also crucial because in a real crisis public pressures will affect the implementation and success of any doctrine.

Any attempt to anticipate authoritatively the character of a future confrontation to suggest how best to prepare for it inevitably involves a certain amount of make-believe. Myth refers here not only to beliefs that have little basis in fact or experience, but also to Plato's conception of myths as convenient stories that might help promote unity in diverse societies.

The myth of flexible response is that if in desperate straits following a Soviet invasion of Western Europe, NATO will take the initiative in going nuclear. Strategists have long criticised NATO for depending on such a threat to a degree that far exceeded the probability of it ever being implemented. The concern has been that once this myth had been recognised by the Soviets they would not be fully deterred. By its nature, however, this myth is one that the Soviet Union must still take seriously, and so its deterrent value remains strong. The real problems NATO faces stem from the fact that those who depend on this myth are finding it increasingly difficult to take seriously. This situation might be awkward enough in times of peace, but it could be downright dangerous at times of crisis when unity is at a premium.

NATO's nuclear strategy is being subjected to intense public scrutiny. The nuclear issue has suddenly returned to the fore in Western political life as a result of such factors as the tense international climate, the publicity surrounding new weapons, and the uncertain course of SALT. It is now an issue that turns politicians out of office and divides their parties, gets people on the streets, animates the media, and brings authors and publishers together. The nuclear issue has emerged in different forms on the two sides of the Atlantic, with a clamour in the United States to bolster the nuclear strength of the alliance and a clamour in Western Europe to do the opposite.

The protest movements in Western Europe have commanded the most attention because of their spectacular rise and radical manifestoes. Their successes have forced NATO to reconsider its strategic nostrums. Quite simply, it is becoming difficult to introduce the weapons deemed necessary to implement NATO's established doctrine. When put on the spot, liberal politicians do not wish to be perceived to be erring on the side of the apocalypse.

The established NATO approach combines defence and détente. Rather than address awkward defence issues, governments have sought to improve East-West relations so that defence itself would become less important. But the main instrument of détente — arms control — is now suspected alike by hawks and disarmers for its failure to stabilise the strategic competition. Even the best conceivable agreements on theatre nuclear forces (TNF) would probably not appease the disarmers because the likely outcome would reduce but not remove the requirement for some new missile deployments by NATO.

In response to protesters' claims, the NATO establishment has sought to educate the public better to the realities of nuclear deterrence. This undertaking has proved to be a difficult task, however. For beyond the undeniable and critical fact that the last 35 years have been remarkably peaceful in Europe, NATO doctrine is not necessarily readily comprehensible even to officials pledged to uphold it. Current doctrine fudges so many issues and places so much weight on increasing uncertainty in the minds of potential aggressors that it cannot create certainty among the potential defenders and therefore does not lend itself to confident exposition.

Finally, many West European officials just hope that the current political fuss will blow over. They may not be disappointed; so-called peace movements are rarely at peace with themselves. Natural divisions exist among the motley collection of worried Atlanticists, neutralists, pacifists, politically vulnerable social democrats, revolutionaries, theologians and others who make up the movement. These groups, currently united in opposition to TNF, may soon divide over defence policy in general, particularly the question of a non-nuclear NATO. Moreover, the deterioration of East-West relations has contributed to the current unease; and if these relations can be improved, the protest movement will lose much urgency and steam. But this last point suggests that NATO's defence strategy remains politically viable only if international conditions do not put it to the test.

The Inadequacies of Flexible Response

Analysts have long recognised the weaknesses of NATO's nuclear strategy. The attempt to deter conventional aggression in Europe with a nuclear arsenal controlled by a non-European power that is itself subject to nuclear retaliation has never appeared to be an example of political or military rationality. Inertia, comparative cheapness, and apparent success have sustained the doctrine despite its evident flaws.

The United States would be irrational to commit suicide on behalf of Western Europe, but NATO has not found this fact a decisive flaw in its strategy. The East may be unsure of the rationality of the United States and find the mere possibility of uncontrolled and unintended nuclear escalation threatening. Thus, deterrence can operate perfectly successfully, but through a general fear of the unknown rather than through NATO's conditional threat. The scenarios of a failure in deterrence have seemed sufficiently implausible to serve as evidence that the strategy in some way worked and to warrant putting off a major reappraisal.

The real value of flexible response is that the doctrine has served as the basis for an Alliance consensus. This contribution to the political cohesion of NATO has been as critical to West European security as the weapons at NATO's disposal. As a partial response to the US belief that excessive reliance on nuclear weapons was reducing the credibility of NATO's deterrent posture, flexible response took the heat out of the US-West European argument over the balance of risks among the Alliance members. The West Europeans had feared that the risk of a conventional war confined solely to the European continent was increasing because of a US desire to reduce the risk of a nuclear confrontation with the Soviet Union. Flexible response offered the notion of a seamless web of deterrence, emphasising the likelihood that conflict in Europe would turn into a superpower confrontation. NATO reached this compromise in 1967 after an exhausting and acrimonious debate that had resulted in French withdrawal from NATO's integrated military command. After concluding the debate, most in NATO seemed content to busy themselves with more mundane matters.

Few are anxious to see the debate reopened. The essential arguments remain the same and the different points of view are as incompatible as ever. Those officials who would have to put together some new doctrine see that pursuit bringing nothing but endless argument to an Alliance already plagued by tensions. As long as they are not actually losing votes and, heaven forbid, wars, government leaders will tolerate strategies that possess weak intellectual foundations and internal contradictions. Changes in both strategic and political environments, however, have now made the inadequacies of flexible response hard to ignore. They myth cannot be sustained.

By the compromise of 1967, West Europeans accepted the need for a serious initial conventional response to Soviet aggression and Americans admitted that continued aggression would eventually necessitate a US nuclear response. Unfortunately, this change was no more than a declaratory gesture: it did not include serious reorganisation of NATO forces.

By 1967 the United States had come to see strategic nuclear forces as a self-neutralising system, with superiority neither available nor attainable. Since then, the growth in Soviet strategic forces and the SALT process have confirmed the existence of nuclear parity. The problem of maintaining a credible US nuclear guarantee to Western Europe was hardly new, having been recognised in the 1950s. But visible parity pushed this dilemma of extended deterrence to the fore.

In the early 1970s, studies in NATO's Nuclear Planning Group and elsewhere concluded that under conditions of parity the threat of nuclear escalation was becoming more dependent on linking first nuclear use to the course of a land war in Europe. Unfortunately, it was hard to see how NATO would improve its position by using existing TNF. Soviet nuclear retaliation would negate any immediate NATO benefits and subsequent TNF exchanges would favour the Warsaw Pact since it possessed numerically superior forces.

The doctrine of selective strategic strikes, announced by Secretary of Defence James Schlesinger in 1974, suggested one way out of this dilemma. Carefully controlled and targeted US strategic systems — intercontinental ballistic missiles (ICBMs) and submarine-launched ballistic missiles (SLBMs) — could be used to help thwart a Soviet invasion of Western Europe. Because the SALT process drew attention to the separateness of US strategic forces and other NATO weapons and because of Soviet moves to modernise its own TNF through deployment of the SS-20 intermediate range ballistic missile and the Backfire bomber, West Europeans found Schlesinger's innovations insufficient. Despite past pronouncements about the so-called indivisibility of deterrence, West European leaders now considered a distinctly West European response necessary.

A Credible Threat

The West Europeans had never really been convinced of the value of battlefield nuclear weapons as supplements to conventional forces. They considered short-range TNF important because the weapons were nuclear and therefore created risks of escalation — not because they appeared usable in a traditional war-fighting sense.

The weakness of TNF, particularly short-range TNF, is that they could never be used as functional equivalents to conventional weapons. If defenders used TNF as their initial response to aggression, the weapons might succeed in stopping the invader in his tracks. But political leaders would never sanction such early use of nuclear weapons. Later in the course of hostilities, political agreement on their use might be achieved, but TNF would then be used in far less propitious military conditions. The enemy would be dispersed, closer to defending forces and, more important, closer to the population to be defended. Moreover, if NATO postponed an initial nuclear response, enemy forces could actually overrun TNF and their storage facilities.

West European leaders have long considered the only real virtue of TNF to be the link the weapons provide to the US strategic arsenal. In this sense, the concept of the balance of nuclear forces in Europe had serious political implications: short-range TNF could then represent the top of an escalatory ladder — the point at which Europe is devastated and the superpowers decide to stop fighting.

This possibility pointed to a critical role for long-range theatre nuclear forces (LRTNF) — which reach Soviet soil — as a means by which nuclear exchanges could both be linked to a land war and involve the superpowers. LRTNF modern-isation was thus requested by West Europeans to increase the risk to the United States. The irony of the debate that has ensued since NATO's December 1979 LRTNF decision is that cruise and Pershing II missiles are being criticised on grounds that only really apply to short-range TNF — that they provide the possibility of fighting a limited nuclear war confined only to Europe.

Improved conventional forces could compensate for weakness in the nuclear component of flexible response, but the reverse is not true. Without a serious conventional response to invasion, NATO's nuclear threat loses even more credibility. The nuclear threat can be implemented only if any breach of NATO territory involves a massive conventional clash that NATO can sustain long enough to leave no doubt about the enormity of the challenge. Only then would NATO leaders have sufficient time to make ready the relevant systems and to undertake the onerous political decision to launch them.

In 1967 the West Europeans did not want to increase their conventional forces to support flexible response, and the Americans were bogged down in Vietnam. The West Europeans accepted the principle that the ability to resist a Soviet invasion at the conventional level for a longer period would enhance deterrence, but not the financial impli-cations of that concept. Having got into the habit of bemoaning an inherent Soviet superiority in conventional forces, the West Europeans could not bring themselves to consider whether a serious conventional option was attain-able and took for granted that it was not. Meanwhile, the impressive improvements in Soviet forces helped to confirm that impression.

The 1978 Long-Term Defence Programme responded to a range of deficiencies in NATO's conventional forces. It was the first attempt in over a decade to get the NATO countries to plan together. The problem now is to resist the corrosive effects of the worldwide economic recession on defence commitments already undertaken. The three per cent real increase in defence expenditures NATO countries agreed to in 1978 will be insufficient to support significant expansion.

British and West German decisions to cancel proposed defence increases indicate the problems NATO faces in holding together its established force structure.

Subversion by the Hawks

NATO'S inability to devise a satisfactory conventional option has kept Western Europe reliant on a nuclear strategy that survives more on its comparative lack of expense than on its substantive merits. NATO has left itself with the problem of convincing the Soviet Union that the West might initiate use of nuclear weapons in response to a deteriorating situation in conventional warfare while playing down this possibility in front of domestic audiences. So NATO does not want the Soviets to believe that they can wage war without the risk of nuclear exchanges; yet NATO does not want to believe that waging war inevitably involves nuclear exchanges. The West acts as if nuclear war would be easier to start on the battlefield, yet dares not claim that it could be contained there, for that might alarm the West European people and tempt the Kremlin with the spectre of a limited nuclear war in which the superpowers might be only barely touched. This strategy is a strange game of bluff and psychology, in which NATO can undermine the confidence of the other side only at a high risk of doing the same to itself.

Flexible response from the start involved an inadequate conventional defence backed by an incredible nuclear guarantee; and with the passing of the years, the doctrinal weaknesses have intensified. Moreover, political problems are making these weaknesses increasingly difficult to ignore. Although the NATO establishment is most aware of the challenge from the disarmers, it is the challenge from the hawks that has proved the more subversive. The disarmers' challenge is blatant and mobilises sections of the public. But the disarmers have had to adopt the mechanisms of popular protest because they lack a point of contact with the establishment, largely because they suggest that the NATO Alliance is part of the problem rather than the solution. The hawks, by contrast, appear to be no more than over-exuberant members of the establishment, just taking the Soviet threat more seriously. Moreover, the hawks are usually technically more competent than the protesters.

For the last 10 years, the hawks have been exposing the underlying incredibility of NATO's nuclear deterrent in the belief that they could devise a technical fix to the problems of deterrence. To demonstrate the need for whatever systems or innovations in targeting doctrine they proposed, the hawks proclaimed the inadequacy of current capabilities and doctrine. They stressed the surge in Soviet capabilities, dismissing the risk of spreading alarm and despondency in the belief that they could stimulate a comparable Western surge. They even questioned the morality of assured destruction more forcibly than some disarmers, believing that strategies that envisioned using nuclear weapons as precision instruments could better conform to Western traditions of warfare by providing some distinctions between combatants and non-combatants. Unfortunately, the proposed alternatives to assured destruction have not demonstrated themselves any more compelling, so the overall effect of the hawks' critique has been to undermine a cherished NATO myth.

The hawks' quest has proved futile because of the misguided notion that there can be a nuclear strategy that uniquely favours the West. In the early 1950s, many already recognised that the superpowers' nuclear relationship would develop into a stalemate. Only the creation of a first-strike capability could prevent this eventuality. Such an achievement was thwarted by the development of virtually invulnerable submarine-launched ballistic missiles and the subsequent inability to develop plausible anti-ballistic missile systems.

Those searching for strategic superiority began to contemplate the development of highly accurate nuclear warheads. The hawks ascribed great significance to topics such as ICBM vulnerability, to capacities for subtle or ingenious forms of weapons targeting, or even to a numerical advantage in one of the many measures of strategic power.

Now, however, the hawks are returning to the ideas of the 1950s. They have lost interest in limited nuclear exchanges and are regaining interest in first-strike capabilities. Some have discovered new potential in ballistic missile defence. Indeed, many hawks are now claiming that if US leaders know they possess a meaningful advantage at the strategic level, they will take escalatory moves with confidence.

The new approaches are as deficient as the old ones. Either they exceed technical or financial capabilities or they make unreal political assumptions about societies' propensities to experience pain and to engage in risk-taking. At no point have the hawks succeeded in breaking the popular association between any nuclear use and utter catastrophe. They had little trouble undermining assured destruction as a military strategy because the doctrine offers no useful guidance on how to cope with a failure in deterrence other than mindless destruction. But they could never dismiss assured destruction as a fact of life. The hawks have underlined NATO's inability to meet previous standards by raising the standards by which the deterrent must be assessed. For example, in arguing over ICBM vulnerability some have suggested that one cannot assume that the President would retaliate after a nuclear strike against America. Yet NATO has relied on the possibility that the President would retaliate after a conventional attack on Western Europe.

New wave nuclear strategists have confused what NATO has always tried to keep separate — the threat of first nuclear use and a first-strike capability. Moreover, they have fostered illusions about future capabilities. Even if NATO devoted all available economic and technical resources to the search, it would still not find a plausible form of nuclear superiority. Because of technical, financial, and political reasons, the Reagan administration is not able to implement the more ambitious plans being proposed by the strategic zealots in its ranks.

Dependence on technological fixes — saying that all will come right once MX (Missile Experimental) or space-based lasers or whatever are deployed — and statements that a safer world will emerge if only NATO can survive the window of Soviet opportunity have always involved risks. When these wonderful machines fail to appear, the only conclusion is that deterrence cannot be sustained. When they appear and the world is still turbulent and uncomfortable, the only conclusions are either that more ingenious machines are needed or that NATO's position is beyond repair. Perhaps most important, the whole preoccupation with complex and fantastic weapons and equally complex and fantastic scenarios scares people and confirms nuclear strategy as the preoccupation of Dr Strangeloves, full of madcap science and devoid of human sensibilities.

This last point is important because, until now, it has allowed the professional and public nuclear debates to operate at quite different levels. Even many who accept nuclear strategy share the view that it is a black science, communicated through euphemisms and equations and best left to those with that peculiar combination of technical competence and abstract theorising. High-sounding institutes and top secret government departments play a never-ending game of chess with real pieces against a real opponent, only they never take enemy pieces nor call a check. They play their moves with untried weapons of uncertain reliability and base their moves on untutored intuition and speculation concerning political responses to extreme and unlikely contingencies.

The political consumers of nuclear doctrine assume it to be vital, if enigmatic. By and large, they find it irrelevant to everyday diplomacy and domestic political debate. Nuclear strategy does not purport to offer advice on general international issues. Moreover, if those extreme contingencies that provide it with its raison d'etre arose, nuclear doctrine would offer no guide to outcomes unless the contingencies happened to conform to the peculiar conditions the doctrine demands.

Perhaps policy makers have preserved nuclear deterrence by disregarding the theology and concentrating on the crude and basic fear of catastrophe, which induces caution in both themselves and the Kremlin. But the theology is of little use for the everyday world of international affairs or for convincing agnostics or debating with the opposition.

The Disarmers

The opposition currently comes from disarmament groups. Given their nature, these groups cannot be expected to contribute to strategic thinking. The subject matter is tainted to them. They see analysis of the details of nuclear strategy as similar to analysis of the smooth functioning of concentration camps. As part of the tribute virtue pays to vice, disarmers often display an unhealthy fascination with the composition and technical details of military inventories, largely prompted by a desire to reveal the depths to which men can sink and the mendacity of official sources.

The disarmament groups have misinterpreted NATO strategy and exaggerated the potential of new weapons to make them more deserving of protest. Despite finding deterrence obnoxious, these groups, to the extent that they have a stategic framework, promote mutual assured destruction. They object to anything — civil defence, counterforce weapons, and counterforce doctrines — that suggests that nuclear war is in any way less than terrible, let alone winnable. They fear that a genuine strategy — ie, one based on a plausible war plan — might prompt nuclear use whereas threats of unrestrained terror are so suicidal that they will be kept for the very last resort.

With this background, the disarmers have watched the push of the US hawks with growing alarm. Instead of exposing the logical flaws and political unreality of the new strategic theories, the disarmers have taken the concepts of nuclear war fighting at face value and have begun to work out the implications of such concepts for Western Europe, the likely testing ground. Thus, the US hawks and the West European disarmers feed off each other. The hawks' reckless confidence in nuclear strategy justifies the disarmers' worst fears. In turn, the disarmers' neutralist inclination justifies the hawks' suspicions of the dire political consequences of Soviet nuclear supremacy.

On a number of key issues, a striking similarity exists

between the hawks and the disarmers. Both groups tend to assume that international tension is increasing to the point that a superpower confrontation is a distinct possibility; that the security interests of Western Europe and the United States do not necessarily coincide; that new developments in precision-guided munitions, anti-submarine warfare, space weapons, and ballistic missile defence are unsettling the superpowers' strategic relationship and raise the spectre of one side developing a usable nuclear superiority; and that unless large-scale reductions can be achieved, arms control talks are a waste of time.

The two groups differ in their assessments of the Soviet Union. The hawks are concerned that the Soviets have cracked the mystery of nuclear strategy and are tempted to derive immense benefits from this achievement. Conversely, the disarmers are convinced that the Soviet Union — a large and overbearing military power, with a troubled empire — need cause no more than minor inconvenience to West European countries, provided they keep to themselves.

Two key assumptions underlie much of the current anti-nuclear agitation. First, disarmers believe the arms race to be the root of most, if not all, international evil. Put the arms race into reverse, they claim, and not only will the world be safer, but Europe will also reunite, Eastern Europe will become democratised, and so on. Second, since the superpowers are the carriers of militarism, they must be expelled from the European continent if it is to be saved.

Much of the approach of the campaign for European Nuclear Disarmament (END) depends upon East Europeans succeeding in expelling Soviet bases from Eastern Europe in the same way that END hopes to expel American bases from Western Europe. Apart from the fact that the Soviet Union would remain pre-eminent in Europe even if NATO and the Warsaw Pact were disbanded, there is no way that East Europeans can protest against Soviet hegemony without courting disaster. A number of East European dissidents have been politely trying to explain this to END.

END and its ilk are essentially offering a radical foreign policy rather than a doveish defence policy. Nevertheless, although anti-Americanism is rife at the moment, END's appeal does not seem to lie in the anti-Alliance aspects of its programme. Instead, genuine fears about nuclear weapons and war, which have been intensified by the international climate, seem responsible for END's current popularity.

All of NATO's political capital in Western Europe is now being used up in support of LRTNF. At least for the next couple of years, therefore, West European politicians will anxiously await visible signs of improvement in East-West relations and will wish to avoid new controversies. This situation explains West European dismay at President Reagan's August 1981 decision to stockpile assembled neutron bombs in the United States and West European apprehension concerning new US studies that point to a need to modernise battlefield nuclear weapons. For the moment, the disarmament groups essentially possess a veto over any new proposals that call for the deployment of additional nuclear systems in Western Europe.

Yet in urging caution on the United States, West European leaders can only plead a sensitive domestic political situation. On the whole, they have refrained from challenging this nuclear bias within NATO strategy that justifies these new weapons, recognising that they themselves are largely responsible for the bias. In response to a crisis in doctrine, they have looked for political compromises, however technically and strategically unsound. If nothing else, the LRTNF experience has helped the current generation of NATO policy makers understand how their predecessors could respond to a similar set of problems with the proposal for a multilateral force. In the 1960s, some American leaders called for submarines with mixed nationality crews in response to the problem of US control of land-based missile systems in Europe. Today, some suggest submarine-launched cruise missiles as an alternative to LRTNF.

In arguing against the protesters' claims, West European governments have pleaded a sensitive Alliance situation — that Americans are tired of Western Europe's indecisiveness and may decide to abandon it entirely. Moreover, NATO leaders have stressed that Western Europe should stick to a decision already made and that without LRTNF modern-isation there will be no arms control and the Russians will get away with an unimpeded LRTNF modernisation pro-gramme of their own. It is not that NATO's December 1979 decision cannot be justified in terms of a theory of nuclear deterrence, but West European governments do not seem disposed to try to formulate this rationale.

If the LRTNF modernisation programme collapses, NATO can recover, but it will hardly be easy. The accompanying mutual recriminations and demoralisation would not provide the most propitious background for a reappraisal of NATO doctrine. Such a reappraisal should begin before NATO falls into disarray.

Many believe that a Soviet intervention in Poland would dispel the anti-nuclear sentiment and knock some discipline into the allies. In fact, much of the anti-nuclear sentiment derives from the combine effects of tension in international affairs and a surge of well-publicised developments related to all aspects of nuclear weapons. So a major international crisis would result in greater fear of nuclear confrontation, not less.

For example, Soviet intervention in Poland followed by US announcements that called for the movement of neutron bombs to Western Europe would not induce a mood of calm determination among the allies. If the situation worsened and NATO began to issue nuclear threats and move the war-heads for battlefield nuclear weapons from storage to the front, anxiety could turn into panic. Prevailing political circumstances and perceptions will determine the response to any crisis, so it could take the form of bravado or apathy as much as fright. Nevertheless, the recent debate over LRTNF modernisation should serve as a warning concern-ing the ability of democracies to sustain a nuclear strategy in a crisis. When deterrence was under greatest strain, it would be necessary either to risk disunity in the Alliance by persevering with preparations for nuclear war or else to accept that these moves would be too provocative and, in holding back, undermine the established strategy.

A More Compelling Conventional Strategy

The criticism is not that flexible response is a myth, for political life depends on such myths. The problem is that the myth no longer performs its function effectively. Instead of reassurance, NATO doctrine offers controversy. Flexible response has finally been nullified by the logic of nuclear stalemate. If war seemed imminent, the strategy could not withstand scrutiny because it offers no plausible war plan. To say that flexible response has worked up to now is not enough because, fortunately, it has been put to only a mild test.

To suggest that it would be far more sensible for NATO to put more emphasis on conventional forces is not at all novel. The normal response to such an observation from the NATO establishment is of the sort that the worldly-wise reserve for those who can answer every question except cost.

Perhaps all that can be posed is a dilemma, a choice between the unacceptable and the unaffordable; but policy makers should at least consider whether the problem is as acute as is often supposed. There has been little debate over what actually can be done with conventional forces. The focus instead has been on how much can be purchased. NATO leaders have seen conventional strategy largely as a resource problem. Given the constraints imposed by national budgets, more efficient uses of resources have had to supply the answer to the conventional problem. Hence, NATO countries have engaged in the never-ending quest for standardisation in weapons procurement or have attempted to reduce military requirements through arms control or by re-evaluating military intelligence information to scale down the Soviet threat.

None of these approaches has proved to be as rewarding as their proponents believed in the early 1970s. Many reasons explain these failures, but in each case the hazy state of thinking on conventional strategy played a part. Efforts at collaboration on equipment were hindered by great variations in defence doctrines; arms control was side-tracked by an over-reliance on the concept of parity; NATO assessments of the Soviet conventional threat were distorted by preoccupations with the highly impausible possibility of impromptu Soviet attacks. Moreover, as the effort to maintain defence spending at established levels became progressively more difficult in a harsh economic climate, the explanations of why it was necessary to keep conventional forces at particular levels became based as much on political relationships within the Alliance as on military relationships with the Warsaw Pact. The same phenomenon affected proposals, such as those for moving NATO bases forward from areas settled in 1945. Such a step would not provide sufficient military benefits to offset the political upheaval that would result.

Whereas nuclear strategy has suffered from an excess of analysis, conventional strategy has suffered from neglect. Although the professional military has been willing to cede nuclear strategy to civilians, as a peculiar specialism that has little connection with the things taught at military staff colleges, it has been reluctant to do the same with conventional strategy. Conventional doctrine is considered to be the professional military's domain, beyond the ken of civilians.

On the whole, civilian strategists have willingly accepted this division of labour. Most of them have been attracted to nuclear issues because the issues offer a first order conundrum of great political significance complicated by a mass of second order technical diversions that appeal to a certain cast of mind. Conversely, in the areas of conventional warfare, civilian strategists often have no military training, do not properly understand things like logistics and lines of command, and tend to get discouraged by the large numbers of bits and pieces of hardware with which they ought to be familiar. Moreover, a civilian is derided when he suggests radical ways of organising conventional warfare, whereas one can suggest quite absurd and terrible things in the nuclear area, and nobody seems to mind at all.

As a consequence, each country organises its conventional military forces along traditional lines. Innovations are rarely allowed to disrupt established patterns. Although there is a fascination with new technologies, the inclination is to improve on the familiar. Military services occasionally challenge one another in the battle for resources, but clear demarcation lines usually control such disputes. The only real stimulus to change is money. Thus far, the tendency has been to adjust to declining resources by shrinkage, making concessions to quantity rather than quality.

Flexible response has allowed this system to continue because its prime political attribute — that it can mean all things to all men — is a serious military failing. It has allowed decision makers to avoid difficult choices in the conventional field by providing a rationale for every type of military capability. The common notion of a so-called spectrum of deterrence in which no gaps dare be permitted to open up is also a recipe for avoiding hard choices. This concept requires the NATO Alliance to prepare for every type of war: short or long, nuclear or conventional, European or more widespread.

The main doctrinal objection to shifting to a strategy that more strongly emphasises conventional forces has always been that such a strategy raises the spectre of a limited war in which Europe serves as the battleground. Those who stress this objection assume that war will appear as a more tolerable option to both superpowers if the war is unlikely to involve much more than fighting with conventional weapons. This view has always under-estimated the deterrent effect of a strong conventional force posture. It also reflects an assumption that conventional strategy concerns fighting in a traditional manner, according to established conventions.

The assumption that the conventions of non-nuclear war remain familiar and workable, simply because the relevant hardware bears some relation to that used by previous generations, may no longer be valid. Perhaps more than is commonly realised, conventional warfare lacks clear conventions and so planning for it is almost as full of uncertainties as planning for nuclear warfare. Most modern weapons have not been tested in combat against similar forces in conditions approximating those in central Europe. Experience offers few lessons on how armies can cope with all-night, all-weather weapons; high rates of attrition;

maintenance of sophisticated electronics in the field; reluctance to move from cover or the inability to find it; excess of information and options; and complications of urban sprawls and refugees.

Even in the unlikely circumstance that NATO totally withdrew its threat of nuclear escalation, aggression would still represent an extremely unattractive and uncertain venture for the Soviet Union. Furthermore, in a crisis pre-planned measures of conventional reinforcements are far more suited to shoring up deterrence because they offer a way of signalling determination and reinforcing military positions without appearing unduly provocative to the adversary or to domestic populations.

To complement a move to a more compelling conventional strategy, it would be necessary for NATO to find some tangible way to demonstrate a reduced reliance on nuclear weapons. The decisive and unequivocal reduction of short-range TNF stockpiles would be a valuable step in this regard. Battlefield nuclear weapons represent current strategy at its most muddled and dangerous because they inhibit the development of convincing tactical doctrines, increase the fears of collateral damage from nuclear explosions and are vulnerable to accusations of NATO preparing for a geographically confined nuclear war or of creating risks of premature nuclear escalation. By removing the warheads for these weapons from their vulnerable storage sites in Western Europe and perhaps stockpiling them with neutron warheads in the United States, NATO would communicate a clear intent to raise the nuclear threshold. This step would also simplify military planning and free dual purpose delivery vehicles currently stationed in Western Europe for conventional purposes.

Such a scheme might even provide a more convincing rationale for LRTNF. If battlefield nuclear weapons were removed, NATO leaders could describe LRTNF as a way to prevent any Soviet attempt to exploit the concept of the non-nuclear battlefield and also as a means to preserve a clear link between a conventional European war and the US nuclear arsenal. The current risk is that West European countries will reject LRTNF and retain short range nuclear weapons. Strategic common sense suggests a political bargain to reverse this possibility.

NATO has maintained battlefield nuclear weapons, despite widespread recognition of their military deficiencies, because they have become steeped in political symbolism. With LRTNF, they are supposed to confirm the American commitment to Western Europe. It is now clear that this symbolism has gone sour. Persevering within the old framework only highlights its inadequacies.

An Alternative Myth

Nuclear strategy has reached a dead end. NATO should recognise the limits of nuclear doctrine and learn to live with them. The legacy of a series of attempts to push doctrine beyond its limits is a security predicament that the Alliance can now solve only through a fresh look at conventional strategy. If a serious breakthrough can be made in this area, it might be possible to forge a new NATO consensus.

A clear doctrine that both redressed the nuclear bias in NATO strategy and provided a new approach to the design and deployment of conventional forces would have a number of advantages. First, it would help identify priorities for the use of scarce resources in the conventional area.

Second, it would provide a rationale for sustaining and even raising defence budgets. At the moment, the reliance on threats of nuclear escalation undermines the case for spending on conventional forces by making such spending appear wasteful and pointless. Of course, attempts to raise defence budgets face political problems of their own, although these problems normally stem more from general economic conditions and competing social priorities than from deep passions and fears. It is by no means fanciful to suggest that with a more compelling rationale and an improved economic climate defence spending could be raised. If the economic situation does not improve, it is unrealistic to expect budgetary pressures to subside. In such circumstances, NATO will still have to rethink conventional strategy because it will become unable to maintain the current range of conventional activities.

Third, the development of a doctrine that stressed conventional preparedness could alter the political balance within NATO. The United States will always be the leading power within the NATO Alliance, but current nuclear strategy accentuates US pre-eminence to a degree that is politically awkward for all concerned. Despite broad equality in most other indices of economic and military power, the striking imbalance in nuclear capabilities creates a sense that the most vital West European interests are utterly dependent on the vagaries of US policy. A NATO defence strategy that placed more emphasis on conventional forces, where the West European members make by far the greatest contribution, would increase West European influence over, and commitment to, Alliance policies.

Fourth, a strategy that was less reliant on nuclear weapons and more specific on how to enhance the deterrent effect of conventional forces would facilitate the development of criteria for arms control. These criteria would help NATO determine what weapons were dispensable, which needed protection, where rigid controls could help, and where flexibility had to be preserved. This knowledge would also help NATO escape from the mindless force-matching enshrined in the concept of parity.

Finally and most important, this approach offers the opportunity to remove strategic doctrine as a source of dispute within the Alliance. The raw military power at NATO's disposal is obviously critical to its ability to offer a credible deterrent, but just as critical is the political cohesion of the Western democracies — their ability to come together at a time of crisis to protect their common values. A consensus on defence doctrine would greatly contribute to this political cohesion.

Nuclear strategy is by no means the only source of dispute in the NATO Alliance. Conflicts of economic interest or disagreements on global security issues might cause as much damage to Alliance unity. Moreover, it is clear that a meaningful reappraisal of defence doctrine will be neither easy nor painless. If not undertaken voluntarily, however, such as reappraisal could be forced upon NATO by either continual arguments on nuclear matters or poor economic conditions. The doctrine of flexible response no longer carries conviction, and attempts to revive it through more variations on discredited nuclear themes serve only to accelerate its decline. If the alliance is not to suffer from doctrinal confusion, an alternative myth must be developed, more in tune with current strategic and political realities.

(First published in **Foreign Policy**, Washington, No. 45, Winter 1981–82)

4 Limited War, Unlimited Protest

My intention here is to put the anti-nuclear weapons movement in Europe and the arguments with which it has become associated in some sort of political context. In particular, an attempt is made to relate the movement to the broad deterioration in East-West relations as much as the specific questions relating to new types of nuclear weapons.

Over the past couple of years, the political opposition within Europe to NATO'S programme of long-range theatre nuclear force (LRTNF) modernisation has become extremely vociferous and active. Observers cannot but be impressed by the commitment and organisation of the new "peace" movements and their capacity to mobilise hundreds of thousands of supporters.[1]

The protest campaign has already had a profound effect on European politics. It has made coalition politics in Belgium and Holland even more difficult than usual; it unsettled Chancellor Schmidt, while in office, in West Germany and has put more strain on his party in opposition; it has affected the British Labour Party sufficiently to influence many not of this persuasion to leave and join the new Social Democratic Party (SDP). The campaign has also had a marked effect on intra-alliance relations. The sight of the mass demonstrations, often with a distinct anti-NATO and anti-American flavour, has confirmed certain American prejudices about the "soft-ness" of contemporary Europeans, but it has also helped to convince key members of the Reagan administration that its reputation is damaged by an excessively bellicose and militant image. It certainly has made visible activity in arms control a political necessity. Finally, the movement has stimulated a public debate about both the specific horrors of nuclear war and the state of European security in general.

The still rather inchoate debate about the fundamental issues of European security is in some ways the most interesting. Questions have been raised about the closeness of the relationship with the United States, about the future of Eastern Europe and about the specific position of Germany. A vague neutralist aspiration can be detected among the banners and the slogans, a sense that the European countries would be far better off if they somehow freed themselves from Soviet and American hegemony and joined together to bask in their common culture, tradition, and mutual interest, possibly even constituting some sort of third force.

All this has undoubtedly been immensely distressing to the members of the NATO establishment. They have not enjoyed the novelty of having decisions that reflect a delicately constructed consensus being so crudely challenged. They do not like being the butt of rude comments and unpleasant insinuations and have been appalled at the misrepresentations of their policies and plans. Their conviction is that this is all helping the Soviet Union, and they are frustrated by the lack of evidence supporting their suspicion that the protest is funded and directed from Moscow.[2] Looking forward, they are nervous about the consequences of protest sympathisers achieving real political power, particularly given the fact that the leadership of these movements is believed to be predominantly neutralist and anti-NATO.

The Need for Debate

Of all the political and strategic issues that have been raised since December 1979, it almost seems now that the least prominent is whether NATO should persevere with the plan to deploy Pershing II and cruise missiles during the rest of the 1980s, subject only to progress in the arms control talks. The LRTNF programme has become a symbol for a generation that has discovered ''the bomb'', in much the same way that a previous generation discovered it in the late

1950s. Both generations have disliked what they have found.

In my view we should regret neither this discovery nor the many difficult questions that it inevitably has prompted. It is very rare that we can make full use of our democratic institutions to have proper debates about basic security issues. Too often legislators and the media are content to leave such problems to an élite of policymakers and specialists who are believed to have mastered the unique complexities of NATO doctrine and contemporary defence policy. If the protesters wish to be taken seriously, however, they must be required to debate seriously and answer hard questions themselves on their alternative vision. In short, to welcome the opportunity for a good and constructive argument that has been made possible by the peace movement is quite different from acceding to all its demands.

Some in NATO might wish that the LRTNF decision of December 1979 could be reversed precisely because it has brought in its wake this lively debate which has raised many awkward questions and heretical thoughts. However, the debate should be fully and actively joined because the issues are so important and because the formulas with which NATO has been working since the mid-1960s are unsatisfactory and need to be scrutinise and reworked.

Other features of the current scene should also be borne in mind by those who wish to calm the passions and return to a quiet life. The first point is that just as LRTNF is a symbol for those who oppose NATO, it has also become a symbol for those who support the Alliance. However foolish the original decisions may be considered now, to retreat would undercut those politicians who, often at great risk to their careers, have been defending the Alliance.

Second, the issue that has been raised, of NATO's dependence on threats of nuclear first use and the forces needed to back up this threat, will not go away. The sacrifice of the neutron warheads to the protest movement in April 1978 did not clear the way for an easy time for LRTNF. It simply whetted the appetite of the movement. Already it is hard to imagine the NATO Council approving any new nuclear (or chemical modernisation) programmes for Europe. Most governments are simply too scared of overloading the political circuits.

The abandonment of LRTNF or the reluctance to embark on similar exercises would not be sufficient to correct the Alliance's nuclear bias. There are still plenty of nuclear weapons around the continent, from the obsolescent to the quite modern. So the result would be votes of no confidence in a nuclear force posture that would still not be wholly dismantled. Neither the protesters nor the establishment would be satisfied, with suspicions rife of either duplicity or lack of political will. If LRTNF is defeated but the short-range systems remain, then the Alliance may be left with the worst possible posture: dubious preparations for nuclear exchanges on the battlefield without the link to the superpower's strategic arsenals ostensibly provided by LRTNF.

So simply letting LRTNF go may not be a way of rationalising a component of the Alliance force structure generally agreed to be in need of reform. This can only be achieved by clear, public, and decisive choices on future military policy.

The Zero Option

Of course, there are other ways to acknowledge the opposition to LRTNF than by acceding to it. Those responsible for the LRTNF programme hoped from the start that the addition of an arms control offer to the force-modernisation plans would be sufficient to deflect the opposition. It was never envisaged that arms control would lead to the abandonment of the plans for 572 cruise and Pershing missiles, but sufficient slack was built into the numbers to allow for substantial reductions in the name of arms control.

Unfortunately, the credibility of the arms-control option suffered from the US Senate's failure to ratify SALT II and then from the marked lack of enthusiasm for arms control evident in the higher ranks of the Reagan administration. This credibility gap has yet to be closed, despite the readiness to begin talks with the Soviet Union and the adoption of the ''zero option'', by which the NATO plans would be abandoned in return for the wholesale dismantling of the

Soviet SS-4, and SS-20 missiles.[3] In part, the lingering suspicions stem from the protest movements detecting political unreality in such a radical proposal. They doubt whether it ever would have been adopted had there been any chance of its being accepted by the Russians.[4] However justified these doubts may be, it is hardly up to unilateral disarmers to pass judgment on what is and is not realistic in bilateral negotiations.

There is actually far more consistency of approach in President Reagan's espousal of the zero option and deep cuts in strategic arms than is realised by many in Europe. The irrelevance of arms control unless ''real reductions'' can be made has been a constant theme of the anti-SALT lobby in the United States, as well as of the pro-disarmament lobby in Europe. An undercurrent in the administration's thinking has been that theatre nuclear forces will be quite unnecessary once the confidence of Europeans has been regained by the programme of rearmament at the strategic level, and by robust leadership in general foreign policy.[5]

The zero option is less a contradiction for the Reagan administration than it is for European governments that have long stressed the essential role of US nuclear forces based in Europe as a mechanism for coupling the defence of the continent to US strategic forces. The ''European view'', by one of those many convenient formulas that are used in NATO as a substitute for fresh analysis, was that theatre forces had to be protected from arms control because they represented a unique requirement for NATO to which there was no Warsaw Pact equivalent. At the beginning of SALT, a conscious decision was made not to press the issue of Soviet intermediate-range and ballistic missiles so that the United States would be able to resist Soviet pressure to include the US forward-based systems (now subsumed under the general category of LRTNF).[6] Similarly, in the discussions within the high-level group that formulated the LRTNF policy, there was resistance to the notion that the new programme was needed simply to match the SS-20. The requirement of a nuclear link between the United States and Europe was not one that would disappear if the Soviet Union could be persuaded to remove all its own intermediate-range missiles.[7]

Yet the logic of arms control always made it likely that this instinct toward parity and trade-offs between Soviet and American systems would prevail. The politicians could not be expected to desist from mentioning the active Soviet modernisation plan in justifying NATO's, and thus a close connection between cruise and Pershing missiles and SS-20s was soon well established in the public mind. In a display of even-handedness, the protest movement called for the prohibition of both US and Soviet systems. As such a prohibition would be far more costly for the East than the West (because the deployment of SS-20s is so well advanced), the temptations for the Reagan administration toward the zero option were enormous. It would not only put the Soviet Union on the spot, forcing it to explain its negative response to the demands of the disarmament movement it had so actively supported; but the option would also disarm the disarmers themselves by appropriating their slogans.

All this was politically very clever, though the influence either on the course of the domestic political debate in Europe or on the arms control negotiaitons was less than had been expected.

The success of the zero option depended on it either serving as the basis of a US-Soviet agreement or as a means of passing the blame for a nuclear arms race in Europe on to the USSR. Both of these possible objectives depended in turn on the Reagan administration managing to give the appearance of taking the negotiating exercise seriously. Unfortunately this was found to be difficult. The initiative was partly lost by the failure to maintain momentum in arms control, with the continual delays in returning to negotiations on central strategic arms. After it had become clear that the zero option could not serve as the basis for an agreement, the administration appeared to have run out of ideas. All it could do was reiterate the first proposal as if the alternatives were "zero or nothing". Towards the end of 1982 in addition to derision from the disarmament movement, there were signs of impatience within NATO at this lack of flexibility (and even within the administration itself). [8]

In the closing weeks of 1982 the new Soviet leader Yuri Andropov provided President Reagan with a lesson in artful public relations.[9] For most of that year the USSR had been pursuing in public its own proposal, which was to cut all medium-range missiles and bombers to 300 for each alliance by the end of the decade. This proposal had not made much impression, as it was based on a highly contrived presentation of the "theatre balance", ignored Soviet systems based east of the Urals and was promising cuts largely in systems that would be expected to be dismantled soon on the grounds of age. In the middle of the year there had been informal hints by the Soviet negotiator that the USSR might be interested in accepting a sub-limit on its modern SS-20s, and the two chief negotiators even appear to have worked out, in as non-committal a manner as possible, the outlines of a possible deal.

In November 1982 the outlines of these ideas were leaked in Washington, after it had also been revealed that the chief US negotiator Paul Nitze had been told not to pursue them, as this would indicate a softening of the zero option.[10] Further signs of deviation in Washington such as hints of new proposals involving 100–200 missiles for each side being canvassed in the State Department and the Arms Control and Disarmament Agency (ACDA) were also stamped upon by the Pentagon. However, the revelation of the Soviet ideas, which were not a formal offer, allowed all the European frustrations in Europe to well to the surface and there was a clamour that it be taken seriously. Andropov quickly exploited this by making the offer firm, and casting it in a dramatic mode by linking Soviet SS-20 numbers with the 162 British and French missile forces. While this was still being digested a Warsaw Pact meeting in Prague came forward with an offer of a non-aggression pact.

Meanwhile Soviet spokesmen were spreading gloom about the future of the Geneva negotiations, in a context which made it clear which side would be responsible for any failure. The fact that the USSR had been the first to reject the negotiators' deal from Geneva and were still vetoing any deal which allowed the United States to deploy *some* new missiles attracted less attention. By early 1983 President

Reagan was forced to acknowledge that an inflexible and dismissive response to Andropov would no longer suffice. Vice-President George Bush was dispatched to Europe to explore the possibility of devising something a little more positive, and the governments of Germany, Italy and Britain prepared the ground by observing that it was now possible to conceive of an interim agreement, prior to the achievement of zero all around, which might allow a little bit for everyone.

The significance of this saga lies in the further evidence it provides of reluctance to address directly the issue of the role of nuclear forces in NATO doctrine. The hope has been that an active and visible involvement in arms control will impress those sections of public opinion worried about NATO's intentions, but there are few clear ideas as to the actual objectives to be pursued within the negotiations. The zero option is at variance with the doctrine that supposedly formed the original LRTNF programme and if, by some mischance, this proposal were adopted, then again the NATO force posture would be rationalised in such a way as would leave it weak where it needed strengthening — with its worse features accentuated. The public negotiating surrounding the talks in late 1982 and early 1983 demonstrated a concern more with the strategic relationship itself. Any prospective agreement would reflect a hard bargain rather than a clear strategic concept.

It can be argued, of course, that NATO doctrine is so confused that it can support a great variety of alternative force postures without any apparent discomfort. Moreover, as the mechanisms of deterrence are so uncertain, it is difficult adamantly to maintain that any particular set of weapons is critical to its effective functioning. By this argument new distortions in the force posture and inconsistencies in its rationale are far less important than the immediate problem of calming public opinion and preventing anti-NATO ideas from taking root. If this requires either complete surrender on LRTNF or some arms control deal to cover the retreat, then that is an acceptable price to pay.

Much can be said for the proposition that public support of the Alliance is of paramount importance and that it would be foolish to jeopardise it by persevering with a patently unpopular military agenda. Nevertheless, to apply this proposition in this case assumes that the current fuss is attributable solely to LRTNF and that it would go away if the plan were abandoned. This conclusion is based on a mis-interpretation of the sources and extent of the divisions within the Alliance.

Prejudices, Fears and Aspirations

Certain features of the LRTNF programme have been highlighted by its oponents. These include the likely proximity of the bases to centres of population and the lack of control over the use of the missiles by the host govern-ments.[11] Nonetheless, US nuclear bases are hardly novelties in Europe. The high accuracy of the new missiles certainly has been a source of criticism. These weapons were believed to be designed for "war fighting". This belief was encouraged by the apparent attraction of US admini-strations to concepts of flexible and controlled nuclear targeting as found, for example, in Presidential Directive 59 (PD 59).[12] The notion that the new technologies were eroding the restraints on nuclear use was powerful among the opponents of LRTNF. These anxieties appeared in the complaints about insidious US preparations for limited nuclear war, which I shall discuss later.[13]

Then there is the fact that many political activists in Europe have been sensitised to the nuclear issue. In Germany in particular there have been large-scale and sometimes violent protests against nuclear reactors, and it does not involve a large conceptual leap to move from worrying about the risk attached to the civilian exploitation of nuclear energy to the far greater risks attached to its military exploitation.[14] The campaigns against the neutron bomb in 1977–8 united those concerned about nuclear weapons and to some extent served as a dry run for the subsequent campaign against LRTNF. All of this made some sort of protest over LRTNF likely but it did not determine the extent of popular support or the distinctive flavour of the campaigns. These factors certainly do not explain the depth of the anti-American or anti-NATO feeling.

There are four possible explanations for this feeling. The first is simply that the Alliance in general, and the United States in particular, naturally will be blamed for military decisions made in their name. The second is that these sorts of feelings are always lurking under the surface in Europe, a consequence of resentment of Europe's dependence on the United States and the "old" continent's lingering disdain for a pushy and somewhat erratic newcomer. Third, it may well be that many now moving into positions of some influence in Europe are more disposed than were their predecessors to think ill of the United States, for they spent their formative political years campaigning against the Vietnam War. Thus, as protest is frustrated, the dislike for those held responsible grows: as a campaign concerned with the whole structure of security in Europe develops, latent fears, prejudices and aspirations find expression.

These points are all relevant, but the real clue to what has been happening may be found in the fourth explanation — that much of what has happened is a response to the hawkish trend in US foreign policy, which has exacerbated all of these other factors. The combination of the excitable reactions to the Afghanistan and Iranian crises, the stress of military responses to diplomatic problems, the failure to ratify SALT II, and, to cap it all, the election of Ronald Reagan as President (and the subsequent demonstrations of "toughness") have alarmed much of the Western European public.[15] At a time when the Soviet Union has been displaying itself in its most menacing and unappealing light, the United States has fallen all over itself to attract its share of the blame for the deterioration in international relations.

The anti-Americanism in Europe is by no means pro-Soviet. Perhaps over-conscious of past accusations, this generation of activists tends to argue for a "plague on both houses". Indeed, the full application of the activists' theories would be far more destabilising to the East than to the West: after all, the movement argues for protest within Eastern Europe to break the grip of the Soviet Union. As a strategy for disarmament, this is a trifle naive. The suppression of Solidarity in Poland, upon which inordinate hopes were placed as a sort of Eastern parallel to the peace movement, has undermined whatever credibility this strategy ever enjoyed. Even so, the predominant view in Western Europe still appears to be that in recent years it has been the West, led by the United States, and not the East that has been accelerating the arms race, and is generally more confrontational (the USSR operating unpleasantly but at least consistently within its own sphere of influence). [16]

It should be remembered that the decision of early December 1979 to deploy cruise and Pershing II missiles in Europe took place in somewhat different political circumstances from the present. The conservative US trend culminating in the 1980 elections was evident, but a reasonable hope that SALT II could be ratified still existed. Indeed, a number of European legislators expected such ratification as the American part of an LRTNF "bargain". The diplomatic hostages had only recently been seized in Iran and Afghanistan was about to be invaded. The representatives of the NATO high-level group can be criticised for a lack of political insight as they contemplated the likely consequences of their determination to deploy new missiles in Europe, though the adoption of the parallel arms control approach indicates that they were not unaware of the need to offer hopes of a diplomatic solution to the problems they had identified. They certainly cannot be blamed for failing to anticipate the imminent crisis in both East-West and alliance relations. Few others were so prescient.

Rather than attribute the neutralist and anti-American sentiments to LRTNF, it may be more accurate to see the agitation over the missiles as a symptom of a general crisis in Atlantic relations. This crisis is over Western policy regarding the Soviet Union and particularly over what is the most appropriate response to turbulence in the Third World. If the United States were to pursue a high-risk foreign policy, then the risks of association with the United States would grow proportionately. Moreover, if the US policy was, in European eyes, misguided and misplaced, then the risks would be incurred on behalf of policies that neither commanded nor deserved allied support.

Such thoughts have not been entirely absent from the minds of elected leaders in Western Europe, even if they are rarely expressed so starkly. There have been well publicised differences over interpretation of Soviet behaviour in Afghanistan and Poland and the value of measures such as economic sanctions to influence this behaviour. In the Middle East, wide differences again prevail over the Arab-Israeli dispute and how best to promote Western interests in the Gulf. The relevant governments of course can keep these differences in perspective and accept the need for compromise but it is not surprising that others take more extreme views. This has happened not only in Europe. In the United States as well, there are clear signs of impatience with the lack of strong European support for policies considered to be in the interests of the entire Alliance.

Returning to the context in which concern was first generated over the theatre nuclear forces, the common description of the strategic problems was that some way had to be found to ''couple'' the United States to Western Europe. Many Europeans saw in SALT signs that the United States, not surprisingly, seemed to assign a lower priority to the strategic problems of Europe than to the US relationship with the Soviet Union. Suspicions were roused by the apparent readiness to tolerate Soviet Backfire bombers and SS-20 missiles only so long as they could not be used against the continental United States, while also accepting restrictions on the ground-launched cruise missiles which seemed to offer a cost-effective means of developing a European response[17]. With SALT II also confirming the strategic parity that many believed to be inexorably undermining the US guarantee to Europe, and Jimmy Carter adding a personal touch of his own to doubts about American intentions by his handling of the neutron bomb episode, LRTNF appeared to be the ideal way to reinforce the links across the Atlantic.

The very fact of agreeing on such a difficult issue could demonstrate by itself that Alliance procedures for consultation and decision making were in good working order. Though it was never put so blatantly, the underlying strategic effect of the programme was to increase the risk to the United States. Reducing vulnerability to surprise attack by putting the missiles out to sea was rejected in favour of placing them firmly on European soil, thus denying US commanders the option of turning around and going home if discretion got the better of valour. The emphasis on being able to attack Soviet territory increased the likelihood of a European war escalating into nuclear exchanges between the superpowers. Some might doubt whether this was good strategic theory. For example, how valid was the assumption that a US president would find it easier to initiate nuclear exchanges with the Soviet Union with weapons based in Europe and as a direct outgrowth of a land war on the continent? The real significance lay in the belief that America's strategic position vis-a-vis the Soviet Union had now reached such a state that Europeans would not feel safe without some local reassurances that there were US nuclear forces committed to their defence. The ingenious targeting strategies devised under the Schlesinger Doctrine of selective strikes in 1974 were insufficient. The coupling would have to be more direct.

Limited War

Given this background, it is not surprising that certain American policymakers have become extremely annoyed at the proposition, common in Europe, that the LRTNF programme was pressed upon the Allies to enable the United States to fight a limited nuclear war, confined to the continent. The proposition on limited nuclear war is easier to refute in principle than it has proved to be in practice. It is, after all, difficult to explain why a US President attempting to fight such a war would start exploding any nuclear weapons on Soviet soil, when everything the Soviets have ever written on the subject confirms that a war will stay limited only if Soviet territory is left untouched[18]. Certainly the excursions by leading members of the Reagan administration, including the President himself, into nuclear strategy hardly helped matters[19]. It is also the case that while the particular charges against cruise and Pershing missiles can be dismissed as unfounded, the accusation might hold against the shorter-range theatre nuclear forces. Perhaps with hindsight the most interesting feature of the campaign against the neutron bomb was the extent to which the limited nuclear war thesis was hardly used at all, with the indictment based more on the immorality of a capitalist-inspired bomb which supposedly could kill people but leave buildings intact.

It is very difficult for NATO to insist that there are no preparations underway for a limited nuclear war. The whole concept of escalation supposes that distinct stages exist in any war, and that if fighting can be kept within one particular stage, then the level and geographical spread of the violence may be contained. However one views battle-field nuclear weapons — as a means of signalling a willing-ness to cross the nuclear threshold or as a war-fighting supplement to conventional weapons — their use would depend upon the hope that further escalation would prove unnecessary.

This is not the place to examine limited nuclear war theory, but there are two criticisms of the concept that must be taken seriously. The first criticism is that the notion that nuclear war fighting can be controlled within predeter-mined limits is an illusion. Indeed, the adjective ''limited'' acts as a narcotic, because no war involving nuclear weapons is likely to be limited compared with any other wars in human experience. The risk is that this illusion might cause nuclear weapons to be used before other options had been exhausted and with disastrous results. The second criticism is that preparations for limited nuclear war inevitably introduce the weapons into a conflict earlier than necessary — that is, on the battlefield — and may even provide incentives for pre-emption.

It may be argued that these criticisms exaggerate the practical problems of limited and controlled nuclear use, and that the alternative of no other option than a swift move to the holocaust is hardly realistic. The basic defence, however, is that it is thankfully impossible to distinguish between myth and reality in nuclear war fighting, and that this uncertainty reinforces deterrence. If the Soviet leaders suspect that NATO is engaging in a sort of inadvertent reck-lessness, so that despite itself it has adopted an unusually dangerous strategy, then they have made an even more per-suasive case against provoking a conflict. The basic problem, of course, is whether it is possible to maintain a posture cal-culated to alarm the Soviets without alarming our own people in the process.

By focusing attention on these issues, the current debate has exposed the weakest point of NATO strategy. Many in NATO are ready to acknowledge the difficulty of justifying dependence on the threat of nuclear first use to the public. The debate at this level is solely about strategy. One may think the doctrine foolish and even dangerous without deny-ing the importance of deterrence or that its achievement is difficult. Yet many of the critiques of theatre nuclear forces developed over the past couple of years appear to be about something quite different.

Let us assume that a limited war of some sort is perfectly feasible under contemporary conditions, but that it is inevit-able that in any European war the European people will suffer far more than any external powers that choose to be involved. In the two world wars of this century, the Euro-pean democracies may have resented the fact that their American allies got off so lightly by comparison, but this was certainly no reason to reject US assistance when eventually offered. National survival was at stake. Whatever its motives, America's entry into the war against Hitler was in support of a European cause. The Allies were in no position to be self-righteous about equality of suffering. Indeed, given the opposition of US isolationists, Europeans could accept that American intervention was more likely in a "limited liability" war for them.

Nonetheless, European attitudes would have been quite different if the United States had picked a fight with Nazi Germany for reasons of its own, perhaps while the other democracies were still practising appeasment, and if battle had been joined on European soil. Thus, the tolerance of limited war depends on political context. Is the external power, for whom the war is inevitably a limited affair, acting to support its own narrow interests or to support the interests of friends in the locality?

The growth in alarm in Europe over the past few years over what are believed to be American plans for limited nuclear war reflects an underlying concern that such a war might be started by the Americans for reasons that have much to do with the US global struggle with the Soviet Union and very little to do with European interests.[02] A scenario frequently mentioned is a superpower clash in the Persian Gulf which would be immediately taken up in Europe, because that is where the two powers are most ready for conflict. The assumption of potential conflicts of interest between the United States and its Allies is therefore crucial to the whole anti-nuclear movement. To explain how the Europeans could allow themselves to be used thus, the literature of the movement suggests that the Western Europeans have lost control of the relevant decisions. Those who make policy are caught up in a NATO culture. There is a horizontal network across the Alliance connecting defence and foreign ministries and military officials that make them neglectful of the true needs of those they are supposed to represent. From this perspective the most outrageous feature of the LRTNF decision was neither the new missiles' capabilities nor the doctrine governing their use, but that they were under US control. If the Americans wanted to start a nuclear war for their own purposes from their European bases, there would be nothing the host governments could do to stop them. (Although in crude, physical terms this is never going to be wholly true.)

So while the European view as late as 1979 stressed the need to ''couple'' the United States more closely to Europe, two years later the question was whether Europe wanted to be so closely tied to the United States. Rather than the missile programme prompting a sudden re-examination of European loyalties, it was the reappraisal of European loyalties resulting from the tension of recent years that cast the LRTNF programme in a new and more ominous light.

The Concept of Coupling

In 1979 the argument in favour of LRTNF was that it

provided a demonstration of an American commitment to the defence of Europe. By 1982 the argument was that unless the Europeans agreed to host the new missiles, the Americans would not consider Europe worth defending. This analysis therefore casts doubts on the view that alliance relationships can be regulated by means of carefully designed missile programmes irrespective of the general political context. NATO policymakers looked in 1978–79 to the concept of coupling to provide them with guidance. To avoid "decoupling", it was necessary not to emphasise the strategic separateness of Europe from America, so there must be no talk of a "theatre" or "Eurostrategic" balance distinct from the central strategic balance. On the other hand, there must be tangible evidence of the US determination to defend its allies and to take grave nuclear risks on their behalf, so some American nuclear weapons must be based in Europe.

It is a matter of fine judgment to discern the point at which a US missile build-up in Europe stops signalling resolve to protect allies and starts signalling a willingness to unload upon Europe all the risks of an East-West confrontation. In practice it has proved extremely difficult to use missile deployments to signal anything very subtle, and whatever messages were envisaged in the 1979 plans, they soon were obscured by the imperatives of the political debate, which led to a close link between NATO cruise missiles and Soviet SS-20s, and the logic of arms control which, in turn, led to the zero option. The zero option is highly decoupling in principle but could be considered perfectly coupling in practice — at least in the short term — in helping to survive a political crisis.

Thus, the strength of the Alliance bond is only loosely related to the pattern of US military deployments made on behalf of NATO. The political symbolism accompanying these deployments is usually of such ambiguity that the impression they make will be governed largely by existing political prejudices and assumptions. When the interest is confined to those specialising in these matters, then the familiar hand-me-down formulas about "coupling" or "nuclear thresholds" or "flexible responses" may serve to shape attitudes, but when people come to the issues fresh, then much more basic and intuitive responses are likely to come to the fore.

To argue that US missile deployments are not a certain cement for the Alliance is not to argue that they must inevitably cause cracks. Anti-American and neutralist sentiments would not disappear if the LRTNF programme were abandoned because they reflect deep-rooted concerns about the hawkish trend in US foreign policy over a range of issues, including the management of relations with the Soviet Union and the responses to sundry Third World crises, from El Salvador to the Middle East. Nuclear strategy is a menacing enough topic at the best of times, and the fears of holocaust that have now been raised will not easily be put to rest. The effect of the hawkishness in US foreign policy has been to add urgency to this debate and to introduce the spectre of a European war prompted by US irresponsibility elsewhere in the world.

This analysis suggests that the problems of the Alliance must be viewed as a whole and that the various sources of division need to be addressed head on. In the process, possibly helped by a toning down of rhetoric and by the energetic pursuit of serious arms control at Geneva, the administration might be able to correct its image of an explosive combination of recklessness in foreign policy and a cavalier attitude about the dangers of nuclear war[21]. While this might remove some of the overlay of anti-Americanism, however, it would not by itself calm the protest movements. Now that the missile issue has reached the forefront of public debate, it will not readily subside, even if the international context becomes less forbidding.

As was seen in the campaigns against the MX missile in Utah and Nevada, opposition to neighbourhood missile sites is not solely a European phenomenon. (Nor is the ability to cloak the selfish, but perfectly understandable, basis for such opposition in lofty-sounding concerns about the immorality of an arms race and of nuclear weapons.) The Reagan administration's response to the anti-MX campaign offers one model for the response to the European protest movements: surrender. Nevertheless, for the reasons suggested at the start of this article, which do not necessarily apply to the American case, simple surrender could only delay necessary considerations of the fundamental and long-term security issues that have been raised over the past couple of years.

What is remarkable is that up to now the response to the debate by the European governments has been presentational and in the realm of arms control proposals rather than in reneging on the modernisation programme itself. The problems in the testing of both the cruise and Pershing missiles have been viewed with mixed feelings, with some hope that a "technical" reason might emerge for delaying the deployments. However, the political investment is such that the missiles would probably be delivered to their sites even if they were nothing but empty shells. The British, German and Italian governments are currently bracing themselves to receive the missiles and the storm of possibly violent protest that will accompany them. The German election in March 1983 and the British election of June 1983 have made it certain that the new missiles will be deployed. Holland and Belgium have still avoided the final commitment. They may never make it, but the striking feature is that they have avoided a definite rejection. The only parliament to have voted against the programme is that of Denmark, which refused, against the advice of the minority government, to contribute to the infrastructure programme. So despite the vast demonstrations, the unfavourable opinion polls and the awkward sense that nobody is "for" the missiles with the same passion and intensity that so many are "against", the governments have stuck to their original positions. Moreover, the main victims of the nuclear debate, the conservative parties who have stuck to NATO orthodoxy, have still prospered electorally, while the social democrats have been torn by their sense of loyalty to the Alliance and the need to accommodate the anti-nuclear movements in their ranks.

Thus there has, as yet, been no surrender. What has begun however is a serious debate on security policy as governments have been forced to explain themselves to their electorates and to confront the possibility that existing

doctrine is flawed. This is healthy. Neither alternative, that
is to "stonewall for NATO" — in order to defend all of its
current force posture from criticism — nor to sacrifice the
most controversial portion of this posture in the hope that
the rest can escape intact, is satisfactory. Both options are
unsatisfactory because the public debate on security policy
is unlikely to stop with LRTNF. If one programme were
turned off because of the accompanying protest, would
NATO dare to initiate other programmes lest the furore start
up again? Or would matters of possible controversy be
handled in a surreptitious manner in the hope that nobody
would notice, with the result that when someone did notice
the uproar would be even greater? In practice, the Alliance
is quite properly incapable of functioning with a consistently
low profile. Even if the nuclear issues are successfully
"managed", other difficult matters remain: the parallel
question of chemical weapons; the possibility of anti-
European sentiment in the United States leading to
demands for troop withdrawals from the Central Front; the
general tensions of maintaining adequate defence at a time
of economic recession; and so on. Unless the Alliance has
clear priorities, then it risks being buffeted by a series of
economic and political pressures, often pushing in quite
contradictory directions.

Neither the modernisation nor the arms control "tracks"
alone can help NATO withstand these pressures. Some sort
of deal with the East on arms control would help if it
encouraged a modest revival in détente, although the
chance of an agreement requires the sort of bargaining that
tends to strain political relations. Anything to emerge from
the Geneva talks will reflect a process more akin to haggling
in a bazaar than the application of some strategic formula.
All available formulas (including a "freeze") would require
quite unequal concessions. At any rate, for the West, a
freeze would be slightly worse in terms of cuts in Soviet
forces than current Soviet offers and would have the dis-
advantages of the zero option in preserving the distortion in
NATO's force structure in favour of short-range forces. The
only real criterion by which many Europeans seem to judge
proposals now is "negotiability". The objective is to repair

the East-West relationship without further damage to tempers within the Alliance. Again we return to the point that military programmes and arms control agreements have to be seen in terms of the organisation of basic political relations as well as in the creation of some sort of notional military stability.

Therefore, two quite separate debates are under way. The first is over the quality of NATO doctrine and concerns such questions as the proper balance between conventional and nuclear forces and the role of arms control. The second is over the fundamental security arrangements in Europe and concerns such questions as the proper relationship between the United States and Western Europe and the future of détente.

The first of these debates is important and deserves encouragement, and is directly linked to the LRTNF programme. It must be widened, however, so that the full implications of the competing arguments can be thought through. For example, how would it raise the nuclear threshold if LRTNF were abandoned, especially if followed by cuts in US forces in a fit of American pique? The result would be to accentuate rather than diminish the role of short-range "battlefield" nuclear weapons which are the real villains of the NATO piece. The second debate brings to the fore questions of Western Europe's dependence on the United States and the possibility of some alternative arrangements with the East. These questions are prompted by much more than LRTNF and will be with us for many years, whatever happens to this particular missile programme.

Notes

1. In June 1982, for example, most European capitals witnessed massive demonstrations. The Bonn demonstration coinciding with the NATO summit involved some 350,000 people. More demonstrations of a similar size are planned for October 1983.
2. For an argument that willingly or unwillingly the peace movement serves Soviet interests see Vladimir Bukovsky, "The Peace Movement and the Soviet Union", **Commentary**, May 1982.
3. The offer was made by President Reagan in a speech to the National Press Club on 18 November, 1981.

4. For example, Herr Wilhelm Born, of the Free Democrats in West Germany and a leader of the peace movement, argued that "the prohibitive conditions which the President set can hardly be fulfilled". Others, however, welcomed the change from "sabre rattling". In Britain, Labour party leader Michael Foot was honest enough to recognise the essential similarity between Reagan's proposal and that of this own party. **The Times** (London), 20 November, 1981.

5. This view could be detected in the speeches of Eugene Rostow while Director of the Arms Control and Disarmament Agency.

6. See Uwe Nerlich, **The Alliance and Europe: Part V. Nuclear Weapons and East-West Negotiations**, Adelphi Paper No. 120 (London: International Institute for Strategic Studies, Winter 1975–6).

7. See the report prepared by the Congressional Research Service for the Subcommittee on Europe and the Middle East of the House Committee on Foreign Affairs, **The Modernization of NATO's Long-Range Theatre Nuclear Forces.**

8. For example, after a meeting of NATO's Nuclear Planning Group in November, Secretary-General Joseph Luns said, "The zero option is the ideal solution, but we never said it was the only solution". British Defence Secretary John Nott added that other proposals should be examined if they were realistic. However, US Secretary of Defence Caspar Weinberger seemed unimpressed. "What we will do in Geneva is not up to defence ministers sitting here". **Washington Times**, 1 December, 1982.

9. "Grab the initiative, take the fight to the enemy, make 'em an offer they can't refuse, dance like a butterfly, sting like a bee. That seems to sum up the style of the new Soviet leader, Yuri Andropov, has chosen for himself. For the 68-year old, scarcely younger than Ronald Reagan, his first seven weeks in office have produced a performance that would put Nijinsky and Nureyev to shame." **Sunday Times**, 9 January, 1983.

10. **International Herald Tribune**, 13 December, 1982.

11. The lack of a dual-key with these systems was partly because it was felt that they would represent a more credible threat if the United States had the only key. A second key was an offer, however, if the relevant European governments had been willing to pay: dual-key means shared ownership. The issue is being reviewed as deployment grows closer.

12. See, for example, E. P. Thompson, the "guru" of the British-based European Nuclear Disarmament campaign: "European war is to be one 'choice' or 'option' for the United States strategists, although what might appear to be 'limited' on that side of the Atlantic might appear to be spasmodic and apocalyptical on this. The cruise missiles which are being set up in Western Europe are the hardware designed for exactly such a 'limited' war, and the nations which harbour them are viewed, in this strategy, as launching platforms which are expendable in the interests of 'Western' defense." E. P. Thompson and Dan Smith, eds., **Protest and Survive**, (London: Penguin, 1980), p.42.

13. See pp. 93–6 for further discussion.

14. For background on the German anti-nuclear movement, see Dorothy Nelkin and Michael Pollak, **The Atom Besieged: Extra-Parliamentary Dissent in France and Germany**, (Cambridge, Mass: MIT Press, 1981).

15. In an opinion poll conducted in Britain in early November 1981, only 14 per cent felt that the US president showed ''sound judgment'' (the figure was 6 for Brezhnev), **The Times** (London), 25 November, 1981. The figures also showed that in Britain, American nuclear bases were far more unpopular (59 per cent) than a national nuclear deterrent (only 29 per cent favoured unilateralism). Another poll of the same month showed that 57 per cent of the population thought that Reagan's policies had made nuclear war more likely. **International Herald Tribune**, November 9, 1981.

16. See E. P. Thompson once again: ''I would hazard that the Russian state is now the most dangerous in relation to its own people and to the people of its client states . . . The United States seems to me to be more dangerous and provocative in its general military and diplomatic strategies.'' **Protest and Survive, op. cit.**, p.49.

17. See Lothar Ruehl ''The Grey Area Problem'' in Christopher Bertram (ed.), **The Future of Arms Control: Part 1, Beyond SALT II,** Adelphi Paper No. 141, (London: IISS, Spring 1978).

18. For Soviet views on these matters see **Soviet Theatre Nuclear Forces Parts 1 and 2** by Stephen Meyer, Adelphi Papers Nos. 187 and 188, (London: IISS, Winter 1983-84).

19. The greatest furore was caused by Reagan's remarks in October 1981, when, in the midst of a rather rambling answer on the inevitability of escalation following initial nuclear exchanges, he said: ''I could see where you could have the exchange of tactical weapons against troops in the field without it bringing either one of the major powers to pushing the button''. This not only confined limited nuclear war fears but also implied that nuclear exchanges in Europe involved something less than ''pushing the button.'' **International Herald Tribune**, October 21, 1981.

20. See, for example, Mary Kaldor, ''END Can be a Beginning,'' **Bulletin of Atomic Scientists**, Chicago, December 1981.

21. I am not assessing whether this image is correct, only stressing that it is widely held.

(First published in **Orbis**, Spring 1982, and revised for publication in **The Nuclear Freeze Debate: Arms Control Issues for the 1980s**, ed. Paul Cole & William J Taylor, Westview, Washington, 1983).

5 The Atlantic Crisis

The political analysis is taken a stage further with a consideration of whether there is anything in the latest crop of transatlantic disputes to suggest that they could really threaten the durability of NATO. The changing international scene and the extent to which economic factors are so critical in many of the disputes have accentuated NATO's traditional security dilemmas.

It is easier to describe the character of the malaise that afflicts the Atlantic Alliance than to explain its origins. The disputes over monetary policy, Middle East diplomacy and all aspects of relations with the Soviet Union provide regular and ample fare for the media. However, it remains unclear whether this conjunction of arguments is a temporary phenomenon brought about by the strains of recession or by the incompatibility of the current crop of political leaders, or whether we are witnessing the symptoms of a much deeper crisis that is unsettling the whole set of assumptions that have governed Western policy-making over the past three decades.

The fact that this question has already occurred to a large number of people is in itself relevant to the answer. The disarray in the Alliance at the start of 1980, caused by the twin crises over the Iranian seizure of American hostages and the Soviet invasion of Afghanistan, stimulated a surge in seminars, conferences, pronouncements and publications of all shapes and sizes, which has yet to subside, and has indeed recently been given added stimulus by the differences over how to respond to martial law in Poland.

Whatever its faults, therefore, the Alliance cannot be accused of sweeping its problems under the carpet. If anything the reverse is true. The foreign policy communities on both sides of the Atlantic ensure that the resources and the personnel are available for instant comment and speculation. The relationship at times suffers from over-analysis which, in turn, carries the risk of justifying itself by over-dramatising the issues. Signs of disagreement lead to solemn warnings that the Alliance will tear itself asunder; minor ailments are diagnosed as symptoms of a terminal illness.

Much of the comment assumes that the Atlantic Alliance is the most fragile and delicate of international relationships, unable to withstand significant tension. Yet NATO has so far survived a stormy three decades in international affairs and any number of internal arguments. The arguments across the Atlantic are rarely as fraught or as bitter as those that take place within the European Communities, yet somehow the European arguments rarely excite the same speculation over imminent fission.

Perhaps this is because the issues at stake in Europe are more tangible. The Alliance has been far less successful in allowing argument to range wide within contained boundaries, because there is not much to argue about but fundamentals. Arguments in NATO are rarely about techni-calities or the handling of specific issues. Or at least, if they start at such a level they soon move on to the first order questions: the nature and thrust of the Soviet challenge and the sharing of the burden in meeting it; the consequences of Europe's dependence on the United States for its security, and its ability or willingness to reduce this dependence. That is, it is very difficult to debate Atlantic relations without debating the underlying structure of contemporary world affairs.

This tendency inevitably induces caution among seasoned observers of NATO affairs. It becomes tempting to dismiss the current fuss as yet another round of a never-ending saga, full of sound and fury but of little relevance to a collection of nations bound together by a compelling and resilient political logic. The arguments are as much a fixture of the international scene as the Alliance itself. The 1973–4 rows connected with Henry Kissinger's launch of the ''Year of Europe'' and the responses to the Yom Kippur War and the OPEC price rises were as great as any that have so far occurred in the 1980s, yet all this passed by remarkably quickly. Nevertheless, merely to say "so what else is new?" when told of another Atlantic crisis is inadequate, for there are elements of the current situation that distinguish it from previous periods.

The Changing International Context

Some argue that the source of the problem lies in the decline of a sense of Atlantic "community" that marked the postwar period. "Atlanticism" reflected a mature idealism or at least an enlightened form of self-interest. This, they fear, is in danger of being lost forever and replaced by an un-enlightened nationalism which will undermine any form of alliance or partnership.

The Atlanticism of the generation of policy-makers responsible for the forging of close United States-European ties in the postwar years was based on much more than an appreciation of the distribution of effective world power. It was often an intensely personal commitment — a legacy of the close working relationships developed during the war which was sustained in the years of the Marshall Plan, the Berlin airlift, and the creation of NATO, and nurtured on a certain vision of how close co-operation between the Western democracies could usher in a new era of peace and prosperity.

It is important not to overstate the ideals and cohesion of that generation. The commitment of those "present at the creation" of the Alliance was to a large extent a function of the political battles waged against others of that generation with alternative views as to the propriety of alliance. In fact, defenders of NATO still tend to see their antagonists as direct descendants of the first opponents. The fear is of "isolationism" in the United States or "neutralism" in Europe. In so far as the arguments against alliance always stress the risk of being drawn into something dangerous or foolish by the partner, then a certain continuity in the forms of opposition is to be expected.

However, opinion polls have not detected any groundswell in anti-NATO feeling in the member states (again the comparison with the European Community is instructive). But the approval is combined with a generally hazy notion as to what NATO actually is. In the United States the lack of media coverage of European affairs has long been noted. This has now been reinforced by a general loss of interest in these matters, as evidenced by the decline in European studies in the universities. The European language most favoured is Spanish rather than French or German, and this reflects preoccupations with Latin America rather than Spain. Europeans often suspect that American uninterest in them is matched by an increasing interest in the Pacific region, as a result of the shift in power and population in the United States from the East to the West coasts and the increase in the proportion of American trade accounted for by Pacific countries. Yet the Japanese claim not to be aware of any surge of interest and knowledge in their affairs. The change may be not so much in a switch of attention from the Atlantic to the Pacific, and so a rival set of attitudes on the international scene, as in a growing preoccupation with domestic affairs and interest in foreigners — whether they be Mexicans or Arabs or Germans — only to the extent that they impinge on domestic affairs. The Eastern establishment that long provided the guidelines and recruits for American foreign policy has never really recovered from the shock of Vietnam but it has yet to be replaced.

Introspection is not unique to the United States. The same phenomena can be observed throughout Europe with the inclination to blame ''foreigners'' for national ills and to concentrate on ways in which the nation can prosper and generally follow its own path, no matter what others may say and do. Moreover, the economic troubles of the past decade have rendered political activity less predictable, though more engrossing. National policy, whether for domestic or external consumption, has become correspondingly less coherent and consistent. This turns into a vicious circle. Introspection and instability at home have a negative effect on foreign policy. With many of the major powers displaying the same tendencies the risk of conflicts of interest, or at least conflicts of perception of interests, grows while any co-operative endeavours falter. The effect of this is to make the domestic problems less tractable and so on. The domestic preoccupations leave politicians with less time and energy to attend to external affairs. In all this the "European ideal" has suffered as much as the "Atlantic ideal".

The problem facing the Atlantic Alliance is therefore nothing so simple as active hostility, led by the twin evils of isolationism and neutralism. Such a view may assume far too much of a positive interest in the actual structure of international relations. The real risk may be of a drifting apart, fuelled largely by indifference and introspection, rather than some dramatic and decisive break in the Alliance bond.

For our earlier generation of policy-makers "the Atlantic" provided a natural point of reference for all international issues. Through colonies and spheres of influence, the politics of the rest of the world was an extension of the politics of the United States and the old European powers (including the old outsider, Russia). Relations between the constituent parts of the Atlantic community were not necessarily cordial — for example over Suez — but one way or another they had to work together. Over the past 20 years other powers have intruded into this framework. The end of the empires has meant that the former colonies have had to be dealt with on their own terms and the "old powers" find themselves competing to gain footholds in each others' ex-colonies; Japan has emerged as a world economic power and other small Asian nations have become industrial trend-setters; the Arab states have been attempting to buy political muscle with oil.

Thus, the quality of the Atlantic relationship can no longer be the determinant of a stable world order. Foreign policy has to be wide-ranging. When political power and economic strength are diffused then policy-makers on the two sides of the Atlantic cannot be forever attending to each other's needs, points of view and sensibilities. Moreover, policy-makers now have to cope with a much more complex set of linkages than before. The days when something called "high politics" could be undertaken as a separate and aloof activity have passed. The economic and political spheres are becoming increasingly merged, which means that the ramifications of all decisions have become correspondingly more complicated.

Thus the strains facing the Alliance reflect fundamental changes in the international system and cannot be eased simply by a reassertion of the Atlantic spirit. An international system that is not working properly is generally unsettling and cannot but affect all relations between states as well as their domestic affairs. Moreover, states are likely to vary in their reactions. An unresponsive international environment can induce a sense of resigned fatalism or of desperate activism. The increased diversity and complexity of the environment creates new interests and preoccupations, cuts across old ties and undermines old assumptions.

In these conditions it is not surprising if the United States and the Europeans develop alternative perspectives on the international system and their positions within it. Apart from anything else, as problems that once might have been quite manageable prove to be intractable, the views taken of each other become less generous. Increasingly behaviour is seen to be unreasonable, unpredictable, and unreliable. Whether or not quite different mind-sets have emerged on each side of the Atlantic is more difficult to say. We talk of the "European" and "American" positions as if they were homogeneous and consistent though, of course, they are not. When governments change rapidly, so do policies. It was not long ago that Europeans were bemoaning the naïve idealism of President Carter. A popular anti-nuclear movement is no longer unique to Europe. If in recent years the United States has tended to take a more hawkish view on challenges than has Europe, the Falklands crisis shows how easily stereotypes can be reversed — with a European country pressing on with a military solution while the United States searches for even-handed mediation. Nevertheless, the Falklands crisis has put extra strains on the Alliance, largely because the United States has not felt able to offer the whole-hearted support that has been expected of the allies when America has faced its own problems, and which Britain, more than most, has tried to provide. This illustrates the basic problem: that in any given trouble-spot it is unlikely that American and European interests will directly coincide.

It also indicates what may be the major divergence of substance: the priority given by the United States to opposing communism as a major foreign policy objective. This is why it was reluctant to come down too hard on Argentina which has supported American policy on Central America. Related to this is Washington's increasing difficulty in accepting the legitimacy of the Soviet Union as a major international actor with a role to play in the settlement of disputes. However, apart from this important divergence in view, the key point of this analysis is to stress the features of the contemporary international situation that make it more likely that the members of the Atlantic Alliance will disagree on a variety of issues, rather than the specific content of the disagreement.

The Economic Malaise

We can take this diagnosis further by examining the economic sphere. In the early days of the Alliance the United States dominated the international economy. The relationship between the United States and Western Europe is now quite balanced. The United States is still the largest economic unit in the world but its GNP is smaller than the combined total for Western Europe. The role of the dollar as a reserve currency has not yet been seriously challenged by the Deutschmark, Swiss Franc, or the ECU of the European Monetary System, which leaves the United States pre-eminent in the international monetary system. However, in trade terms the United States has become more dependent on Western Europe. Its general dependence on trade has grown (to around 12 per cent of GNP), and in its pattern of trade Europe assumes a critical role as the only major region with which it enjoys a consistent surplus, thereby offsetting the deficits with OPEC and the industrially dynamic countries of Asia, and as the area most able to absorb extra exports when American competitiveness increases. In addition, nearly half the earnings from America's direct investment come from Western Europe.

Even measured by extra-Community trade the Europeans are still twice as dependent on trade as the United States. However, for Western Europe the United States is declining as an export market. There has been a shift toward intra-European trade — in the broadest sense. Trade with the centrally planned economies, although this may now have passed its peak, is nearly as important to Western Europe as that with the United States (this is particularly true for West Germany with the high levels of intra-German trade).

The United States and Europe are in quite different positions when it comes to supplies of raw materials. In neither oil nor non-fuel minerals is the United States as close to self-sufficiency as it once was, but the dependence is still less than that of Western Europe. For example, America's dependence on oil imports was down to 42 per cent in 1980 (a significant decline since the peak of 50 per cent in 1977) while European dependence still hovers at close to 90 per cent. Thus, trouble in the resource-rich areas of the Third World has graver implications for Europe than for the United States. As American dependence remains substantial, serious risk is not absent. So the importance of the differential dependence may be less the actual difference it makes than that which it is widely believed to make.

All this provides good reason for close co-operation in the formulation of economic policies but it also reinforces the impression of a drifting apart, as each of the partners tries to sort out its position in a complicated web of relationships. Furthermore, the continuing sense of economic uncertainty and the bouts of deep recession that have afflicted Western economies since the early 1970s have encouraged calls for more nationalistic economic policies and, in a more general sense, have encouraged the preoccupation with domestic issues which can soon turn into insularity when it comes to considering the interests and sensibilities of foreigners.

In the past, and simplifying somewhat, the United States was in a position of slight dependence on the international economy while exercising substantial influence over its managment and behaviour. It was able, in the 1950s and 1960s, to regard the international economy as an extension of the American economy and proceed on the assumption that what was healthy for the latter was healthy for the former. There was some validity in this approach in that the size of the American economy had (and to some extent still has) a major influence on the world economy, and in that all the developed economies enjoyed an unprecedented period of economic prosperity. Since then there have been two related changes: the relative decline of America's economic power; and the slowing-down (or stoppage altogether) of the pace of economic growth. The Europeans now feel that the United States ought to be more willing to co-operate on an equal footing, and that they are no longer obliged to accept whatever economic pressures flow across the Atlantic as some force of nature.

Transatlantic arguments are therefore likely to be frequent and substantial. The particular sources of controversy may vary — high inflation one moment, high interest rates the next. The main point is that significant interdependence without effective forms of co-operation and co-ordination (or one party being in a sufficiently dominant position to impose his will) means that domestic economic policies and trends in the key countries of the Alliance are rarely mutually supporting. One pursues tight money policies while another dashes for growth; one trusts the market, another is more dirigiste. Increasing public frustration in the West at the inability of governments, of whatever complexion, to find an optimum mix of economic policies has led in many countries to regular changes of government and correspondingly regular shifts of policy. France now has succumbed to this trend, and Germany may soon follow.

Need regular argument on economic matters undermine the overall Atlantic relationship? The only comfort to be found is of a negative kind. First, while the two sides may blame each other for a part of their economic woes, they are likely to blame Japan and OPEC even more. International economic problems cannot be properly understood let alone solved, on a transatlantic basis. However, what can be done on a transatlantic basis may be less difficult than other forms of co-operation. Secondly, the United States put its allies on notice a decade ago that it could no longer sustain the post-war economic arrangements. The 1971 collapse of the Bretton Woods system provided a severe jolt to America's allies, and it has complicated life ever since, but it did not lead to a collapse of the Alliance nor, for that matter, to a collapse in the international economy.

So the 1971 experience suggests that a major economic row need not have a direct impact on the Alliance, certainly not in the sense of causing a dramatic rupture. That being said, the indirect effects can be significant and in the long run possibly as damaging. With the generally weak economic performance since 1971, and the more nationalist inclinations this has encouraged, there has been an erosion of shared rules and conventions, in particular in GATT and the OECD, which has in turn made it more likely that specific trade disputes (for example over steel or textiles) will get mixed up with general arguments over the regulation of economic interests. Not only is squabbling over economic relations not going to make it easier to cope with differences over security policy, but it is difficult to confine such erosions in Atlantic understanding to the economic sphere alone.

Factors Undermining the Alliance

The Atlantic Alliance is essentially about security. Even much of the stimulus to the post-war economic arrangements came from a fear that unless the Western world could be reinvigorated the challenge from the East might prove to be irresistible. If the basic logic of NATO remains valid then the Alliance may hold irrespective of the disagreements between the member countries on economic matters.

However it is impossible to isolate the military side of the Atlantic relationship. The most obvious reason for this is the high cost of defence. The economic troubles of the past decade ended the surge in public expenditure that had marked the 1960s. Now defence spending either has to be made a special case (with an obvious potential for arguments based on "guns versus butter") or else, if it too is held back, it is necessary to tolerate a diminution in the overall defence effort (given that spending must rise annually by a few per cent in real terms solely to keep pace with the higher inflation in defence goods and services than that obtaining in the civilian sector). Most likely the relentless pressure on spending priorities will lead to a gradual reduction in national contributions to the collective defence effort. Despite current appearances, the United States cannot be excluded from this prediction, but there is a clear potential for argument if the Europeans' defence effort is being cut while that of the United States (for the time being) is undergoing expansion, and if subsequent American cuts are justified by European failings.

An added twist to this developing debate on burden-sharing illustrates the connection between the erosion of understanding in the economic sphere and the loss of cohesion in the security sphere. The Reagan administration's attempts to combine high defence spending with lower taxes in the absence of high rates of economic growth, has resulted in an interest-rate regime which represents a set-back to European economic hopes (or at least has been described as such in Europe). This in turn makes it unlikely that the Europeans will feel willing or able to respond to calls for increases in defence spending comparable to that planned by the United States.

There is another, and probably more fundamental sense in which the changes in the economic sphere influence those in the security sphere. The diffusion of economic power over the past two decades, largely away from the United States, means that Western Europe is now in a stronger position vis-a-vis the United States but has to take account of other important groupings, of which the oil producers and the East European economies are politically important while the newly industrialising countries (NICs) play an increasingly prominent role in trade. The United States can no longer ignore these groupings, but it is still relatively self-sufficient so that it imports proportionately much less of its oil requirements from the Middle East than does Western Europe, and conducts a remarkably small amount of overseas trade with the Soviet Union and Eastern Europe. During the 1970s the Middle East and Eastern Europe became politically more sensitive — a shift that explains more than variations in the actual trading relations. Western Europe has much more at stake in its economic relations with both than has the United States and this puts a cloud over all Alliance diplomacy. The Europeans feel that they are being asked to bear the brunt of any high-risk American diplomacy, particularly if it is based on economic sanctions, while the Americans suspect that the weakness in the European stance on many issues reflects their economic dependence.

To appreciate the significance of both these types of arguments we must now turn to the security debate itself. My point is that the logic of the current debates, within NATO, and especially of the European position within these debates, is accentuating the importance of the issues of defence spending and the relative dependence of the United States and Western Europe in the international economy.

It is probable that the NATO arrangements themselves are far more resilient than is often supposed because if the allies want to sort out their problems they have the means to do so. If the Alliance can hold together and sustain a serious military capability, even if this capability does not meet the most exacting standards, then it probably can keep the Soviet Union in check. There is probably more freedom of manoeuvre available than is normally admitted in shaping NATO's overall deterrent.

The asymmetrical nature of the relationship ensures continual tension, in that the Europeans will always be nervous about being sold out or subjected to undue risk, and the Americans will grumble about shouldering dispro-portionate burdens. Nevertheless, it is unlikely that any party to a NATO debate will feel that its security position will actually be improved by the break-up of the Alliance.

If it is not quite so easy in practice this is not only because the Soviet military build-up has undermined confidence in NATO's position. The basic problem is that NATO has allowed itself to put at the centre of its strategic doctrine the dubious proposition that an American President would authorise first use of nuclear weapons in response to a Warsaw Pact conventional invasion of Western Europe that looks like succeeding.

West European dependence on this myth has become one of the more unsettling features of United States-European relations. Yet although it is intellectually unconvincing, in that it requires the United States to threaten suicidal action on behalf of its allies, it is politically viable, in that the Soviet Union is unlikely to wish to try to call America's bluff. It is an act of faith for the United States to offer, and the West Europeans to accept, a nuclear guarantee which can be sustained so long as both sides engage in an elaborate process of mutual reassurance. Because of this, Alliance doctrine has acquired a heavy overlay of symbolism. This is one reason why discussions of Atlantic relations soon get down to fundamentals, for every move in the security sphere is immediately treated in symbolic terms.

As this symbolism has had to accommodate changing political and strategic circumstances it has become extremely complicated and is therefore imperfectly understood, even by the NATO establishment. The fierce debate surrounding the introduction of long-range theatre nuclear weapons illustrates what happens when unchallenged presumptions of NATO orthodoxy are submitted simultaneously to public questioning and a new strategic situation. The same confusion can be seen with conventional forces: in the first half of the 1960s Europeans saw America's stress on improving conventional forces as evidence of a willingness to deny Europe the best available means of deterrence; by the end of the decade they had come to see threatened reductions of conventional forces as evidence of a willingness to desert the continent altogether. Now, as noted below, many Europeans are coming round to the view that, in principle, a greater conventional emphasis may be sensible after all.

It is common to blame the current confusion in NATO strategic doctrine on the Soviet Union's achievement of parity in nuclear capabilities with the United States. But the prospect of a nuclear stalemate has figured in Alliance calculations since the first Soviet atomic test of 1949, and the state of mutual assured destruction was proclaimed in the mid-1960s. It has certainly become more evident in a strictly numerical sense but the real change is in the judgement of the consequences of parity.

In the 1960s only the French argued that parity had rendered America's nuclear guarantee worthless. The rest of the allies took the view that it was not necessary for there to be a certainty or even a likelihood that the United States would wage nuclear war on Europe's behalf — only a risk just large enough for no Soviet leader to ignore it. This begged the question of what actually could be done to remedy the situation if deterrence failed, but only because it was felt that there was no pressing need to pose the question. During the 1970s this question became difficult to ignore. This was in part a result of the loss of confidence in détente and a concern that, at least in the Third World, the Soviet Union was willing to take higher risks in its foreign policy.

Also, American strategists, displaying a rather clinical and apolitical approach to their subject, became preoccupied with the question of what happens if deterrence fails. Unless a satisfactory answer can be found, it was argued, then the whole edifice of deterrence itself will collapse — for the threats upon which it depends will be exposed as worthless. To remedy this position either American superiority must be regained, or NATO's position at the lower levels of the escalation ladder reinforced. Otherwise a gradual but inexorable process of accommodation to Soviet power has to be accepted.

The strategic logic of this line of argument is not matched in political logic, for it could lead to a self-induced crisis of strategic doctrine quite out of proportion to the actual state of East-West relations. Yet once the process had begun, and the sense of strategic crisis was beginning to grip the United States, the Europeans could not avoid the argument. In the first instance this was simply because this approach was so influential in the United States.

This can be illustrated by reference to the ''European

view" on the Strategic Arms Limitation Talks (SALT) because SALT provided the focal point for American critics of strategic parity. Around 1977–8, it was not unreasonable for conservative critics of SALT in the United States to assume that their fears were shared by the allies. The most visible European input into the debate was a series of worried queries on the impact of particular constraints on weapon systems and mooted non-circumvention clauses. What the conservatives failed to realise was that not only did the European governments lack a thoroughgoing critique of SALT, and so could be satisfied on these various queries, but that their concern for the health of détente meant that they had a positive interest in the talks succeeding. When this became apparent in 1979 the conservatives had to insist that the official European voice now being heard was quite different from that of *their* European contacts and so not truly authentic. The suspicion grew that the allies had been "got at" and so spoke only under duress.

In 1981, the new Reagan administration soon discovered that the allies' view of arms control was more firmly based than it had suspected and that they would not be reassured by American displays of military preparedness. When Secretary of Defence Caspar Weinberger spoke in February 1981 about the likelihood of the "neutron bomb" being reinstated he thought this would be welcomed by the Europeans who had been let down so much by President Carter's abrupt change of policy in 1978, and so must have been surprised, if not persuaded, by the European anxiety on this matter.

To the Reagan administration this sort of reaction, and the evident second thoughts in Europe over the advisability of the long-range theatre force modernisation programme, confirmed the impression of an appeasing and neutralist trend. Given the frames of reference of many of the key American policy-makers and strategists, a likely explanation for the European, and particularly the West German, position was that the gradual process of accommodation was underway. The attempts to shore up nuclear deterrence by new programmes and strategies had failed to convince the Europeans who were now in danger of slipping away.

For the West European governments the real problem was that the attempt to solve a crisis in NATO strategic doctrine that had been largely self-induced, by playing around with all sorts of American nuclear options, had turned into a genuine crisis. Articulate sections of European public opinion came to agree with the American view that the real question, to which the state of East-West relations added urgency, was what happens if deterrence fails. The answer was inevitably unappealing, and NATO's large arsenal of theatre nuclear forces made it more so.

West European leaders found themselves accused by Americans of succumbing to Soviet power, because of their inability to accept what is necessary to make deterrence work, and accused by many of their own people of succumbing to American power by accepting, via nuclear weapons, all the risks of a hawkish American foreign policy. To argue back to both that the likelihood of deterrence breaking down in the form of an all-out war in Central Europe is too remote to warrant all this tension within the West and expenditure of so much nervous energy, hardly seemed adequate.

It might be possible to restore some faith in deterrence by calming East-West relations and the associated arms race by effective measures of arms control, but it is difficult to be optimistic on this score. So, despite themselves, European governments are being forced to address the crisis of doctrine. Political circumstances and, it so happens, strategic logic dictate only one response: to raise the nuclear threshold and, by improving conventional forces, rid the Alliance of the burden of having to threaten nuclear first use. This has in the past generally been considered to be preferred American approach, and certainly many involved in the current European debates see it as a likely compromise.

The economic logic, unfortunately, is not so compelling. The long-standing European preference for nuclear deterrence has been based on an unwillingness to fund a much more expensive conventional defence. It is not inconceivable that substantial improvements in the quality of conventional defences could be achieved by more efficient use of existing resources, but the resources are becoming more scarce. Unless the economic performance of NATO countries improves markedly, hard choices are going to have to be made between, on the one hand, holding down defence expenditure and so increasing NATO's nuclear bias with all the associated political problems, or, on the other, redressing the bias by raising expenditure with unfortunate consequences for other social and economic objectives with their own associated political problems.

Divergences in Global Perspectives

Even if the doctrinal issue could be solved there is no reason to suppose that the current disquiet in Europe on American security policies would quickly evaporate. Part of the critique of the anti-nuclear movement, which finds resonance in polls sampling European public opinion, concerns the combative approach of the Reagan administration to its foreign policy problems. Again this is something that might be remedied by a less assertive American diplomacy or possibly by international developments that might convince public opinion of the need for a certain degree of toughness. However it may also be that there is a longer-term generational factor at work. The incitement to the anti-nuclear movements in Europe was undoubtedly the publicity surrounding first the neutron bomb and then cruise missiles, but they were given direction by leaders whose inspiration draws as much from suspicion of the United States as from any coherent theory of the arms race. These leaders gained credibility from American behaviour during 1980 and the election of Mr Reagan with his entourage of zealous hawks. If East-West relations improve then these movements may subside, even if the objects of their protest remain. The long-term implications of these movements is the growing influence of activists who developed their beliefs during the days of student radicalism and anti-Vietnam War protest in the late 1960s and are now moving up the political, academic, media and bureaucratic hierarchies. The fading away of the generation whose

Atlanticism was based on the intimate co-operation of the Second World War and post-war reconstruction has been noted. What may now be the case is the ascendancy of a generation with an in-built suspicion of American foreign policy.

This has clear implications if the centre-piece of American foreign policy over the coming decades is going to be a robust and indiscriminate stance against all manifestations of communism. For the new European activists, the critique of NATO military doctrine only gains force because of a prior critique of the risks of American foreign policy in the Third World. If deterrence fails, it often appears to be assumed, this will not be because of a political breakdown in Central Europe but because of superpower conflict in the Third World that will then spill over into Europe.

While few West European leaders would endorse the more sinister interpretation, it is the case thay they have on occasion been unnerved by elements of American policy. Certainly, the "Vietnam syndrome" by which one legacy of the sorry Indochina experience was believed to be an unnatural reticence in the conduct of American foreign policy, was always much more of an American than a European diagnosis. By and large the Allies have been far more concerned about the Americans rushing in to new foreign escapades than holding back and, while never quite sure about the proper mix of military muscle and diplomacy, are still happier when the error is on the side of soft talk rather than big sticks. Nevertheless, as has already been pointed out, the Falklands crises reminds us that simply to pose American militarism against European restraint is to caricature both parties. But the crisis has underlined the way in which America's sense of its global role — and in particular its desire to line up anti-communist coalitions — can give it a different set of interests to even its closest ally.

If one looks back over the episodic crises of the past decade there is a recurring theme of an effort by the current generation of European leaders to encourage the United States to keep a sense of perspective about left-wing successes in various parts of the world. They recall how the rise of Eurocommunism and the Portuguese Revolution was going to lead to the collapse of NATO's southern flank; then Angola and Zimbabwe were going to be the means by which the Soviet Union could control the Cape route; next the invasion of Afghanistan was the first stage en route to the Gulf; and more recently insurgency in El Salvador was adding to the communist outposts in America's own back-yard.

From an American viewpoint such an impression is hope-lessly exaggerated. It is arguable that had not Washington made a fuss there could well have been a complacent drift into a dangerous situation because of the cumulative effects of developments that might each individually appear to be of only marginal importance. The American complaint, voiced with as much if not more vigour during and after the 1973 Yom Kippur War as in the early 1980s, was that Europeans had lost their global vision for regional blinkers and that they were unwilling to see the links between their own security and events outside Europe. This, the Europeans insisted, was unfair. They just had differing perspectives.

The frequency of controversies over developments out-side of the Atlantic region (even when broadly interpreted) has been sufficient to make this a distinctive feature of the relationship. Arguably, it is *the* key divergence, for by contrast the security arrangements within Europe still appear to be remarkably stable, and, as noted above, much of the questioning in Europe of the advisability of such close links with the United States stems from concern over the consequences of what is perceived to be a certain American recklessness in its dealings with the Third World.

The divergence over security challenges in the Third World has three main causes. First, there are so many parties involved and the issues are so complex that the potential for miscalculation is enormous. Second, the differential dependence on key raw materials, notably but not exclusively oil, means that the Europeans are willing to take fewer diplomatic risks. Third, the incentives for low-risk policies are intensified by the decline in the ability of European countries to project significant military power outside the continent, although it is of note that since

Vietnam, British and French forces have seen more action outside of Europe than those of the United States.

The point is that the United States, alone among the Western nations, has both the self-sufficiency and military strength for global assertions of power, and a competitive relationship with the Soviet Union that is qualitatively different from relations between any other pair of countries. The United States sees the increased military visibility of the Eastern bloc countries in the Third World over the past decade as a challenge to a previously dominant American position. The Soviet Union as an outsider trying to get in primarily as a promoter of communism is regarded as inherently subversive of the international order and so an unlikely partner in the resolution of regional disputes.

As the Europeans are out of this competition and can do little, as contributors on the Western side, to influence its course, they tend to see the single-minded concern with United States-Soviet relations as a distraction from the complexities of most regional conflicts. From the perspective of neighbours, they tend to view the Soviet Union as an unpleasant fact of life which cannot be excluded from international affairs and whose interests and view must be recognised if there is to be any sort of peaceful co-existence.

The Soviet Union and its allies are getting more involved in the Third World and their involvement does have a military bias, largely because they have so little to offer in the economic sphere. This has led to an attempt to extend deterrence beyond Europe. There has been a debate within NATO as to whether or not it is appropriate to prepare for large-scale military intervention in the Third World in general, and the Gulf in particular, to counter any Soviet adventures; and, if so, how these preparations should be made.

This debate involves Europeans in yet another of the discussions of ''what do we do if deterrence fails?'' Only this time it is in the context of areas of the world where disorder is only too regular and where military intervention by the West is extremely unattractive. The Europeans are faced with the dilemma of wishing to maximise their influence over the use of such intervention forces (because they are worried about hasty and ill-considered use) while minimising their actual contribution to a level tolerable to the United States (because they doubt that this would be a useful way to use scarce resources). They would prefer to keep out of local controversies and concentrate on what is believed to be the real Western interest of preserving steady markets and raw material supplies by encouraging regional stability and a general sympathetic attitude towards the industrialised countries.

This may be fine as a general inclination, and can obviously be supported by generous policies on the whole gamut of North-South issues from aid to commodity agreements but it leaves little scope for active diplomacy. It becomes risky to offend key states by talking too loudly about their more dubious internal practices or local external adventures. It may make sense to follow the line of least resistance and accept the dominant regional view on controversial matters or attempt to keep out, and might even be justifiable according to our principles (opposing apartheid in South Africa) or our notion on another's self-interest (warning Israel of the consequences of ignoring the Palestinians).

A cautious arms-length diplomacy has much to commend it, for if one cannot meddle effectively it is best not to meddle at all. It may even work in most places for most of the time. Unfortunately, there are always exceptions, as Britain has recently discovered, where key interests are at stake in some local turbulence and the West needs to act. The Europeans are therefore prepared to go along, at least verbally, with American proposals such as those for the Rapid Deployment Force. The hope is that, as with other forms of deterrence, the possibility of a Western response will ensure that the Soviet Union avoids getting into a position that might result in a serious military confrontation.

The result may well be to neutralise the military instrument as a means of solving Third World crises with an East-West dimension. In these circumstances a different, if less dangerous, problem opens up for Europeans. If it is the case that the best approaches to Third World crisis involve political and economic means of persuasion then these means are as available to the Europeans as they are to the United States. As the limits to military power are acknowledged then the potential of economic power has to be explored. If international diplomacy is to move in this direction, and the Europeans have to consider greater use of economic sticks and carrots, the higher profile will lead to an expectation of a greater say in determining the overall Western "line". A more active European diplomacy inevitably will result in arguments with the United States. Already significant strains are developing over Southern Africa and the Middle East. This suggests that questions of boycotts and sanctions, subsidies, and grants, are going to increase as contentious issues. To this can be added questions relating to economic relations between North and South and the political strings attached to development aid. This politicisation of economic life brings new problems: doubts over the actual efficacy of sanctions and generous aid or credit provisions; resentments resulting from the differential impact — Europeans feel themselves more vulnerable to loss of oil supplies; in trade with Eastern Europe embargoes on grain hurt American farmers while those on industrial goods hurt the Europeans.

Thus, despite the current preoccupation with improving the means of overseas intervention, few security issues can be resolved on this basis — because except in rare cases applications of military power tend to be too dangerous or inefficient or simply impractical. The price that might have to be paid to avoid excessive militarisation of global diplomacy is an increased politicisation of the global economy. This will mean that disputes which one might have been dealt with by traditional means of diplomacy backed by threats of military force will now be played out in the economic sphere. In each of the recent crises — Iran, Afghanistan, Poland, El Salvador — the lack of credible military options soon led to demands for economic sanctions or, if the recipient was not too large, generous offers of aid. Even with the Falklands crisis, where military options seemed more appropriate, the first instinct of many was to seek economic forms of pressure.

It is arguable that there are as many, if not more, limits to economic intervention as there are to military intervention. Few countries will be willing to make sacrifices for extended periods. At times of recession it seems foolhardy to forgo trade in order to make a political point, or to subsidise credit or improve general aid to gain fairweather friends. As an indirect form of pressure economic sanctions can usually be resisted by a moderately determined country with a relatively self-sufficient or resourceful economy. Even where this pressure can make a difference it will take time to have effect, while the short-term consequences of exercising it can cause great disruption to international trade and finance. Moreover, while economic sanctions are often assumed to be more humane than direct military action, they can result in immense distress to vulnerable sections of the community.

All that having being said, contemporary crisis management seems to require economic sanctions as an obvious first step in signalling displeasure — something between inaction and the horrors of military action. In time it may be felt that regular resort to economic sanctions has led to far greater costs than gains, and that such political intervention should be held back for only the more extreme contingencies. Then the question will have to be asked as to whether there is any other form of pressure that is appropriate to modern conditions that can back up diplomacy. Until then, politicians are likely to find it difficult to resist the temptation of looking to the economic sphere for their sticks and carrots.

International economic policy already involves hard bargaining over divergent interests, is becoming dependent on the decision-making procedures of awkward coalitions such as OPEC or the EEC, and is influenced by the grievances of the South against the North. These issues are now being complicated even more by linking economic concessions to political favours and considering punitive economic measures to signal displeasure or force reversals of transgressions. It is hard to believe that this will do anything other than render the underlying economic backdrop for defence policies and international diplomacy even worse.

Prospects: Rupture or Readjustment?

To return to our original question: should we view the current set of trans-Atlantic troubles as just another episode in a continuing story or are there deeper factors that will severely test the durability of the Alliance?

The difficulties in agreeing on a coherent set of Alliance policies reflect the difficulties in establishing a coherent political structure within the Alliance. The pressure of economic circumstances is forcing governments to be more inward-looking. The complexion of individual governments and their policies change regularly. All this is largely a consequence of instabilities and uncertainties in the larger structure of international relations. The Atlantic Alliance remains a crucial feature of the structure, but its relative importance has declined. The challenge for the Alliance therefore is to organise itself so as to be able effectively to influence the factors shaping the rest of the structure. To some extent this has already been recognised in calls for Alliance-wide consultations (including Japan) to co-ordinate responses to crises in the Third World as they arise.

However, the analysis of this article argues that we must move beyond the recognition that the security problem involves more than the Soviet military threat to Central Europe. The economic dimensions to the problem must also be acknowledged. Otherwise there is a risk that attempts to deal with the dissatisfaction in Western Europe (and increasingly in the United States) with the nuclear bias in NATO strategy, or to develop an effective diplomacy towards the Third World will falter through a lack of funds to support them or get caught up in the spillover from arguments on trade or monetary issues.

The issues which currently exercise NATO — on nuclear strategy and arms control, and on burden-sharing — are new variations on old themes and ought in principle to be manageable. This long-standing question of how best to organise the defence of Western Europe is, however, being complicated by outside factors and unless these factors are addressed the original question will get progressively harder to answer. When West German politicians doubt whether the close association with the United States is so wise and their counterparts in Congress wonder why the United States continues to spend so much to help wayward Allies, their queries have often been prompted by arguments about how to handle crises outside the NATO area. And whether the issues are related to East-West security relations in Europe or to troubles in the Third World, the economic issue is looming larger as a disruptive and complicating factor.

It is therefore becoming increasingly difficult to solve specifically NATO issues on their own terms, while the wider issues cannot be handled readily within an Atlantic framework. Too many other countries and international groupings and institutions need to be involved. The first requirement for the Atlantic Community is therefore to recognise the linkages between its more immediate problems and these wider issues. In particular the importance of world economic recovery cannot be stressed too much. Nothing is so corrosive of Atlantic relations as the current recession and the accompanying arguments over the allocation of responsibility. The second, and inevitable, requirement is to improve mechanisms of consultation and co-ordination not only on security questions but also on general economic policy, and to extend them to include the relevant outside parties.

These sorts of institutional improvements are difficult enough when the very international conditions which make them so necessary also create an indifference and impatience towards multilateral diplomacy. They are also insufficient unless those involved operate with a clear sense of what is at stake and where they stand. In this sense the current crisis is more troublesome for the Europeans than for the Americans. They are increasingly being forced to question the economic policies and global diplomacy of the United States. They bring to the arguments considerable experience in Third World diplomacy and substantial economic strength, so that in many areas economic levers are as available to them as they are to the Americans.

The risk is that, faced with this challenge, the temptation for the Americans will be to draw the Europeans' attention to their dependence on the United States for their own security. In the sort of conditions that I have been describing, the Europeans are unlikely to be quiescent on contentious economic matters because of security considerations. This will be particularly so if they feel that the United States is over-stressing security and if they feel that the Americans are making dangerous and mistaken calculations in their dealings with the Third World. In such circumstances, it is going to be extremely difficult to protect the special and largely successful security arrangements in Europe.

This logic now takes us full circle for it may be that only if these arrangements are adjusted can the European dialogue with the United States be on equal terms. If NATO can reduce its dependence on nuclear weapons then Europe can reduce but not remove its dependence on the United States. Perhaps only by doing this can the Alliance be turned into a more mature relationship between countries aware that traditional ties and common interests require them to stay close together, but also that differences in perspectives and interests must mean that they bargain and argue as much with each other as they do with everyone else.

(This Essay was prepared in connection with the Royal Institute of International Affairs' research project on US-European relations and was first published in **International Affairs**, London, Summer 1982)

6 Flexible Response and the Concept of Escalation

This is a critical analysis of NATO's doctrine of flexible response and the concept of escalation which underlies it, at least as they are commonly understood. It is argued that even if the intention is to improve the credibility of nuclear threats, far more attention needs to be given to all aspects of conventional deterrence. More positively, a full consideration of the political aspects of conventional deterrence might make allowance for reduced dependence on nuclear threats.

This concept ... is based upon a flexible and balanced range of appropriate responses, conventional and nuclear, to all levels of aggression or threats of aggression. These responses, subject to appropriate political control, are designed, first to deter aggression and thus preserve peace; but, should aggression unhappily occur, to maintain the security of the North Atlantic Treaty area within the concept of forward defence.

Communiqué, Ministerial Meeting of the North Atlantic Council, 14 December 1967.

NATO's doctrine of flexible response is a testament to the influence of the concept of escalation. It cannot be considered a strategy in the traditional sense of seeking to achieve objectives by means of a decisive military outcome. Instead it seeks to influence the opponent's decision-making by facing him with the consequences of his actions. The doctrine requires of NATO that it convinces the Soviet Union that any aggression directed against Western Europe — however limited initially in means, location and objective — could set in motion a train of events that would conclude with the destruction of the centres of Soviet power.

The fact that the same process would also in all probability conclude with the destruction of the centres of Western power has led many to question the validity of flexible response. Either it is a bluff and will one day be exposed as such; or it is not, in which case it is reckless and irrational. Here, I am seeking to address this debate and move it beyond the point where it appears to be stuck at the moment. The issue has got bogged down in the question of whether or not it is feasible or even desirable to raise the nuclear threshold. The issue that set off this debate was what, if anything, useful could be done once the threshold had been passed, especially with regard to the limited employment of nuclear weapons. It is my argument that to shore up NATO strategy we need to give far more attention to what we would be doing before the passing of the nuclear threshold. This must include consideration of periods of tension as well as the earliest stages of a conflict, and not simply the point at which a massive battle is underway in the centre of Europe and there is much agonising over whether to ''go nuclear''.

Because flexible response is so bound up with a view of the dynamics of escalation my argument shall be based on a critique of this concept. As a concept, escalation is highly suggestive. It clearly relates to processes that can be identified in most wars and, indeed, in other types of conflicts from lovers' tiffs to industrial disputes. However escalation can come in a variety of forms and it is not necessarily as powerful an influence on the course of wars as is often supposed. NATO has found it convenient to work with a rather formalised model of the likely stages of escalation in an East-West conflict; yet this provides little guidance as to the course that a conflict might follow and therefore may be an unreliable source of policy.

I shall argue that:

> Much of the debate within NATO on strategic doctrine can be seen as a contest between two opposed views, labelled here *dominance* and *uncertainty*.
>
> The debate has led to the development of an excessively systematic model of the escalation process that has been adopted by most participants in the debate.
>
> This model is flawed largely in its attempt to mark out definite steps in the period after the nuclear threshold has

been passed, while being remarkably vague on the distinctive forms of escalation that might be found during the conventional stage.

The frustrations in NATO doctrine can be traced to the readiness to treat nuclear hostilities in a self-contained manner with regard only to the failure in but not the character of the prior conventional hostilities. Rather than a nuclear strategy offering an alternative to conventional weakness, a nuclear strategy with any hope of success depends on conventional strength.

Even with conventional strength, any nuclear strategy still carries far too many risks for it to appear convincing in peacetime — though it cannot be ruled out that it might actually succeed in practice. Any success must ultimately depend on the political response of the opponent to nuclear use and this cannot be forecast with confidence prior to the event. Any nuclear strategy must therefore involve a political gamble of a sort that few politicians could commit themselves to beforehand.

The flaws in NATO strategy would be felt most keenly at those times of tension when there would be a need to fortify deterrence in the face of some sort of challenge by warning the Soviet Union of the dangerous consequences of a resort to armed force. No doubt the ultimate risk of all-out nuclear war would be stressed, but NATO might well find it difficult at a time of acute public anxiety to dwell on a specific and deliberate intention to initiate nuclear hostilities.

On the other hand, NATO is unlikely to embark on a substantial improvement in its conventional capabilities. Just as in the nuclear sphere the Alliance has been forced to rely more on a sense of uncertainty on the Soviet side that NATO *might* ''go nuclear'' rather than a certainty that it *will*, so its best hope in the pursuit of deterrence may well be to attempt to draw on uncertainties in the conventional sphere, which has been somewhat neglected in the pre-occupation with the nuclear sphere.

Escalation — Two Views

Escalation refers to a qualitative transformation in the character of a conflict towards increasing scope and intensity. It describes not just an expansion of a conflict, but a movement across a limit that had been previously accepted by both sides.

Developments in any conflict which can be described as an *act of escalation* are usually easy enough to identify. A *process of escalation* may be more difficult in that this implies a series of developments inexorably following each other, and only resisted by acts of restraint of a sort that are rare in wartime. The assumption that escalation is a tendency affecting all warfare is one that needs examination.

To identify a process of escalation we need to have some sense of the critical thresholds which would be recognised turning points in the war. The second question, after identifying the salient thresholds, is whether the passage through them is likely to be deliberate or involuntary, the result of a conscious political choice or a consequence of the confusion, chaos and uncertainty of war. To assume a process is to imply a series of involuntary escalations, and this has been the view of many commentators on a future world war, especially once the nuclear threshold, the most readily acknowledged threshold of all, has been passed. Those who believe that a credible operational nuclear strategy can still be developed, argue that it would even be possible to control a nuclear conflict to the extent of not being forced to accept an unacceptable level of damage while still meeting strategic objectives.

Happily there is a lack of experience to help us discern the likely course of a major East-West confrontation in the nuclear age. This is why the views on the existence and probable shape of an escalation process have been formed through theoretical speculation rather than empirical observation. Two basic views, of which there are many variants, have been influential within NATO — categorised as "dominance" and "uncertainty".

The first involves an attempt to prevail in a conflict by dominating at a particular level of escalation and putting the onus on the other side to move to a higher and more dangerous level. The second involves drawing on the un-certainties inherent in the escalation process to achieve deterrence through warning the other side that things could get out of control. They can best be understood by considering the views of two outstanding theorists — Herman Kahn and Tom Schelling — who were responsible for the intellectual development of these two approaches.

Kahn assumed that a nuclear conflict could be conducted in a controlled and discriminating manner. At each stage of the movement up the escalation ladder — on which Kahn identified 44 rungs — one of the two sides would feel better equipped to fight. During a stage in which the enemy enjoyed the advantages it would be necessary to decide whether to accept an unsatisfactory settlement or raise the stakes by moving to the next stage. This stage would be more violent and dangerous and perhaps less controllable, but the advantages might begin to flow in a more favourable direction.

This decision would become progressively more difficult the further up the escalation ladder it was necessary to travel to have a reasonable chance of success. The ultimate logic pointed towards a "spasm war" in which both sides would lose all. By manipulating a margin of superiority at lower levels an intolerable burden could still be put on the side forced to raise the stakes. Kahn described such a condition as "escalation dominance":

> This is a capacity, other things being equal, to enable the side possessing it to enjoy marked advantages in a given region of the escalation ladder ... It depends on the net effect of the competing capabilities on the rung being occupied, the estimate by each side of what would happen if the confrontation moved to these other rungs, and the means each side has to shift the confrontation to these other rungs. [1]

However, as an escalation ladder was unlikely to appear as clear in practice as in theory, what would happen if one side tries a move which the other did not recognise in terms of an orderly movement up the ladder or if a communications failure led to a substantial overestimate of the scale of the other side's activities? If it could not be guaranteed that the situation could be kept under control, then an involuntary escalatory process could take over and the two sides could find themselves involved in massive exchanges of nuclear weapons against their better judgement. Kahn's approach depended first, on the presumption of control, even after the point when it might be expected that the forces of irrationality would have completely taken over; and second, on the possibility of clear-cut margins of superiority and even victory at the various stages. Without these the conflict was always likely to get bogged down at an intermediate stage and the incentives would be insufficient to warrant the high risks attached to escalation.

An alternative method of exploiting escalation sought to draw on the uncertainties inherent in the process. This was developed most effectively by Tom Schelling. Schelling argued that even after deterrence had failed in its primary task to stop the outbreak of war there would still be a possibility of retrieving the situation. A nuclear threat would be most credible either if not matched by a counter-threat (no longer possible) or if implemented automatically by the adversary's misbehaviour. But neither side was likely to follow the second course if the first did not obtain. The threat therefore risked being exposed as a bluff — especially if it had not already been implemented following enemy aggression.

But nuclear exchanges might be initiated whether or not either side considered this to be a rational step in the circumstances. Schelling did not expect escalation to develop as a result of deliberate steps taken by calculating governments fully aware of the consequences of their actions:

> Violence, especially in war, is a confused and uncertain activity, highly unpredictable depending on decisions taken by fallible human beings organised into imperfect governments depending on fallible communications and warning systems and on the untested performance of people and equipment. It is furthermore a hot-headed activity, in which commitments and reputations can develop a momentum of their own.

There was an unavoidable risk of things moving beyond responsible control in the move from limited to general war. Drawing attention to this possibility could reinforce deterrence; if necessary, allowing the situation to begin to slip away would force the adversary to confront the possibility of matters getting completely out of hand. This might make him more accommodating. If deterrent threats in or out of war could not be credible so long as the threatener was in full control, then it would be necessary to relinquish some control in order to achieve credibility. Schelling called this ''the threat that leaves something to chance''. He explains: ''The key to these threats is that, though one may or may not carry them out, *the final decision is not altogether under the threatener's control*''. [2]

The approach was to create a situation in which only the other's compliance could relieve the shared pain and remove the shared risk. This, of course, assumed that the adversary would be sufficiently in control to be able to comply. The dangers of handing over to the adversary the responsibility for the course of the conflict would be enormous, involving the abdication of responsibility at the most critical time in a nation's history. As a prescription for the conduct of war — and thus for what was described as ''intra-war deterrence'' — Schelling's analysis had obvious drawbacks. Moreover, as a warning about what might happen in a war yet to start, this approach offered a real insight into how deterrence could operate in peacetime; as a function of the fear of the unknown rather than of the specific threats of the potential enemy.

Of these two approaches, dominance was the most appealing to stategists because it provided a clear goal for the development of forces and plans; despite this NATO has continually fallen back on uncertainty.

Flexible Response

The basic dilemma that continues to vex NATO planners stems from the belief that a Soviet conventional attack on Western Europe cannot be thwarted without resort to nuclear threats that themselves lack credibility because of the extent of the Soviet counterthreat.

One approach to this dilemma has been to challenge the

defeatism on the conventional situation. If the conventional option could be shown to be more promising then it might be possible to reduce the dependence of NATO on the threat to use nuclear weapons first. President Kennedy was tempted by this approach in 1961. However, he was held back by the fact that the major crisis of that year was over West Berlin which was the only part of the Alliance indefensible by conventional means. In the course of the conflict Kennedy was obliged to reaffirm the commitment to the first-use threat.

Having acknowledged that the West might be forced to escalate into use of nuclear weapons, the United States toyed publicly with, and began privately to develop, a strategy based on attacks on military targets and the avoidance of cities. The military targets in mind related as much to a land war in Europe as to the Soviet Union's strategic nuclear assets.

The construction put on the new strategy by the Soviet Union, combined with the apparent desire by the United States Air Force to confirm this construction by preparing for a full first strike, led Secretary of Defence Robert McNamara to abandon this approach. He became far more concerned with ensuring that the nuclear threshold was not passed than with what could be done afterwards. The lack of confidence in the exercise of responsible control over events once nuclear exchanges had begun was expressed through the concept of Mutual Assured Destruction (MAD). The adoption of this concept by no means precluded the development of targeting options that fell well short of MAD, but at least in public the model of the escalation ladder became somewhat truncated. Nevertheless, McNamara was still operating within an "escalation dominance" framework, especially in terms of his stress on the nuclear threshold and on maintaining second-strike forces in reserve, to warn the Soviet Union of the dangers of escalation to that level.

His growing determination that the nuclear threshold should not be passed led to arguments with the West European allies. The Europeans, of course, were not anxious to pass the threshold but they were worried about the implications for deterrence in the American position. They were dependent on the United States for their nuclear protection, yet understood only too well the element of irrationality this required on the American side, given the arrival of a full-blooded Soviet retaliatory capability. The more the Americans talked about the need to avoid "going nuclear", the more the Europeans suspected that the nuclear umbrella was in the process of being removed. The Americans might reduce the risks to themselves inherent in a European war but, by confirming the unlikelihood of nuclear escalation, they would also reduce the risks to the Soviet Union of aggression.

More robust conventional forces for NATO might deny the Soviet Union a victory but it still might calculate that the cost of failure would be slight. Soviet territory itself would remain unscathed. Without a need to worry about nuclear catastrophe, Soviet risk assessments would be dangerously simplified. To the Europeans all war, not just nuclear war, had to be deterred and deterrence required at least some prospect of a resort to nuclear weapons. The European complaint therefore was that the United States was in effect withdrawing its nuclear guarantee by its continual stress on the need to stay well clear of the nuclear threshold.

In the end a compromise was reached, to some extent made possible by the withdrawal of France from NATO's Integrated Military Command. In 1967 NATO adopted the strategy of flexible response. The new strategy was more a form of words than a carefully worked-out plan of action and was thus subject to a variety of interpretations. This was inevitable as it was an attempt to reconcile opposing views. Such flexibility has since made it difficult to object to the doctrine: it is hard to object to the idea of responding to aggression in a flexible manner.

The nod towards the American position was the acceptance of no automatic nuclear response to conventional aggression. The attempt was to be made to hold back the aggression with conventional means. Should that fail there would be a move to tactical nuclear weapons. If this did not terminate the conflict on satisfactory terms there would be recourse to the US strategic nuclear arsenal. This was no more than a restatement of the accepted and simplified view of the escalation ladder. The question was whether progression up this ladder would be deliberate or inadvertent, whether NATO was relying on dominance or uncertainty.

It was the second approach that was adopted, to some extent by default. The Europeans were resistant to the American conviction that a feasible conventional option was readily available. One European condition for adopting the new strategy was that there would be no expectation of higher expenditure on ground forces. By this time the United States army was bogged down in Vietnam and there was less interest on the American side in adding to the European commitment. (Indeed the debate in Washington had by this time moved on to demands for troop withdrawals from Europe). There was thus little chance that NATO was going to feel able to dominate at the conventional level.

Nor was there optimism that dominance could be achieved at the tactical (battlefield) nuclear level by turning a land war in Europe in favour of the West. By this time there was only a slight belief in the possibility of fighting a limited nuclear war. To the Europeans, indicating their preference for the uncertainty principle, the importance of these weapons was that they *were* nuclear; not that they might be used as if they were conventional. Their value was not to prevent escalation to the strategic level but to create a risk of exactly that. According to the doctrine, these weapons coupled the US strategic arsenal to a land war in Europe. The Soviet Union could not avoid the risk of all-out nuclear war should it contemplate localised conventional aggression.

The adoption of flexible response and assured destruction together demonstrated a lack of confidence in the possibility of establishing and sustaining distinctive thresholds once nuclear weapons were in use. At the same time, there seemed to be no pressing need to delve too deeply into the awkward question of what would be done if deterrence failed because there seemed to be little reason to believe that deterrence would fail. This was a period of détente.

During the 1970s this relaxed attitude was subject to

increasing criticism. The deterioration in international relations made the question of what to do should deterrence fail seem more relevant and immediate. If eventual hostilities could not be ruled out, then relying on a threat that left things to chance seemed like the abandonment of strategy. It provided no guidelines for the design of forces or for the preparation of targeting options. Although American planners did not envisage an all-out attack on cities as the one and only option, the stress on assured destruction was widely taken to imply as much.

The United States, it was argued, was relying on the overbearing threat of mass destruction, yet the Soviet Union had an altogether more sophisticated concept — and even an operational doctrine to match — for actually fighting a nuclear war. NATO's military forces would provide the targets, with the objective of at least limiting their ability to damage the Soviet Union and its strategic assets and at best preparing the ground for a traditional military victory.

Developments in weapons technology encouraged the view that complex and discriminating nuclear tactics were becoming realistic. These developments included multiple warheads; the reduction of yield to weight ratios; the ability to tailor nuclear effects; the growing capacity of communications, command, control and surveillance systems; and, most of all, the ability to hit quite small and protected targets with astonishing accuracy. They all contributed to a sense that nuclear weapons were increasingly becoming precision instruments. The task was to develop an operational nuclear doctrine for NATO that could exploit this precision.

Another factor was the impact of the various arms control negotiations. The negotiating activity of the 1970s was concerned with establishing parity between the two superpowers. Negotiations on this matter inevitably led to debate on the meaning of particular disparities and encouraged a more intensive examination of the significance of specific aspects of the force structure than might otherwise have been deemed necessary, or even healthy, given the enormous quantities of redundant offensive nuclear power available to both sides. When hard bargaining is underway there is a tendency to assume that the subject of all this bargaining matters! The organisation of arms control in the 1970s and 1980s also encouraged a perception of distinct categories of nuclear weapons — the strategic, the intermediate, the short-range. One reason for this was the simple problem of dividing up the negotiations into manageable areas, but an important consequence was to reinforce a concept of a graded escalation ladder.

Return to Dominance

All these factors worked together to encourage a return to strategies based on the principle of dominance. The process began in 1974 when Secretary of Defence James Schlesinger announced plans to develop a range of selective nuclear options to reduce dependence on threats of assured destruction. The trend continued under the Carter administration. Secretary of Defence Harold Brown unveiled the counter-availing strategy (PD-59) in 1980. This took the development of options further, including an investigation of the possibilities of fighting a protracted nuclear war and targeting key Soviet political and economic assets. However, the basic concept was that should the Soviet Union move up the escalation ladder the United States would be able to respond effectively at each level.

In 1981 the Reagan administration took the process a stage further. It claimed to be doing no more than developing the forces necessary to implement the doctrine of the previous administration. But there was a definite change of tone. There was still the argument that flexibility was necessary should the Soviet Union force the pace of escalation, but there was now the suggestion that Western Security would be immeasurably strengthened should the United States feel able to force the pace. This line of argument had been developed by a number of civilian strategists who had pointed out that as the United States had committed itself to initiating nuclear hostilities in support of its allies, it needed to have some idea where these hostilities might lead. It might be argued that President Reagan's Strategic Defence Initiative (more popularly known as ''Star Wars'') followed through this logic. One interpretation (and there are many) of its objectives would be to deny the Soviet Union its targeting options, including ultimately the ability to attack cities, in the hope that the United States would maintain at least some of its own.

During the 1970s and 1980s the possibilities for actually exercising dominance at different levels of the escalation ladder were discussed exhaustively, often in connection with proposals for specific weapons systems: moving up the ladder, and mentioning only the most controversial proposals, we find enhanced radiation weapons (ERW), cruise and Pershing missiles, and the MX ICBM. At each stage the more the problems have been analysed, the more the awareness of the obstacles facing any attempt to achieve and exploit dominance. The more the Reagan adminis-tration persisted with the suggestion that there could be an operational nuclear strategy favouring NATO, the more sceptics reaffirmed that in the end the West was still relying for its security on the threat that leaves something to chance.

By the early 1980s, the doubts about nuclear strategy, particularly in Western Europe, had developed to such an extent that there were widespread calls for a renewed emphasis on conventional strategy to reduce dependence on nuclear weapons. In turn it was pointed out that conventional forces are more expensive and that it was therefore unrealistic to expect to raise the nuclear threshold too high — deterrence still depends on a prospect of this threshold being passed. This is about as far as the debate has got for the moment. In an attempt to take it further let us now consider the adequacy of the conceptual framework within which it is taking place.

The Stages of Escalation[3]

Although the two concepts of dominance and uncertainty are quite distinct, both in their assumptions about the character and dynamics of a conflict and their policy require-ments, they have been developed in the West on the basis of a shared model of the escalation ladder. This model is based on five key thresholds. When these thresholds are passed the conflict is transformed in the direction of greater and more widely-spread violence and is less easy to control. The passing of each threshold is assumed to have, at the same time, both military and political connotations. This model has been found valuable because it imposes some order on what would otherwise be a mass of uncertainties. The five thresholds are:

1. From Peace to War, normally assumed to be marked by a large-scale conventional invasion across the East-West divide.
2. From Conventional to Nuclear war, normally assumed to be marked by the employment of battlefield nuclear weapons.
3. From Battlefield to Continental nuclear war, normally assumed to be marked by attacks well to the rear of the front-line, including on Soviet territory.
4. From Continental nuclear to Intercontinental nuclear war, normally assumed to be marked by strikes launched from or against North America.
5. From Counterforce to Countervalue intercontinental strikes, normally thought to be marked by direct attacks on the socio-economic structure rather than against military targets such as missile silos or submarine pens.

At issue has been whether these thresholds represent natural firebreaks; that is would the opposing forces be driven over them by the dynamics of warfare — involuntary escalation — or would the passage require, or at least allow for, deliberate political decision — voluntary escalation. Particular weapons are often discussed in terms of whether they would support or undermine the setting up of firebreaks. For example, enhanced radiation weapons were criticised and promoted as blurring the line between conventional and nuclear weapons. At issue with cruise missiles was whether they would inevitably take a conflict into the realm of superpower exchanges or whether the conflict could still be contained in the European theatre. In other words, does stage three inevitably merge into stage four? The anxiety over ICBM vulnerability revolves around the possibility of large scale attacks against North American targets being experienced as something less than all-out nuclear war.

These thresholds are important as political constraints, whatever their relation to military practice. It is generally assumed that, all things being equal, there are no incentives to escalate for the sake of fighting at a higher level. The incentives must be found with those things which are not equal. The side taking the fateful decision expects either to lose if he does not escalate or to win if he does. NATO insists that it would only be the prospect of conventional defeat that would lead it to escalate. However, although NATO does not discuss positive reasons for employing nuclear weapons, such reasons might be found if it were believed that at the first nuclear stage all the advantages would flow in its direction.

If one side is aware that the other is likely to dominate more as escalation progresses then it will wish to keep the conflict at as low a level as possible. So long as a prospective war will not touch home territory, for example, then it might be contemplated with greater equanimity than one which will involve its cities being bombed within minutes of the start of hostilities.

To different members of an alliance the same act of escalation has therefore quite different implications. This helps to explain the distinctive attitudes of the West Germans and the United States to the prospect of hostilities breaking out in the middle of Europe. The Germans cannot view any war with equanimity; they therefore stress its escalatory potential so as to ensure that the superpowers also feel fully at risk.

It is generally agreed that the superpowers have the greatest interest in establishing firebreaks. However, this interest is preordained by a framework which defines the highest stage of escalation as attacks on superpower cities. For the same reason, those thresholds which have exercised the most powerful hold on the American strategic imagination are found at the higher levels. The most recent example of this has been the concern over ICBM vulnerability and the political benefits the Soviet Union was expected to obtain through its comparative advantage in counterforce capabilities.

While American strategists were wondering whether the United States would be able to bring itself to retaliate in the event of a nuclear attack on its own territory, Europe's interest was in guaranteeing an American reponse to a conventional attack on the Allies. The focus in Europe has therefore been on the earlier stages. Once the war threshold has been passed the consequences would be so catastrophic that the interest lay in demonstrating the fragility of any subsequent thresholds so as to attach a clear risk of unavoidable escalation to the opening shots of any war. (It would also be in Europe's interests to pass over the earlier stages as quickly as possible, on the presumption that the later stages would be taking place over their heads.)

The logic of geography gives the United States an interest in defining the escalation process in terms of a succession of firebreaks, with the presumption that at each stage it might be possible to impose dominance. The West European interest lies in stressing the difficulty of establishing firebreaks and the consequent uncertainty as a source of deterrence.

The identification and ordering of strategic choices within the framework outlined above reflects, as much as anything else, the peacetime debate within the Alliance. That is, the framework as developed above has been shaped by understandings concerning the rights and duties of the various NATO members, and also the appropriate distribution of risk. This means, of course, that the consequences of any shift in NATO's strategic policy, including a revamping of flexible response, may well be more substantial within the Alliance than within East-West relations. Opponents of nuclear bases in Europe may feel that there is a sufficiency of nuclear capability directed against the Soviet Union from the other side of the Atlantic. However the issues raised by their removal would be the impact on the US nuclear guarantee if the Allies felt unable to share the risks associated with this guarantee, or the political consequences of the link between the US nuclear arsenal and the defence of Europe becoming attenuated.

Statements about nuclear policy are made with regard to

their immediate political consequences. This is seen in the desire to couple the two halves of the Alliance together through doctrine and force structure. This attempt has suffered because of a lack of clarity over what precisely does the coupling. US bases in Europe can be seen as a demonstration of commitment to Europe or an attempt to export the risks of a nuclear confrontation. In practice, rather than serve as the cement by which the Alliance is held together, NATO's strategic policy has served to express a link that is, and ought to be if it is to endure, much more rooted in a shared political outlook and deep economic and social connections. The point is that strategic doctrine — and the conceptual framework within which it is understood — is a dependent rather than an independent variable in Alliance relations.

This should warn us against treating the framework too uncritically. It has developed as a politically convenient way of ordering the debate and not as an attempt actually to predict the course of an East-West conflict or to identify the precise times when NATO leaders will face their moments of truth.

War-fighters and Signallers

Before moving on to consider the adequacy of the model taken as a whole, let us look closer at the one aspect that has been clearly identified: the nuclear threshold. The issue at this, as any other, threshold is whether the fateful steps will be taken deliberately, as a result of confidence in the next stage and in the expectation that any further escalation will be a matter for considered choice, or inadvertently as part of the confusion and fury of war. These alternative views lead on to the adoption of policies based on escalation dominance or on the threat that leaves something to chance (uncertainty).

We have seen the extent to which the United States has tended to work on the principle of dominance and the West Europeans with that of uncertainty. This, and the problems with both approaches, can be illustrated further by looking at the debate that has developed in NATO in the past over the best way of passing the nuclear threshold.

The first major studies completed in NATO's Nuclear Planning Group (NPG), which was established in December 1966, concerned the question of the initial use of nuclear weapons. According to MC14/3 (the flexible response document) such use had to persuade the invader "to cease his aggression and withdraw". The debate within the NPG in 1969–70 revolved around a paper written by the British and West Germans which came down firmly in favour of the view that any nuclear use would be fundamentally political in purpose, warning the enemy of the dangers of further escalation consequent on persisting with his aggression; in other words, signalling. Although individual weapons might have military targets, the overall purpose of their use would not be military. They would not be expected to turn the course of a land battle, for such an attempt would not only fail in the face of Soviet counterattacks but also, in requiring large-scale initial employment, would obscure the political signal. So the conclusion, accepted reluctantly by the United States, was that initial use would involve tens of low-yield weapons rather than hundreds of high-yield. This would be accompanied by clear declarations of restraint.

The Americans' preference was to delay any nuclear use but, once it appeared unavoidable, not to rule out the possibility of obtaining some military advantage. Some in the United States argued that new technologies were making possible forms of nuclear employment that could hold and repel a Soviet invasion without necessarily resulting in a nuclear counterattack. This approach came to be known as war-fighting.

Later studies in the NPG on "follow-on" use provided a forum for a debate between the signallers and the war-fighters. The conclusions of these studies, with only a few minor exceptions, pointed in the same direction. If the Soviet Union responded in kind, without raising the stakes, neither side would have gained a significant military advantage. At best a pause in the fighting might result, allowing both sides to take stock and wonder about a political settlement. At worst the Warsaw Pact would find itself in a more favourable position because it would be far better placed to take advantage of its reserves.

This pointed to a reinforcement of the initial signal even though the problem of follow-on use had only come about because the initial signal had not been received or acted upon as intended. Persistent aggression would be met with a persistent signal. So long as the objective remained one of reinforcing a crude and desperate political message it was unlikely that much of military value would be achieved.

The difficulty lies in trying to warn in a controlled manner that a situation is getting out of control. The limited initial strike would certainly signal a willingness to use some weapons but the evidence of deliberation and control would also signal a profound reluctance to slide into suicidal exchanges. The failure to derive any military benefits might signal no more than that NATO was confused and was not attempting to achieve a decisive victory. If NATO wants to make a threat that leaves something to chance then a part of the signal must be an indication that control is being relinquished, for example by decentralising decision-making to field commanders. However an emphasis on continuing political control is proper: democratic societies could expect nothing less. The dilemma is that exercising control through and after the passage of the nuclear threshold undermines the stress on uncertainty and indeed makes most sense in terms of an attempt to exert dominance.

If control was being exercised and if we accept that the only circumstances in which NATO would consider nuclear use would be those of an actual or imminent conventional defeat, would it be possible to ignore any chance of retrieving the position?

The problem was that neither the signalling nor the war-fighting strategies appeared convincing. Signalling was adopted because it was the most politically satisfactory of the two. It satisfied the need for a first-use option without appearing reckless. It could create uncertainties for Soviet planners, if not certainties for NATO planners. The war-fighters wished to dominate at the battlefield nuclear level but could not demonstrate that they would be able to do so. The signallers wished to emphasise the threat that leaves something to chance, but could not bring themselves to follow through the implications of the fact that the political leaders would already have had to take a chance in making a deliberate decision to push things into the nuclear sphere.

It proved difficult to plan for a collective show of irrational temper. All that could be done was to create options that could allow for such an exhibition, or alternatively for just a mild show of displeasure, according to the perceptions and requirements of those taking the decisions at the time. If NATO is to base its threat on sliding into nuclear war, then it cannot at the same time set up firebreaks to ensure that there is no inadvertent slide.

The nuclear threshold is now part of our strategic culture, political rhetoric and military preparations. Whatever the claims of doctrine, NATO is organised so as to ensure that passing this threshold would be a deliberate political decision. This can be seen in the guidelines for consultation on nuclear use, the special command structures controlling nuclear release, the promises made with ERW (neutron bombs) and other potentially ''threshold-transcending'' weapons, and the general treatment of the nuclear issue in public debate. It is likely that during the course of a serious international crisis there would be even more stress on the threshold, and the desirability of staying beneath it. The fatal flaw that many have detected in NATO's dependence on the threat to use nuclear weapons first is that this would be a source of division within the Alliance at times of tension. At the very point when it was necessary to rely on the quality of NATO's deterrent posture it would be subjected to vigorous challenge, to the extent that unity might only come at the expense of the disavowal of the established doctrine.

The threshold may exercise a firm hold on policy-makers and, because of the horrendous risks involved, there will be powerful pressures at work to stop it being violated. But this is not the same as saying that the threshold is inviolable. Circumstances might arise of extreme desperation (or even sudden military opportunity). The overwhelming dis-position of the belligerents would be to avoid passing the threshold but nevertheless, because of the extreme pressures to which it had been subjected, the threshold might none-the-less be passed. This would be true whether or not declarations of no-first-use had been made.

The nuclear signal warns of a situation getting out of control before control has actually been relinquished. But consider the circumstances of an enfeebled and panic-stricken coalition contemplating such a signal. Their quandary would be that passing the nuclear threshold would provide genuine evidence — a convincing signal — that matters were getting out of control and for that very reason they would be unwilling or simply unable to take the decision. If a deliberate decision to escalate is unlikely at this point, escalation may still take place because in a sense matters are already out of control; the furies of war may have built up to such a pitch that the resultant momentum smashes through the firebreak. A major clash of arms in Europe might indeed create such a momentum: a Soviet walk-over would not. What this suggests is that the credibility of the signalling strategy depends on the intensity of the preceding fight at the conventional level.

The same point holds for the war-fighting approach. The escalation dominance approach suggests a war passing through neat and self-contained stages as if on the passing of each threshold the contest takes on a completely different character, even to the extent that those in the ascendant suddenly experience a descent. It is, in practice, difficult to imagine a strategic inferiority giving way to a sudden superiority at a new and much more hazardous level. Armies that become used to being defeated decline in morale and efficiency. They are unlikely suddenly to become brave and well-organised on being told that they are about to employ nuclear weapons, however superb the munitions and brilliant the concepts. The best prospect for a successful nuclear campaign would be to wage it from Day One, while NATO armies were still fresh and enemy forces were still concentrated and not spread over allied territory. Of course, the problem of retaliation would still loom large (not to mention awkward little things like fall-out) and the political authorisation would not be given.

The conclusion of this section is that if NATO wishes to

rely on deterrent threats based on either escalation dominance or leaving things to chance then these must be established during the conventional phase. Both approaches would look more credible if they were not burdened by the presumption of a prior conventional collapse. It is not good enough to see this phase as simply a time for doing the best we can while mentally preparing ourselves for the big nuclear question. The character of the conventional war will determine when, if and how we move into nuclear hostilities.

A Soviet Model

To assess the possibility of a war-fighting approach based on conventional strength we can consider a Soviet model, which has been adopted by many of those advocating such a posture for NATO (even though they often neglect the conventional prerequisites for its success). What follows is not claimed to be an accurate representation of Soviet thinking. Indeed the most recent analyses of Soviet doctrine suggest that the flaws in the approach outlined below have become all too evident to the Soviet General Staff, so that the trend now is towards a greater emphasis on conventional operations. So the main value of this alternative model is the light that it may enable us to throw on Western rather than Soviet thinking.

According to this model the transformation of a war from the conventional to the nuclear is seen not as an act of last resort but more as a deliberate initiative, a means of delivering the coup de grace. Conventional operations are not conducted in the hope that nuclear warfare will not take place but to prepare the way for more effective nuclear warfare; the involvement of nuclear weapons does not signal the end of attempts to achieve a military victory worthy of the name; the success of the nuclear operation will pave the way for conventional forces to return to the fray to complete the job and occupy the contested territory. Failure in the conventional sphere might therefore even make nuclear use less rather than more likely (subject to the observation made earlier concerning the implications for the nuclear threshold of the intensity of the fighting at the conventional level).

A conventional phase geared to an eventual nuclear phase would not simply be a case of attempting one type of warfare before turning in frustration and desperation to something different. The objective would be to shift the NATO-Warsaw Pact nuclear balance in the latter's favour prior to the firing of any nuclear shots. This would be achieved in two ways. First, conventional war serves as a cover under which Soviet nuclear forces could be prepared for a strike; the weapons would be distributed to the relevant units, the targets would be defined and assigned to the units. Second, the conventional campaign would have, as its first priority, the destruction of enemy nuclear assets to reduce the risk of their being used either in a first strike or in retaliation.

The first nuclear strike is expected to be decisive, so the timing and design must be just right. The primary objective is to destroy NATO's remaining nuclear assets within the European theatre, leaving the surviving conventional forces extremely vulnerable. In a simple, almost mechanical formulation the best time for a nuclear strike would be the point at which the preparation of Eastern, and the attrition of Western, nuclear forces achieved during the conventional phase would allow for the remaining Western forces to be wiped out in a Soviet strike. There is no requirement that US strategic forces be wiped out in this attack. The whole concept is highly dependent on the belief that, when it came to the crunch, the Alliance would not be coupled, that Washington would refrain from retaliation so long as American territory was not touched. Some retaliation within the European theatre may be unavoidable but the United States has to be warned that any attack on Soviet territory would lead to direct relatiation against North America. If Soviet territory can be preserved as a sanctuary, the easier it becomes to mount nuclear operations within Europe.

There are a number of problems with this approach (which is why it is no longer in favour in Moscow). The first is that it reduces the likelihood of victory being achieved by non-nuclear means. Dual-capable aircraft, for example, cannot be fully committed to the conventional battle if they must be held in reserve for nuclear operations. The single-minded pursuit of enemy nuclear assets may mean that dangerous groupings of conventional forces have to be by-passed, even while they gain in strength. The precaution of dispersion might make it even more difficult to organise assaults against enemy conventional units that cannot be ignored. Any intermingling of friendly with enemy troops hampers the execution of a nuclear strike. The massing of forces in the rear has to be limited because of the choice targets they might present to enemy nuclear strikes. Problems such as these become progressively more manageable with even stronger conventional forces but they can never be wholly eradicated — even if there is no intention of going nuclear.

A second set of problems concerns the risk of pre-emption. While the Warsaw Pact was waiting for a favourable balance NATO might get in first. Indeed, if NATO commanders observed the steady attrition of their nuclear forces then they would be under some pressure to gain authorisation for nuclear release before the position had become completely hopeless. Evidence, or even rumours, of a NATO strike might force the Soviet hand before it was ready. Such a race to pre-empt would mean that some of the advantages of surprise would be lost and more enemy forces might survive.

Third, there is obviously a high risk involved in leaving US strategic forces unscathed. The whole approach is dependent upon sanctuary status being accorded to super-power territory, but there is nothing that the Soviet Union can do to ensure that this would be observed. One might add that its opposition to cruise and Pershing may, in part, be based on the recognition that it makes the observance of its sanctuary status even less likely.

The point is that while it cannot be ruled out that one side would achieve a nuclear victory, and forces of a certain quality and quantity, organised in a certain way, may be a necessary condition for such a victory, they cannot be sufficient. A successful strategy must depend on a political assessment of what is at stake for both sides which might affect their respective risk-taking and the likely effects on the enemy of the first blow; whether, for instance, it would be shocked into a stunned passivity rather than into frenzied revenge.

In terms of force structure all one can say is that it becomes easier to make the best of a bad job in the design of an effective war-fighting nuclear strategy if one can presume conventional superiority. However even this assumes that the situation as hostilities move into the nuclear phase is one that is essentially under control. Any debate on what might be possible in a strategic sense after the passing of the threshold is based on assumptions concerning the state of affairs which precedes the passage. The case for those who argue for deterrence through uncertainty must be based on the proposition that the course of conventional hostilities would be sufficiently difficult to predict for there to be little confidence in the prospect of dominance being established by either side.

Escalation in the Conventional Phase

To develop this point further we need to return to our model of the escalation process. The lack of attention to the conventional phase in our model of the escalation process can be illustrated by the supposition that the geographical extension of the conflict and the movement from counterforce to countervalue targeting will only come once the nuclear threshold has been passed. There is no reason in principle why either of these thresholds should not be passed prior to the use of nuclear weapons. Indeed if the enormity of these thresholds derives largely from an assumption that the war has already "gone nuclear" then it might be easier to pass them if the conflict is still well within the conventional sphere. With a wide geographical spread and civilians already at risk the enormity of the act of passing the nuclear threshold becomes even greater.

It is easy enough to see how civilians might get involved early in any war in Central Europe. Many urban areas would be in combat zones and civilians, either caught in their homes or fleeing as refugees, could soon appear as military obstacles. At some point a target essential to the military effort will appear in the middle of a civilian population. Or measures ostensibly intended to harm enemy forces, such as opening dams, will cause immense civilian harm.

The question of the geographical spread of the war is of course extremely sensitive. For perfectly good political reasons, NATO must plan on the basis that a Soviet attack would include the Northern and Southern flanks as well as the Central Front (which is clearly nonsense) and that neutrality would be respected (which is not the way the last two world wars started). In contemplating any aggression, the Kremlin would probably hope to be able to concentrate its efforts on the major areas of contention rather than become involved in battles all along its periphery. On the other hand it might be tempted to gain an advantage by violating Austrian or Swedish neutrality.

It also tends to be assumed that the two alliances would maintain their peacetime composition. This latter assumption has major consequences for analysis of the subsequent battle, yet all historical experience tells us that this is the point when alliances fall apart or are cobbled together with disturbing rapidity. Indeed, it is extremely difficult to develop a scenario for the outbreak of a European war which is not dependent on the collapse of one or other alliance. The first requirement for any alliance strategy must therefore be that it can serve as a source of unity rather than division at a time of crisis.

Once a war is started it is unlikely to follow the path anticipated in peacetime. Moves which at first glance might appear quite innocuous come to be recognised as politically loaded, likely to effect which countries will be dragged into the war and which will stay on the sidelines, or the economic viability of the belligerents. Should the territory of a non-belligerent be allowed to serve as a route of attack against the main enemy? What will be the consequences of energy installations (for example in the North Sea) being attacked?

The orthodox expectation is of a determined Warsaw Pact

assault against NATO's Central Front. The normal pre-sumption is that this will succeed. If it does not then it tends to be assumed that Warsaw Pact forces would conduct an orderly retreat, perhaps waiting to fight another day. How-ever, it is doubtful that Soviet rule could survive a military defeat of this nature. The retreat would be disorderly and there would be opportunities for NATO to exploit the dis-array. Sending forces into the East would involve passing a different sort of threshold and the way it was handled would again reverberate with political implications. An alternative possibility might be a stalemate, with NATO just holding on and/or a Soviet attack faltering with both sides desperate to find a non-nuclear way of breaking the dead-lock. In these circumstances the movement of reserves and raw materials will become critical, with implications for the geographical spread of the conflict.

The simplest model of escalation as graded steps of increasing violence does not correspond with the experience of war. Such a model implies a steady loss of control as the process picks up speed. As each stage is passed the pace increases so that eventually it becomes impossible to apply the brakes. For conflicts to take the form of a series of definite steps through known boundaries normally requires one side to have sufficient military superiority to control the pace. When one or both belligerents fear that delay or restraint could lose them victory or cause them defeat, they will be unwilling to forgo opportunities to obtain a strategic advantage. Another factor that will interfere with attempts to control escalation will be our old friend "the fog of war": a local commander feeling his hand forced by an enemy presence; failures of communication or intelligence; an in-advertent attack on the assets of a neutral.

Experience suggests that wars rarely follow a straight-forward path. In the early stages a military logic can suddenly let rip after being held in check by a political logic. Fighting will be fast and furious, with probing actions serving to set the parameters of the conflict. After that things may settle down while both sides take stock. The first engagements may be among the bloodiest, while some set-piece encounter designed to make a political point might go terribly wrong with such a loss of life that a new edge is immediately added to the dispute. The standards set in the early stages are likely to influence the readiness to consider restraint later on. If atrocities are believed to have occurred and peacetime agreements ignored then there is unlikely to be much response to calls for restraint and magnanimity.

Another critical factor is the extent to which the fighting is clearly linked to a serious political bargaining process. So long as military moves are expected to have their main impact as a form of pressure in the search for a settlement there is hope of controlling escalation. This argues for ensuring that there are robust international institutions or at least lines of diplomatic communication available to sustain a search for a settlement not only at times of tension but also during the early stages of a war.

Conclusion

All these factors add up to a substantial mixture of confusion and uncertainty. My main argument is that we should learn to draw on these as important sources of deterrence. If the adversary is reminded of all the things that could go wrong in the early stages of war he might be further discouraged from attempting anything foolish. We also need to be sensitive to these factors in preparing our forces and political leaders for the management of tension and war. Forces that are designed solely with some setpiece battle in mind, along lines that are appropriate to peacetime exercises and raise few political hackles, are likely to be inappropriate for the more complex sets of moves that may need to be made in such periods of tension and war.

It is no part of my argument that NATO might simply rely on the fog of war to sustain deterrence, in the hope that the adversary will flounder around and grind to a halt for reasons related solely to its own incompetence and confusion. The stronger NATO's forces, the more the adversary must be uncertain about the outcome of any encounter, the more his planners are taxed and the more he may be, if not deterred, forced into clumsy opening gambits. What is being suggested is that in judging the adequacy of NATO's forces, criteria different from — or at least additional to — those normally employed might be useful.

The argument as developed thus far does not lead to a call for a revision of flexible response, simply because that term allows for so many alternatives. Flexible response is little more than a form of words; it is not a strategy in the sense of providing guidance to those who would manage a crisis or a war. It allows those responsible to choose from whatever military options can be made available at the relevant time.

The somewhat vague and indefinite quality that would render it virtually useless at a time of serious confrontation does have value in peacetime, reminding a would-be aggressor that there can be no certainties as to how apparently rational governments would act when they found themselves in an utterly irrational situation. By helping to create an artificial sense of strategic unity within NATO it serves a useful political function.

In strategic terms, the only distinctive feature of flexible response is the refusal to come down firmly on behalf of the conventional or the nuclear spheres, offending those who argue that true deterrence must threaten an almost automatic and immediate nuclear response to any aggression as well as those who argue that all nuclear threats are inherently incredible against a conventional challenge.

Short of these two extremes a multitude of positions — often self-contradictory — can be accommodated. A continuing and often quite heated specialist, and occasionally public, debate revolves around the alternatives. For much of the time this debate is in a sense irrelevant because deterrence depends less on a set of specific threats and capabilities than on a general sense that war would be an unwise and foolish act. The weaknesses of flexible response are unlikely to be put to the test unless a political dynamic develops within Europe capable of throwing the continent into the sort of crisis that would force both sides to look harder at their military options. Quite rightly, force planning cannot proceed in such a way as to create the sort of disruptive political dynamic that needs to be avoided. That is, care should be taken to ensure that it does not take on an aggressive character; nor is allowed to take precedence over responsible forms of arms control and confidence-building measures; nor is so expensive as to lead to domestic upheavals; nor is so controversial that it threatens alliance unity.

However, a political crisis might still develop despite the best efforts of diplomacy and then the movement and disposition of military forces and associated declaratory statements will have to be related very closely to a developing political situation. This is the point when the limits of flexible response will be exposed and it will be found necessary to fashion a strategy suitable for the circumstances, drawing on much capabilities as are available at the time.

Only one part of flexible response is likely to be of value in such a case: the not-too-specific sense that if things get out of control it could all end up with a nuclear disaster. To attempt to turn flexible response into something more specific would as likely as not merely expose its inherent weaknesses. For example, a promise of no-first-use of nuclear weapons would contradict the inherent sense of nuclear risk that ought to provide a source of sobriety in crisis diplomacy. On the other hand definite threats to use nuclear weapons first would also be difficult to sustain, given the probable public unease and the desire to appear responsible.

Reminders of the dangers of all-out nuclear war are important features of crisis diplomacy but are unlikely to be sufficient as a means of fortifying deterrence at a time when it is under the most severe pressure. Moreover, there will probably be only a few nuclear actions and declarations that will be of such practical help in this area. In my view, therefore, it is necessary for NATO to concentrate on conventional forces in its strategic planning. This is essential both to give credibility to the nuclear risk — because without a major clash of arms at the conventional level, nuclear escalation is highly unlikely — and to ensure that practical measures are available with which to back up crisis diplomacy. The important thing in developing conventional strategy is to recognise the profound uncertainties that must face any planner contemplating a conventional war and ensure that the uncertainties facing Soviet planners are unbearably great. In the recent surge of interest in conventional strategy there has been too much of a willingness to assess conventional forces by standards that have long since been abandoned when assessing nuclear forces, and to ignore the prevailing budgetary realities. The task remains one of deterrence not of ensuring military victory, and it is now time to give due weight to the role played by conventional forces in fulfilling that task.

Notes

1. Herman Kahn, **Escalation: Metaphors and Scenarios** (New York, Praeger, 1965).
2. Thomas Schelling, **The Strategy of Conflict** (New York: Oxford University Press, 1963): **Arms and Influence** (New Haven: Yale University Press, 1966).
3. For an earlier version of some of the ideas developed in the following paragraphs see my essay "The no-first-use debate and the theory of thresholds" in Frank Blackaby, Jozef Goldblat and Sverre Lodgaard (ed), **No-First-Use** (London: Taylor and Francis, 1984).

(This paper was prepared for the Royal United Services Institute, Nuneham Park Conference).

7 Negotiations on Nuclear Forces in Europe, 1969–83

European-based nuclear weapons only began to play a prominent role in arms control negotiations at the start of the 1980s. They had been relevant to the course of negotiations on strategic arms, however, since the talks began in 1969. An examination of this history illuminates the origins of the current impasse in the negotiations.

My object in this Essay is to provide a history of the arms control negotiations on nuclear weapons in Europe since the Strategic Arms Limitation Talks (SALT) began in November 1969. The story ends with the 1983 impasse. It points to a way out of the impasse — along lines which are hardly original — but the main value may be in suggesting how to avoid reaching a similar impasse in the future.[1]

There may be some impatience with a backward look during the course of a forward-looking debate. However, there is a need to keep the current arguments in perspective. First, it is easy to believe that the current problems are simply the result of an inflexible American or Soviet stance. However, there is no evidence that negotiators operating in a more favourable political environment found the problems — albeit in a different form — much less intractable. Secondly, and more optimistically, the history of shifts and turns in negotiating positions reminds us that what seems fundamental at one moment is disposable the next although it still must be admitted that it is normally the other way round!

The history of the arms control negotiations might make one optimistic or pessimistic about the prospects for a deal. It certainly encourages the view that if a deal is struck it is going to be less radical than the rhetoric surrounding the negotiations might lead us to believe. The overall effect of the history, therefore, might be taken as casting doubt on the role that arms control negotiations can play as a means of rationalising force structures.

SALT — Agreeing the Limits

When SALT began in November 1969, there was every reason to believe that the question of nuclear weapons based in Europe was not going to loom large as a basic issue. During the 1960s both superpowers had put their greatest stress on intercontinental systems. The United States had begun the decade by removing Thor and Jupiter missiles without replacing them with systems of comparable range and, a year before SALT opened, removed from Germany 90 MACE-B cruise missiles capable of reaching the Soviet Union. While long-range systems were thus out of favour, the United States still doubled the number of short-range systems (from 3,500 to 7,000 warheads), but these could not reach Soviet territory and were generally not given much prominence in US pronouncements.

In the Soviet Union there were signs of a continuing, but not desperately successful, research effort on medium-range missiles. Systems for Europe seemed a low priority as against the massive investment of the late 1960s in ICBMs and SLBMs. Moreover the particular concerns that had animated Warsaw Pact proposals in the past, such as the various schemes for "atom-free zones", had been eased by other means. The signing of the Non-Proliferation Treaty and the demise of the plan for a NATO Multilateral Force had calmed worries concerning German access to nuclear weapons, while the agreements and Treaties on Berlin and Soviet-West German relations made it unnecessary to secure recognition of the territorial status quo via indirect means.

Nevertheless, while there were grounds for believing that the importance of nuclear weapons in Europe to the strategic calculations of both superpowers was small and declining, these weapons raised a series of awkward questions that made it likely from the start that they would complicate the negotiations.

The first question they raised was that of the scope of the talks. In any agreement some restrictions have to be placed on weapons just outside the formal scope in order to prevent circumvention. In this case there was a difficulty in limiting the formal scope. Was the concern with weapons of a particular range, able to travel intercontinental distances, or with weapons capable of reaching a particular target, that is the territory of a superpower? Taking the first view allowed for a cut-off point by range, with due allowance for submarine-launched systems. This was favoured by the United States but was unacceptable to the Soviet Union which felt directly under threat from British, French and Chinese systems, US weapons based in Europe, as well as from US intercontinental systems.

This raised the question of responsibility to allies. The Soviet view of the scope of the talks challenged the United States to negotiate on behalf of other countries in bilateral talks, to accept restrictions on weapons which played a major role in the basic security guarantees it had made to its allies, while not obtaining restrictions on Soviet weapons which directly threatened these allies. In principle these were issues also of concern to the Warsaw Pact. However, the Pact's comparative compactness, which meant that the same weapons tended to threaten all members, including the Soviet Union, the lack of Soviet nuclear weapons based in Eastern Europe, and a political structure which assigned overwhelming priority to Soviet interests, kept any East European fears below the surface.

Thus once the negotiations began to drift towards those systems based in and targeted upon Europe, it was going to be very difficult to contain them. Instead of bilateral discussions concerning clear categories of weapons, SALT would get entangled in the overall strategic relationship between the two alliances. An added disincentive was the knowledge that the numbers and types of European systems were of a sort that would frustrate negotiations.

At the start of SALT neither side accepted the difficulties of setting limits to the negotiations. Both proposed partial limits on some of the other side's European systems. The initial American SALT proposal developed prior to the start of the negotiations advocated a freeze on medium-range ballistic missiles (which only the Russians still maintained) and a ban on mobile versions thereof. This was not fundamental to the American proposal and was largely motivated by a desire to make any agreement on intercontinental missiles easier to verify. However, it did serve to placate those who argued that, if Alliance unity had any meaning, weapons aimed at London and Bonn were as strategic as those aimed at Washington and New York.

As the American team presented their initial ideas, they were taken by surprise by the Soviet Union's own proposal. The Soviet team claimed that American fighter-bombers in Europe had the range to reach the Soviet Union and so were strategic and should be withdrawn before the talks could proceed. On similar grounds, it argued for the removal of American forces in the Far East and on aircraft carriers. The exclusion of the Soviet Union's own theatre forces was justified on the grounds that these could not reach the United States and were needed for defence against third countries. [2]

This latter point, of course, made it difficult for the Soviet Union to argue for inclusion of third-country forces. It nevertheless did so, in a muted way. The lack of conviction behind the effort was illustrated by the concentration on only submarine-based forces and the neglect of British and French aircraft.

The US and Soviet proposals on theatre forces led to an impasse and was responsible for a lack of progress at the talks. The Americans eventually proposed, in August 1970, that forward-based systems (FBS) and medium-range missiles both be excluded to allow for progress on the basic issue of central strategic systems. This was supported by the Allies. Whatever the West European view a decade later, at that time far greater priority was attached to keeping the US forward-based systems out than getting the Soviet missiles in. [3]

The Soviet Union dropped only its demand for the withdrawal of forward-based systems, but still insisted that these systems be properly taken into account in the main agreement.

This was not explicitly granted in the SALT I agreement of May 1972, and the issue itself is barely discussed in many accounts of the accord.[4] However, a number of tacit concessions may have been made by the United States in return for Soviet deferral of the FBS issue: the agreement was far more limited than originally proposed and allowed the Russians numerical superiority in offensive missiles. One of the arguments used to justify this imbalance to domestic critics in the United States was the lack of constraint on US systems based in Europe. The Russians also seemed to think that they had been given some allowance for British, French and Chinese systems. In a unilateral statement of May 1972, which was not accepted by the United States, the Soviet team argued that any additional British or French missile-carrying submarines in addition to the nine then deployed or planned would justify a comparable Soviet increase in submarine numbers.[5] One direct consequence of the inequality embodied in the 1972 agreement, which made it possible for the Soviet Union to make this argument, was that the US Senate passed the Jackson Amendment which required future American-Soviet agreements to be based on strict equality and so made it extremely difficult for the Soviet Union to be given any allowance for the forces of small nuclear powers in the future.

As the FBS had not been formally included in SALT I, they were still available as a Soviet bargaining chip in the subsequent SALT II negotiations. Once again the Soviet Union raised the issue. The November 1974 Vladivostok aide-mémoire between Presidents Ford and Brezhnev excluded FBS, and Kissinger suggested that this made the US Soviet agreement possible,[6] but once again there were suspicions that some form of quid pro quo had been obtained by the Soviet Union, including the acceptance of high force ceilings,[7] the inclusion of heavy bombers, and the abandonment of attempts to reduce the Soviet heavy-missile arsenal.

Throughout this period, the issue of nuclear weapons in Europe was not dealt with head-on. It was seen as peripheral to the main concerns of SALT and the weapons themselves were viewed rather as relics of a bygone age. For the Russians, leaving the FBS issue unsettled and deferred for future talks, kept it available as a bargaining chip, while formal agreement might legitimise the US presence in Europe and draw attention to the imbalance in theatre forces. The fact that NATO had stressed short-range "battlefield" nuclear weapons, where NATO itself did enjoy an advantage, while the Soviet Union had focused on the FBS issue, meant that there was remarkable ignorance at the time of the extent of the Soviet numerical lead in medium-range aircraft and missiles. The Americans for their part wanted to keep FBS out of the talks because of potential difficulties with allies. While justifying the exclusion of FBS by reference to the Soviet position on its own theatre forces there was little disposition to push the linkage so as to achieve a clear trade off between the Soviet missiles and the American aircraft. Thus, over the first few years of SALT, the issue declined rather than grew in importance.[8] The Soviet Union had seemed to have a better case through the direct threat posed by the US aircraft in Europe to Soviet territory. However, with the deferral of this issue at Vladivostok, which was to provide the framework for a 10-year SALT II treaty, it might have been hoped that the issue was no longer going to haunt the negotiations.

SALT II — the Grey Areas

At Vladivostok the superpowers had excluded their existing theatre arsenals from the SALT II talks. Despite the fact that these negotiations continued for five more years, the exclusions were not seriously challenged, though threats to revive the FBS issue became a frequent Soviet tactic[9] when the Americans tried to go back on other aspects of the Vladivostok accords. The United States, similarly, abandoned its tentative efforts to restrict Soviet theatre forces, and concentrated instead on those systems which could reach American itself. Indeed, the vulnerability of the national homeland began to obsess Americans even more than Russians.

The advent of new weapons which cut across the boundaries so laboriously established in the early 1970s ensured that theatre nuclear weapons would remain a major issue throughout the SALT process, even after the Vladivostok accord.

The weapons which caused these problems were described as "grey area" systems, in that they could not be properly described as either strategic or theatre systems.[10] The principal weapons in this category were the Backfire bomber and the cruise missile. Each side also had a lesser candidate, in the form of the SS-20 and the FB-111 aircraft respectively. The SS-20 was rarely thought to have an intercontinental capability per se.[11] However, many Americans were disturbed by the technical compatibility of this missile with the truly intercontinental SS-16, and continued to urge its inclusion in SALT until the Soviet Union virtually abandoned its SS-16 programme in October 1977.[12] By that time, there were more direct reasons for the United States to pursue SS-20 constraints. The arms control impact of the FB-111 was very different. Since this aircraft was inferior to the Backfire in both numbers and capability, the Russians did not press for its inclusion in SALT.

Backfire was the oldest of the grey area systems, becoming known in the United States in the late 1960s. Its SALT involvement, however, did not start until 1974, when a debate began about whether it counted as a heavy bomber under the Vladivostok accords. It seems that Kissinger deliberately failed to mention Backfire at Vladivostok, and that the Russians took this as a guarantee of its exclusion.[13] The Backfire problem was rather like that of FBS in reverse, in that the aircraft was primarily intended to fulfil a theatre mission but was technically capable of striking the opposing homeland.[14] Throughout 1975, the United States pressed for Backfire to be included in SALT, while Russia remained adamantly opposed.

At the same time, the other main grey area system was also making its presence felt. The modern cruise missile programme was sponsored by Kissinger in the early 1970s, at least partially to provide a bargaining chip in future SALT negotiations.[15] However, more primitive cruise missiles still lingered from the early stages of the nuclear race and prompted some ironic exchanges in SALT before the modern potential of the weapon was recognised. In 1969, the United States proposed a freeze on submarine-launched cruise missiles, which only the Russians then retained. The Soviet Union, no less short-sightedly, refused. The chief Russian negotiator, intent on ridiculing the American concern, compared cruise missiles to "prehistoric animals of the Triassic period".[16]

The new cruise programme in the 1970s was focused initially on a qualitative upgrading of the US strategic arsenal with submarine-launched cruise missiles, comparable to those of the Soviet Union. This soon was overtaken by the air-launched programmes.[17] It soon became clear that the new weapon could have an independent role in the theatre context, delivering nuclear or conventional munitions from a variety of platforms and with phenomenal accuracy. What had been conceived as an expendable bargaining chip grew into a highly desirable and versatile weapons system.[18] A worse complication from the arms control point of view was that the range and payload of any given type were impossible to verify. The cruise missile was, in short, a grey area system par excellence.

The SALT involvement of cruise in the mid-1970s centred on the twin issues of range restrictions and counting rules. Russia used an imprecise statement in the Vladivostok accords to press for a ban on all cruise missiles over 600 kilometres in range. The United States, while prepared to forgo systems which had intercontinental range in their own right, was wary of any greater constraints. However, American was more concerned about the stand-off capabilities of its heavy bombers than about independent cruise platforms, and in the compromise proposals of 1975 and 1976, the future of cruise as a submarine-launched system appears to have hung upon the edge of a knife.[19]

In 1976, concerned about the possibility of a negotiating sell-out and a budgetary veto, the US Navy reclassified its planned cruise missile submarines as theatre weapons, needed to match the Backfire and the SS.20.[20] The classification stuck. When the new *ground*-launched cruise missile first entered the SALT negotiations soon afterwards, the submarine version was classed with it, and so shared the protective unbrella of European concern.

The issues of Backfire and cruise were the principal obstacles to progress in SALT II for nearly three years after the Vladivostok Summit. This being the case, it was natural that a trade-off should be attempted to break the deadlock. On two occasions, once in February 1976 and again a year later, the United States proposed that the twin problems be deferred to SALT III to enable an interim agreement to be reached. The Soviet Union, however, was not prepared to leave cruise missiles unconstrained, even for a ransom of strategic concessions.[21] It became obvious that some more complicated solution to the grey area problem was required.

In January 1976, Kissinger had tried to arrange a positive linkage between Backfire and cruise in the form of mutually acceptable restrictions on the two systems. His attempt foundered on the unwillingness of both sides to accept real constraints on their own weapons programmes. There were many later US ideas for a deal along similar lines, but they were all defeated by a combination of domestic resistance and Soviet intransigence. Positive linkage between Backfire and cruise provided no more of a solution than had negative linkage.

The dilemma was eventually solved by indirect means. The final outcome of the SALT II talks was that each side gave as many concessions as it could afford on its own grey area systems, and the agreement was then balanced by informal trade-offs at the strategic level. The real question is why the limited concessions made on Backfire and cruise proved acceptable to the opposing blocs, which had originally demanded so much more.

Backfire was not made subject to major constraints. The Soviet Union had steadfastly resisted American demands that it should count as a heavy bomber, or that its deployment should be limited to ''peripheral'' areas such as Europe.[22] All the United States obtained was a written promise not to increase the Backfire production rate from 30 per year (a level which it has not always met in recent years) nor to convert the aircraft to an intercontinental role. One way in which America reconciled itself to this setback was to assert its right to counter the Backfire by a similar US system, namely the FB-111. This assertion was not, however, sufficient to prevent the issue of Backfire exclusion from becoming a prime target for critics of the SALT II treaty. It is worth noting that many in the US arms control community were highly dubious of the suggestion that Backfire deserved inclusion in SALT. The range and purpose of Backfire became an annual source of dispute in the formation of the national intelligence estimates. The push to include Backfire in SALT (which is still relevant in the subsequent US-Soviet Strategic Arms Reduction Talks — START) was not successful yet must be blamed for blurring the boundaries of the negotiations.

The issue of cruise missile restrictions was less straightforward. The United States accepted substantial limits on the air-launched version of this missile, in terms of numerical ceilings on its deployment. The ground- and sea-launched versions, however, remained effectively unhampered. This was despite the fact that the Soviet Union viewed the ground- and sea-launched versions as being much more threatening than the air-launched cruise missile, and at one point even offered to abandon restrictions on the latter in order to get stricter controls on the former. A written protocol which prohibited their deployment, along with the MX, for three years did no more than state a physical fact. This protocol served as a device to put off difficult issues for future negotiations, while putting down a marker for the content of those negotiations, reinforced by a declaration of principles on SALT III. [23]

The Russians expected or at least hoped that the protocol would set a precedent for the future. Realising that the growing pressure from both European and domestic quarters would prevent the US administration from granting real concessions on ground-launched cruise missiles, the Soviet Union settled for a seemingly innocuous arrangement which might covertly influence later American decisions. The Soviet Union also failed to make much headway on the non-circumvention issue. In 1975, Russia had proposed a definite clause forbidding the transfer of cruise missile technology to third countries. The United States refused to go this far, and in April 1978 a compromise was reached by which both sides made a general undertaking not to circumvent the SALT II treaty in any way.[24]

Even those concessions which the United States hailed as meaningless (such as the non-circumvention clause and the three-year protocol) were regarded by Europeans with grave foreboding. US critics of SALT were quick to seize on European anxieties as a stick with which to beat their own government. President Carter was forced not only to renounce any substantive restrictions on the ground-launched cruise missile, but also to give a positive assurance that the weapons could be deployed in Europe once the three-year protocol expired. Far from setting a precedent as Russia had hoped, the protocol actively precipitated the modernisation decision.[25] More paradoxically still, the European worries over cruise helped to prejudice the very arms control process which was fast becoming a political necessity for the success of the theatre nuclear force (TNF) programme.

The real root of the increased NATO sensitivity was the shift from stagnation in the theatre stockpiles to an accelerating arms race. The Europeans did not want SALT to prejudice any weapons system which might conceivably be needed to counter the new Soviet build-up. This meant, in effect, the cruise missile. NATO solicitude for cruise was at first incoherent, framed in terms of conventional requirements or the potential modernisation of national nuclear forces. Then, in October 1977, Helmut Schmidt publicly spoke of a fear that he had been expressing privately for some time, concerning an unfavourable ''Euro-strategic balance''.[26] The Europeans were worried that, through its preoccupation with the vulnerability of the United States, America would leave the theatre capabilities of Backfire and SS-20 unconstrained by SALT, while bargaining away any Western response. Meanwhile, by codifying a sort of symmetry at the strategic level, SALT was enhancing the importance of asymmetries lower down the line. Last, but by no means least, it was believed by many defence planners that, irrespective of what the Russians were up to with the SS-20, NATO had to improve its own theatre forces because of the age of the existing capabilities, in particular the F-111 and the Vulcan bomber.

The problem was more than the ''greyness'' of the weapons. The two superpowers did not waste so much time and effort on the issues of Backfire and cruise simply because of an inability clearly to distinguish theatre and strategic weapons. The submarine arsenals displayed an even greater technological ambiguity which was overcome without such distress. What gave impetus to the disputes over Backfire and cruise was that these systems were exhibiting a dynamic that was not evident, for example, with diesel submarines. The very momentum of the grey area programme would have attracted arms control efforts, regardless of the technological ambiguities which the weapons possessed. Systems with a more precise role would have produced concerns which were less universal, but no less vociferous. Excluding a stable TNF situation from the SALT process at Vladivostok was one thing: excluding what appeared as a growing theatre arms race was quite another.

SALT II to INF

There was a growing consensus in the late 1970s that theatre nuclear weapons should be directly involved in future arms control negotiations. The development which forged this consensus was that the two blocs at last became prepared to pay for restrictions on opposing TNF by accepting constraints on their own arsenals. A new readiness among Western leaders to countenance positive arms control linkage between opposing theatre systems first became apparent during 1977.

NATO certainly soon got into the habit of pointing to the SS-20 as a menacing feature of the Soviet military build-up, but failed to develop a consistent proposal for its restraint or a clear sense of the Western programmes with which it should be linked. Thus, in February 1977, President Carter offered to halt the development of the MX missile if the

Soviet Union would agree not to deploy any mobile missiles of its own.[27] The Russians appear to have deduced (correctly) that the MX programme was in trouble, and so refused to go along. A year later, the United States announced that it would make its final decision on the neutron bomb dependent upon Soviet concessions with regard to the SS-20.[28] By now, however, the political liabilities of the neutron bomb were evident. Russia preferred to reject any idea of a trade-off, and to work instead for a mutual ban on this devilish new weapon (for which the Soviet forces had conveniently little use).[29] As we shall see, it was not until NATO came up with a programme that the Soviet Union found genuinely threatening — the cruise missile — that a trade with the Soviet medium-range missile force became possible. Then the Soviets took the initiative. In mid-1979, Brezhnev declared that Russia was now willing to include its medium-range weapons in any future talks. For the first time, there appeared to be a bilateral acceptance of TNF arms control in its own right.

One principal reason for this development was that both sides feared the unrestrained theatre arms race which seemed the most likely alternative to TNF negotiations. There were also more specific reasons:

1. The Americans were concerned that the technological ambiguity of grey area systems, together with the resurrection of the FBS issue on the expiry of the Vladivostok compromise, would prevent any further progress in SALT unless the TNF problem was tackled head-on.[30]
2. The Europeans wanted to remove or to counter the growing threat posed by Backfire and SS-20, and had learnt from the furore over the neutron bomb that any programme for new nuclear deployments had to be accompanied by substantive proposals for arms control.[31]
3. The Russians were extremely worried about the military and political implications of having cruise and longer-range Pershing missiles stationed in Western Europe.

In the development of the approach to this problem, the West made nearly all the running. Soviet proposals in this period were concerned far less with the actual form of theatre negotiations than with delaying the NATO decision on TNF modernisation. Western thinking, also, was heavily bound up with the cruise and Pershing programme. In late 1979, there was a strenuous debate within NATO about whether TNF talks should be pursued before or after the deployment decision was made.[32] The final outcome, in December, was that a "two-track" policy was announced, with modernisation and arms control strategies tightly linked.

In December 1979, NATO ministers approved a programme to base 464 Tomahawk cruise missiles and 108 Pershing II ballistic missiles in Europe during the 1980s. The Soviet SS-20 missile, which had first attracted public notice in 1976, was used by Western leaders to assign responsibility for any arms race to the East. This new missile, with its accurate, multiple warheads, also put at risk facilities connected with NATO's theatre nuclear system. The opportunity to justify the modernisation programme by reference to the SS-20 was too good to miss, and the future of the two programmes was seen to be linked.

This encouraged the view that it was necessary to produce an arms control proposal in parallel with the plans for force modernisation. NATO planners worked within a range of 200 to 600 missiles: the fact that the final figure of 572, agreed in December 1979, is near the top of the range can, in part, be seen as anticipating some future cuts in the programme out of deference to arms control. The actual proposal agreed in December 1979 involved the following principles:

(a) Any future limitation on US systems designed principally for theatre missions should be accompanied by appropriate limitations on Soviet theatre systems.

(b) Limitations on US and Soviet long-range theatre nuclear systems should be negotiated bilaterally in the SALT III framework in a step-by-step approach.

(c) The immediate objective of these negotiations should be the establishment of agreed limitations on US and Soviet land-based long-range theatre nuclear missile systems.

(d) Any agreed limitations on these systems must be consistent with the principle of equality between the sides. Therefore, the limitations should take the form of de jure equality both in ceilings and in rights.

(e) Any agreed limitation must be adequately verifiable.[33]

Adopting SALT as the most appropriate forum acknowledged that cruise missiles were already bound up with SALT. Completely separate talks on central and theatre systems could symbolise a break in the link between the major US nuclear arsenal and the defence of Europe.[34] Already, however, by December 1979, the possibility of having to conduct separate talks on theatre forces if SALT II was not ratified had been considered.[35] A number of European politicians had made their support of the decision dependent on the ratification of SALT II, but this point was not pressed home, possibly because of the international circumstances prevailing at the time of non-ratification. It is of note that the NATO communiqué linked deployment only to a negotiating effort. The presumption was that deployment would be limited, but not abandoned in successful negotiations, and only Belgium and Holland linked their participation explicitly to the quality of NATO's negotiating effort. No timetable was insisted on. The deadline, if any, was not the December 1983 initial deployment of cruise, but the December 1981 expiry of the protocol of SALT II.

It had once been assumed that a prominent role for theatre systems would necessitate European representation at SALT, in order to watch over the local interests, but this turned out not to be so. As a practical matter, the experience of the multilateral Mutual and Balanced Force Reduction (MBFR) talks in Vienna suggested there was an advantage in keeping the negotiations bilateral. Confusion could result from involving all interested parties. The unwillingness of the British and French to expose their small nuclear forces confirmed the bilateralism. Only American missiles from the NATO side were to be discussed. Restricting future negotiations to ''land-based missiles'' reflected the popular perception of the issue at hand.[36] It would also keep matters simple by excluding aircraft. However, there was a disposition against regional ceilings, on the grounds that only a global ceiling could take in most of the relevant SS-20s.

The actual substance of the proposal reveals the preoccupation with parity. Condition (d) spoke only of de jure equality, which was meant to indicate that NATO would be more interested in establishing a right to equal ceilings than in actually creating an equality in practice. The problem was in combining two contradictory objectives. The culture of arms control and popular perceptions of the issues stressed the importance of missile parity. Yet the military require-ment had not been to match the SS-20, missile for missile, but merely to provide a credible response, reflecting established requirements. More important, in doctrinal terms, the notion of a separate regional balance implied by parity reflected exactly the sort of uncoupling from the central strategic balance that West Europeans had been trying to prevent.

In practical terms, condition (d) above meant using up negotiating capital to establish a right to systems beyond NATO's requirements, which if exercised, would run counter to received doctrine.

To add to the problems, the Soviet position was at vari-ance with that of NATO. On the formal completion of SALT II in June 1979, the Soviet Union quickly placed European-based systems on the agenda for SALT III. Meeting with the Press on 25 June, Soviet Foreign Minister Gromyko suggested the possibility of drawing other countries and their weapons into SALT and also covering the FBS issue.

A willingness to negotiate on missiles based in Europe had been indicated by Brezhnev as early as March 1979, but the most direct appeal was made in his speech by 6 October. After insisting that the number of ''medium-range nuclear delivery vehicles on the territory of the European portion of the Soviet Union'' had been reduced and not increased (which is true but ignores the extra range and warheads of the MIRVed SS-20), Brezhnev spoke of a readiness ''to reduce, compared with the present level, the quantity of medium-range nuclear missiles deployed in the western parts of the Soviet Union: but, of course, only in the event that there is no additional deployment of medium-range missiles in Western Europe''. In the period leading up to 12 December, this offer was stressed, although its ambiguities were never clarified, particularly as to whether the SS-20 was to be included. It is now widely felt by participants in the NATO policy-making of the time that had Brezhnev offered to freeze the number of SS-20s, it is unlikely that the Alliance would have gone ahead with the December 1979 decision.

After the NATO decision, the main question was whether the Soviet Union would agree to talk at all. The initial reaction was that the "basis" for talks had been destroyed, but by July, and Chancellor Schmidt's visit to Moscow, a new basis had been found. The new Soviet position was stated in **Pravda** on 7 July 1980:

> Without withdrawing the proposals put forward earlier, [the Soviet Union] could also agree to a discussion of issues relating to medium-range weapons even before ratification of SALT II. At the same time, the discussions must involve not only medium-range missiles, but also US forward-based nuclear weapons. Both these problems must be discussed simultaneously and in organic connection. ... Possible accords could be implemented only after the SALT II Treaty comes into force.[37]

In terms of the subject matter of the negotiations, therefore, the key difference between the two sides was the FBS question. The other long-standing Soviet objective, the inclusion of British and French forces, appeared to have been postponed.

INF Talks — Problems of Definition

From October to November 1980, preliminary discussions between American and Soviet teams on theatre nuclear arms control took place in Geneva. In May 1981, Secretary of State Alexander Haig agreed in Rome that negotiations should resume before the end of the year, the timing to be settled when he met Soviet Foreign Minister Andrei Gromyko at the UN General Assembly in September. The unpromising nature of the whole enterprise was illustrated by the difficulties found in describing the 1980 talks. To the USSR, they were "Discussions of Questions related to Nuclear Arms in Europe", which, for the West, begged the question of Soviet weapons that could attack Europe from bases in Asia. The American alternative, ''Discussions of Questions related to the Limitation of Certain US and Soviet Forces'', did not convey even a vague sense of an agenda.

Prior to the start of the negotiations proper in November 1981, it was possible to identify the main problems that were going to create difficulties. First, there was the NATO desire to concentrate solely on missiles, whereas the Soviet Union wished to include aircraft. The **Pravda** editorial of 15 July 1980 stated that ''hundreds and hundreds of various American carriers of nuclear weapons and bases at which they were deployed are involved''.

The United States argued that its F-4s and carrier-based A-6 and A-7s were dual-capable and generally unsuitable for strikes into Soviet territory. Verification would be very difficult. For example, once the carrier-based aircraft were included, there would have to be some rules as to the patrols and composition of the US fleets in the Mediterranean and the Atlantic.

Another problem was that the Soviet Union wished to confine discussions to forces actually based in Europe, while the United States could not accept that. At a minimum, the SS-20s able to cover both Western Europe and China in sites just east of the Urals would have to be included. NATO also envisaged limitations on relevant systems currently facing China. From the Soviet perspective, these SS-20s and bombers have nothing to do with the European theatre; from the NATO perspective, these systems could be turned against it, either as a result of a Sino–Soviet rapprochement or just through reinforcement measures in an emergency. It has been suggested that SS-20s could be transported to new sites by air. (There are obviously no problems for the Soviet Union in moving aircraft from its eastern to its western front.)

A basic problem lay behind these attempts to impose limits, of either geography or weapons, on the scope of the negotiations. The Soviet Union had always seen itself as demandeur on the issue of nuclear weapons in Europe, because of the greater importance it attached to weapons that could attack Soviet territory as against those which could merely attack the territory of its allies. If, however, Soviet weapons of comparable range to the US FBS were included, then a comparison of the US and Soviet inventories put the Soviet Union far ahead in numbers. If the argument was going to be phrased in terms of equality then the Soviet Union would have to make all the concessions. It was too much for the Kremlin to move from a situation where the United States had to make all the concessions to one where it had to make the concessions, so instinctively the Soviet leadership argued that the basic position was equal and that therefore the two sides should make equal reductions and eschew one-sided increases. Parity existed and had to be preserved.

NATO had, in the past, resisted notions of separate European balances, but the culture of arms control and the logic of its own arguments was forcing it towards such a balance. The initial negotiating offer reflected the history of European systems being seen as complicating factors in the central strategic balance, to be dealt with either as part of a broader deal or as a one-off trade between two equally awkward (if not strategically comparable) systems. This depended on being able to view cruise/Pershing and the SS-4/5/20 in isolation from other systems in Europe. This might have been possible while negotiations on central systems provided the dynamic to arms control, but was hopeless once these theatre negotiations had to stand on their own. Given the long-standing Soviet position on FBS, the inclusion of aircraft was inevitable (even if, as noted below, this was double-edged for the Soviet Union). NATO, too, was being forced to argue for equality in Europe, despite all its doctrinal misgivings about such a course. To justify extra missiles coming in on the NATO side, it could not be accepted that parity existed. For NATO, parity was now desirable, but had to be created.

So during 1981, as the two sides prepared themselves for the start of the formal negotiations, they were drifting in uncharted waters. The Intermediate Nuclear Force (INF) negotiations, as the Americans now dubbed them,[38] were the orphaned child of SALT. Without parental guidance they had to stand alone. But neither the United States nor the Soviet Union had a concept for dealing with this situation, as arguments in the past had been subsidiary to arguments on central forces. Both constructed new positions which were, in practice, rootless and bore little relationship to past positions. Unfortunately, when the two sides constructed their positions they came out with completely opposing versions of the existing states of affairs. It would have been easiest if the Soviet Union had been right and there had been a prior equality. Basic equality makes negotiating easier. It was doubly unfortunate that the Americans were right, in that there was inequality, and that even if agreement could be reached on the existing state of affairs, there would then have to be an argument on creating equality.

Negotiating to Public Opinion

Negotiations began in November 1981. The course of these negotiations has been extremely complex, and I do not wish to go over the twists and turns.[39] Before examining the basic positions, it is important to note a key feature of the situation that has influenced both sides' behaviour. It has become a truism that the United States and the Soviet Union have been gearing their statements as much to Western public opinion as to the other side.[40] The Soviet Union has had grounds for hoping that the cruise/Pershing programme would be scuttled through domestic opposition — so obviating the need for concessions on its part. The United States, for its part, assumed that it was only when it seemed likely that the NATO programme would go ahead that Soviet concessions would be forthcoming. Its positions have thus been designed to secure support from domestic opinion, even if they were unacceptable to the Soviet Union.

Obviously, there was always the possibility that in the effort to demonstrate reasonableness in public either side might actually become more reasonable. However, despite initial promises from the negotiating teams of discreet, business-like diplomacy, the continual playing to the gallery by the national leaders has undercut traditional diplomacy. Bold statements demanding quick rebuttals are rarely conducive to the solution of complex issues. In fact, the process of public debating has served to reinforce the original positions which can now probably only be reconciled, if at all, through intensive private diplomacy.

The opening American position was the so-called "zero option" by which NATO would forgo the cruise/Pershing programme if the Soviet Union abandoned all of its SS-4s, SS-5s and SS-20s, including those in the Far East.[41] For anyone familiar with the background to these matters this was a complete reversal of traditional NATO thinking, which stressed NATO's unique requirement for some "coupling" intermediate nuclear forces — irrespective of the number of Soviet missiles. For those concerned with the short term, the zero option was politically clever in that it disarmed the disarmers by appropriating their slogan. An earlier version of this option, which would also have banned the SS-22, a shorter-range missile but still capable of hitting deep into Western Europe, was rejected after European representations that this would be so one-sided as not to be taken at all seriously.

The episode showed up the European governments' pre-occupations with getting the Americans to provide a negotiating spectacle, without devoting much thought to the content of the negotiations. At some point the spectacle has to move to a finale, and the lack of thought on the content meant that the West European approach was always vulnerable to a Soviet veto, which could deny any position the image of "negotiability". This fate befell the zero option and is now likely to be suffered by the new compromise — the "interim solution".[42] The interim solution, by which both sides have equal numbers of missile warheads, at a level as close as possible to zero, is more acceptable in doctrinal terms but no more negotiable because it still depends on the assumption that parity must be created in the negotiations largely through Soviet concessions. It also lacks the political advantage of the zero option in that it carries with it the strong suggestion that somewhere, some-how, cruise and Pershing missiles will remain deployed.

The Soviet position is stronger in that its weapons are in place. Furthermore, its negotiating positions have not been scrutinised for their ''negotiability'' as much as those of NATO. This is surprising for the basic construction of the Soviet position is quite bogus. It claims an existing equality of aircraft and missiles in Europe — at just under 1,000 apiece. However, it can only construct this equality by disregarding its own counting rules at difficult moments. Thus it imposes a geographical restriction to keep out its own aircraft and systems facing China (which could be moved to face Western Europe in a crisis), yet wishes to include US FB-111 aircraft and A-6/A-7 aircraft or carriers, both based outside of its own guidelines area. It has a minimum range of 1,000 kilometres, which would exclude US F-4s but include its SU-19 Fencer, yet it tries to being in the former and keep out the latter by playing games with calculations of combat range (essentially by suggesting that the US F-4s need have no worries about Soviet air defences so that it could fly at a continual high altitude, while the Soviet SU-19s *would* have to worry about their own defences and fly continually from base at a low altitude!). Lastly, it wants to include British and French submarines, despite the fact that, by its own previous arguments as well as those of the countries concerned, these should be discussed, if at all, as strategic forces.

The Soviet position as laid down in a draft treaty of May 1982 would have the two sides going down to 300 within five years of the treaty coming into force. The form of the Soviet calculation would mean that it could keep a reasonably healthy SS-20 and Backfire force while all US aircraft would be expelled from Europe and there would even have to be a reduction in the number of US-based FB-111s.

In December 1982 Mr Andropov modified the formula to allow for a specific deal, relating the number of SS-20s to British and French missiles (162). The offer underlined the Soviet preoccupation with getting the Americans out of Europe rather than cutting the European forces, and it did for the first time offer a specific limit on numbers of SS-20s, but it did not involve a move away from the previous position which included aircraft. Aircraft would still have to be reduced.[43] A later amendment, of May 1983, made a concession that would have been important in the context of US–Soviet missile comparisons, but with the background of the Soviet draft treaty it was merely mischievous. Andropov agreed to count warheads rather than launchers, but when note is taken of the assumed numbers of warheads on current British and French missiles, the net result is the same as the previous offer with the Soviet Union still allowed some 160 SS-20s.[44]

Conclusion — Lost Opportunities

This saga provides an illustration of how not to go about arms control. The issues surrounding nuclear weapons in Europe would be intractable at the best of times. The weapons perform quite different political functions within the two alliances and are held in such different ways and in such different numbers that they defy neat categories and attempts to impose some formal equality. It might have been best not to touch them with arms control but that option was not available as soon as the SALT process embraced a concept so all-embracing as parity. Once one starts to count offensive systems it is difficult to stop, because there will always be something or other that will blur the boundaries.

This particular problem might have been more tractable in the early 1970s when the forces seemed reasonably settled. Whatever opportunity there might have been was lost through the natural disposition to put off awkward issues of low salience. By the time it had become impossible to defer the issue any more, the political, strategic and arms control context had become much less propitious. As with many other areas of political activity, attitudes are often struck more with regard to immediate pressures and short-term effect than with regard to longer-term considerations. The history of arms control is littered with lost opportunities, as weapons still at the early stage of development or issues of great potential relevance but of slight contemporary interest pass by.

It may be that until arms control can escape from the dead hand of parity then there is always the possibility of a repeat performance. Already many in the field hanker after entangling battlefield nuclear weapons in the arms control net. It is not that these weapons are wholly benign and deserve protection from interference but that arms control, as now conceived and practised, is the least promising method for addressing the problems that they create.

It is not possible to turn the clock back and restart the arms control enterprise on the basis of more modest and clearer ambitions. With the INF negotiations now being forced to carry an enormous political burden — for the state of Alliance cohesion as well as of East–West relations — there is a need for a ''fix'' of some sort.

It is unlikely that the formal position of either side can serve as a basis for an eventual agreement. If matters are expected to proceed from highly publicised offer to equally highly publicised counter-offer, with long gaps for tortuous internal negotiations in between, then, at the current rate of concessions, agreement might just about be reached on the completion of the NATO programme in 1989. At some point, somebody must be given the authority to do a deal. Such a deal could be most readily struck at foreign minister level. Only when there are signs of active diplomacy at this level can one be at all optimistic.

The structure of an eventual deal is not hard to work out as it would be likely to follow the famous Nitze–Kvitsinsky ''walk in the woods'' compromise of July 1982.[45] The basis of that deal was that the Soviet Union gained the cancellation of Pershing and a freeze instead of a reduction in its Far Eastern deployments while the United States was allowed some 300 cruise missiles in Europe with a reduction of SS-20 to 75 (225 warheads). Whether such a deal could be replicated in a Shultz–Gromyko meeting, or endorsed by the National Security Council/Senate or Politburo, is another question. The Americans might be tempted to offer discussion of the British and French systems in START, which would be a much more natural home, but this idea is unlikely to find favour in Paris or London. Past experience suggests that the Soviet Union could move off the inclusion of British and French forces as easily as they moved on to them.[46]

Conceding the introduction of any new NATO missiles will be difficult, as will tolerating a further delay in dealing with the aircraft (although here the Soviets must be aware of the shaky foundations of their position). At the very least there will have to be some non-circumvention clause to fix the number of aircraft. For the Americans the main difficulty may be in accepting the abandonment of Pershing: it is a better missile though not as dramatic in its implications as suggested in Soviet propaganda,[47] and there are awkward implications for the role of Germany in the NATO programme if deployment of cruise missiles in Italy and Britain is going ahead while nothing is happening in Germany because of the need to switch construction from the Pershing to the cruise missile sites. It will need to be recognised in both the construction and selling of an agreement that the key achievement may be less one of fixing the number of existing missiles and more one of ruling out future generations of advanced cruise missiles or follow-ons to the SS-20.

A deal is not impossible but a political judgement at the highest levels will be necessary for one to be struck. There is no evidence that such a judgement has yet been made by either side. If a deal were to be struck then it must be realised that this would not be equivalent to a treaty. Given the vexed issues of definition, non-circumvention and verification which will all take months to sort out, all one can hope for in 1983 is an agreed framework, à la Vladivostok, with a promise to expedite consideration of the details. As with Vladivostok the risk will be that the apparently subsidiary issues will become points of deep principle and we will be left with more incomplete agreements being tacitly observed!

A deal which links numbers of cruise to those of SS-20s would be in keeping with similar ideas for such a trade in the 1970s when the two systems first achieved prominence. It has always been the natural "fix" to the problem. It does not, however, offer a means of constructing a complete arms control framework into which nuclear weapons in Europe can be easily placed.

As I have argued, the attempt to construct a separate

framework for a European nuclear balance was, if anything, an aberration. It was a result of the exhaustion of the negotiations on central strategic systems, political enthusiasm for an INF negotiation effort, doctrinal absent-mindedness by the West Europeans and a crude misrepresentation of the existing balance by the Soviet Union.

If the attempt is sustained then there are many years of fruitless wrangling ahead, continuing to poison European politics, in order to achieve an elusive and artificial construction of minimal strategic significance. Battlefield systems will inevitably get drawn in. Transposed into the world of commerce, this would be the sort of exercise in which only lawyers and accountants could hope to prosper.

For the longer term, therefore, the need is to draw a clear line to avoid further complications from further systems. The Americans should acknowledge that F-111s, FB-111s and sea-launched cruise missiles will have to be accommodated somehow, in return for the inclusion of the Soviet Backfire, Badger and Blinder aircraft. Having identified these extra systems (along with GLCM and SS-4s, SS-5s and SS-20s), it should be made clear that all other systems are unsuitable for traditional methods of arms control. The designated systems should then be put back into the strategic arms pot where they have always belonged.

Although it is possible to design schemes for this re-merger[48] the position has been greatly complicated by the sorry state of strategic arms control and the various complicated formulas being advanced by the United States at the START negotiations (now being revamped following the Scowcroft Report on the basing of the MX ICBM). It is possible that warheads will emerge as a sole unit of account which is fine for missiles but causes immense problems for aircraft. Although the asymmetries in START are by no means as marked as in the INF negotiations, each specific issue tends to carry with it great domestic baggage in the United States. There can thus be no confidence that INF or START can be merged with, as it were, balanced books on either of the sides, let alone both sides. Whether a merger between two confused and incomplete negotiations would intensify or ease the agony will depend on the political circumstances of the time. It is not a matter for dogmatism. What is clear is that if nuclear arms control is ever again to prosper, some overall framework must be found.

Notes

1. The author wishes to acknowledge the considerable extent to which he has drawn on original research by Philip Sabin of the Department of War Studies at King's College, London.
2. John Newhouse, **Cold Dawn: The Story of SALT,** New York, Holt, Rinehart & Winston, 1973, pp. 174–5; Gerard Smith, **Doubletalk: The Story of the First Strategic Arms Limitation Talks,** New York, Doubleday, 1980, pp. 88–91.
3. Smith, op. cit., pp. 146–7. For discussions of the role of European-based systems in SALT I, see Ian Smart, 'Perspectives from Europe' in Mason Willrich and John B. Rhinelander (eds), **SALT: The Moscow Agreements and Beyond,** New York, The Free Press, 1974. Also Uwe Nerlich, **The Alliance and Europe: Part V, Nuclear Weapons and East–West Negotiations,** Adelphi Paper 120, London, IISS, Winter 1975/6.
4. Gerard Smith clearly believed the issue to be important but it barely rates a mention in the memoirs of both Kissinger and Nixon. Henry Kissinger, **The White House Years,** London, Weidenfeld & Nicholson, 1979; Richard Nixon, **Memoirs,** London, Sidgwick & Jackson, 1978.
5. This was rejected by the US delegation.
6. 'The progress that has been made in recent months is that the Soviet Union gradually gave up asking for compensations for the forward-based systems partly because most of the forward-based systems, or I would say all of them, are not suitable for a significant attack on the Soviet Union.' Press Conference of Secretary of State Henry Kissinger, in Roger Labrie (ed.), **SALT Handbook: Key Documents and Issues 1972–1979,** Washington, D.C., American Enterprise Institute, 1979, p. 285.
7. Strobe Talbott, **Endgame: The Inside Story of SALT II,** New York, Harper & Row, 1979, p. 33; **New York Times,** 3 December 1974.
8. For an example of the view that obsolescence would eventually take care of the FBS and medium-range missiles issue, see Denis Healey, 'Confrontation: Can this Peace last?', **Sunday Times,** 14 March 1971.
9. See, for example, Talbott, op. cit. p. 72.
10. For a full discussion, see Lothar Ruehl, 'The "Grey Area" Problem', in Christopher Bertram (ed.), **The Future of Arms Control, Part 1, Beyond SALT II,** Adelphi Paper 141, London, IISS, 1978.
11. Although some conservative opponents of SALT did suggest that the SS-20 could be given an intercontinental capability. For example, C. A. Robinson, 'Another SALT violation spotted', **Aviation Week & Space Technology,** 31 May 1976.
12. Talbott, op. cit., pp. 71–2, 133–4.
13. **Washington Star,** 4 December 1974; **Washington Post,** 5 December 1974.
14. One of the difficulties of the United States and the Soviet Union in

the varying arguments over Backfire and the FBS is that claims made in one context could rebound in another. The Soviet Union ceased to suggest that the FBS could be used on a "one-way mission" when it realised that this method might also be used to cover Soviet medium-range bombers attacking the US.

15. Henry Kissinger, **The Years of Upheaval,** Boston, Little, Brown & Co., 1982, pp. 273–4.
16. Smith, op. cit., p. 130.
17. For background to the cruise missile programmes, see R. Huisken, 'The History of Modern Cruise Missile Programs', in R. Betts (ed.), **Cruise Missiles: Technology, Strategy, Politics,** Washington, D.C., Brookings Institution, 1981.
18. For an example of the growing reputation of cruise missiles, see Richard Burt, 'The Cruise Missile and Arms Control', **Survival,** Jan/Feb 1976, pp. 10–17.
19. Gerald Ford, **A Time to Heal,** London, W. H. Allen, 1979, pp. 303, 357.
20. Huisken, op. cit., pp. 90–1.
21. Labrie, op. cit., pp. 420–1, 439; Ford, op. cit., p. 358; Zbigniew Brzezinski, **Power and Principle: Memoirs of the National Security Adviser, 1977–81,** London, Weidenfeld & Nicolson, 1983, pp. 153–4.
22. The unfortunate phrase "peripheral" is revealing. See Henry Brandon in **Sunday Times,** 2 November 1975.
23. The declaration committed the US to the resolution of the issues contained in the protocol. The Russians had wanted a specific commitment to discuss TNF but this was resisted by the United States. Talbott, op. cit., pp. 309–10.
24. Ibid., pp. 149–51.
25. However, this is not to argue that cruise and Pershing would not have been adopted in the absence of SALT. See Greg Treverton, "Alliance Politics", in Betts, op. cit., p. 426.
26. Helmut Schmidt, 'The 1977 Alastair Buchan Memorial Lecture', **Survival,** Jan/Feb 1978.
27. Labrie, op. cit., p. 42.
28. **Washington Post,** 11 March 1978; **Financial Times,** 7 April 1978. See also Brzezinski, op. cit., p. 303.
29. **New York Times,** 12 March 1978.
30. V. A. Johnson (Rapporteur), **Arms Control and Gray Area Weapons Systems,** Washington, D.C., Atlantic Council of the United States, 1978.
31. Greg Treverton, "Nuclear Weapons and the Grey Area", **Foreign Affairs,** Vol. 57, No. 5 (Summer 1979), pp. 1075–89.
32. For the case of postponing the NATO decision see Klaas de Vries, "Responding to the SS–20: An Alternative Approach", **Survival,** Nov/Dec 1979, pp. 251–5.
33. NATO communiqué, Special Meeting of Foreign and Defence Ministers, Brussels, 12 December 1979.
34. The demise of SALT meant that it came to be forgotten that the United States was negotiating on one of its proposed theatre systems prior to December 1979. The innovation of Brezhnev's October 1979

speech was not that theatre nuclear forces should be discussed, but that *Soviet* theatre nuclear forces should be discussed.

35. **The Guardian,** 14 November 1979; the idea of bilateral talks on TNF alone had been rejected by the Atlantic Council Study of July 1978 (fn. 27), p. 15.

36. It is of note that this narrowness went against much of the academic writing on the subject at the time which tended towards a broader scope, even including short-range systems. For example, Christopher Makins, "Negotiating European Security: the next steps", **Survival,** Nov/Dec 1979, pp. 256–63. However, even many writers who advocated a more comprehensive negotiating framework suggested that cruise and SS–20 were obvious candidates for an initial trade-off. For example, Greg Treverton, **Foreign Affairs** (Summer 1979), p. 1087; R. Metzger and P. Doty, "Arms Control Enters the Grey Area", **International Security,** Winter 1978/9, pp. 46–7.

37. The Soviet Union argued that this was an alternative to previous proposals: the reduction of its medium-range weapons if no additional US weapons were deployed in Western Europe, or else a discussion in the framework of SALT III after the SALT II treaty entered into force. **Pravda,** 15 July 1980.

38. By not talking any more of "theatre" systems, by insisting on a world-wide "balance", and by avoiding debate on the make-up of a "European balance", NATO still hoped, against the odds, to preserve some sort of doctrinal integrity. Another advantage of no longer talking of 'theatre' systems was that it removed the implication of preparation for a limited "theatre-wide" European war.

39. An impressive amount of information on the early positions is found in a briefing by a team led by Paul Nitze to the House Committee on Appropriations, **Department of Defense Appropriations for 1983,** 97th Congress, 2nd Session, May 1982 (declassified September 1982).

40. These gestures did not work out as well as had been hoped. In March 1982 Brezhnev offered a moratorium on new missile deployments. Then SS–20 were at 204 facing Western Europe. Another 54 SS–20s became operational during the following months. These had been under construction prior to March 1982, and the Brezhnev moratorium appears to have only applied to "new starts". The Reagan Administration picked on the "new completions" to demonstrate Soviet bad faith. See Raymond Garthoff, 'That SS–20 Moratorium. Who is Telling the Truth?', **Washington Post,** 26 April 1983. In early May 1983 it was reported that new sites were under construction in Central Asia, to take the total above the then deployment of 108 in Soviet Asia. **International Herald Tribune,** 2 May 1983.

41. Announced by President Reagan to the National Press Club 18 November 1981.

42. Announced by President Reagan to the Los Angeles World Affairs Council, 31 March 1983.

43. For more details, see Lawrence Freedman, "The great missile gap — between Andropov and his generals", **The Times,** 19 March 1983.

44. See John Barry, "Exposing Russia's Arithmetic", **Sunday Times,** 8 May 1983.

45. See **Washington Post,** 20 January 1983. For further background see John Newhouse, "Arms and Allies", **New Yorker,** 28 February 1983.
46. However, the May 1983 Andropov proposal keeps the British and the French at the centre and is thus making it difficult to back off. The nature of the proposal which would make it enormously difficult for either of the European countries to modernize their missiles without providing an excuse for a massive expansion of the SS−20 force made it even less likely that the British and the French would tolerate Andropov's proposals.
47. Ironically enough, one of the motives behind the Pershing programme was that this system threatened arms control less than cruise missiles. Cruise had already become controversial in SALT while, it was thought, Pershing II could be presented as merely an improved version of Pershing I. After the Nitze−Kvitsinsky episode, the US position hardened on Pershing, but there has been some evidence of a recent softening.
48. I have discussed one such scheme in Lawrence Freedman, "The Dilemmas of Theatre Arms Control", **Survival,** Jan/Feb, 1981, pp. 2−10.

(First published in **The European Missile Crisis,** ed. Hans Henrick Holm & Nikelaj Petersen, 1984 London, Frances Pinter).

8 The Four Stages of Arms Control

In this article I attempt to explain arms control problems in the context of developments in strategic theory and East-West relations since the 1960s, when the concept of arms control first became fashionable. The fourth stage is said to be the one in which we clear up the mess! A degree of unwarranted optimism may be detected here.

The acute sense of crisis that currently surrounds arms control could already be sensed in the late 1970s. The negotiating effort had shown itself to be arduous, yet the results were meagre. Acrimony rather than goodwill appeared to be the most notable political result. Instead of serving as a worthy exercise, to which all could declare allegiance, it was a source of bitter domestic argument. Although the proposed remedies for this unhappy state of affairs varied greatly, there was a common thread in all the critiques concerning the extent to which arms control had been allowed to become detached from the overall national security policy.

For example, in the magazine **Foreign Policy** in 1979, Leslie Gelb argued that arms control negotiations "should be conceived and carried out as an integral part of US foreign and defence policy". In the same issue, Richard Burt, who went on to play a part in the Reagan administration similar to the role Gelb had played in the Carter administration, suggested that "one reason that arms control has become such a dominant factor in national security planning is that in many areas negotiations have often become a substitute for serious thought about defence problems". Overdependence on arms control reflected the lack of a "general doctrine around which to organise defence policy''. With such a doctrine, arms control would not have to carry an unrealistic burden and those areas in which it might truly be of value could be more readily identified.[1]

Following the November 1980 election, members of the Reagan administration insisted that arms control in the future would at last reflect a coherent overall security concept. Thus the director of the Arms Control and Disarmament Agency warned of the need to "discipline ourselves to view arms control as an integral part of our foreign and defence policy but not a magical substitute for it".[2]

In practice, most analysts have found it easier to relate arms control to defence policy than to foreign policy. Because so much arms control activity attempts to reconstruct the East-West military relationship along more satisfactory lines, it requires some military-related criteria with which to assess the relationship and the prospect that something even more satisfactory can be achieved by means of unilateral force planning initiatives. The objectives are normally framed in terms of a stable military balance rather than a favourable political climate. It is therefore just possible to imagine weapons, doctrines and arms control being brought together to form a "seamless web", although this would require some delicate and intricate weaving. What is much more difficult is to relate arms control, along with weapons and military doctrines, to foreign policy. Now the tapestry has to become much more complex. Foreign policy disrupts all attempts at coherent and lasting military guidelines, for here leaders must be responsive to immediate, diverse and often transient pressures.

US arms control policy has often been criticised for being too technical, with unfavourable comparisons being made with the Soviet approach, which is said to be much more self-consciously "political".[3] It has been argued that the Americans are consistently bound up in attempts to define strategic stability and the details of verification, whereas the Soviets never let opportunities for securing political objectives slip from view.

This argument does little justice to the extent to which US

arms control policy has actually been shaped by foreign policy factors in the past, or the extent to which the priorities in Soviet policy have been determined by doctrinal considerations. Nevertheless, the prevalent conceptual frameworks, within which arms control policies are conceived in both academic and official circles, have not given due weight to foreign policy. This means that when foreign policy begins to drive arms control, professionals view it as unwarranted meddling rather than as a natural and unavoidable condition. The doves object strenuously to the idea of ''linkage''; the hawks complain bitterly when constraints on force planning are tolerated in pursuit of détente.

Indeed, it may be possible to maintain confidence in the fact that full account has been taken of foreign policy only through adoption of an extremely simple view of the relationship between defence and foreign policy. In the early stages of the Reagan administration, for example, it was suggested that foreign policy, and indeed arms control, could be effective only if backed up by substantial military strength. A sound defence policy was the prerequisite for everything else. [4]

The relationship turned out not to be so simple. As we shall see, in both foreign and defence policy, coherence proved to be an elusive objective. In fact, it may be delusionary even to aspire to some grand synthesis. The aspiration soon collapses when confronted with the real world of hard political choices. Theorists are often tempted by the prospect of reconciling what turn out to be mutually exclusive goals by means of some ingenious formula, thereby almost removing the necessity for choice. My assumption is that it would be wiser to content ourselves with a sense of perspective, so that we can at least judge the complex interactions between weapons, doctrines, arms control, and foreign policy and then assess the options available. We may not be able to put together much of a tapestry, but at least we can understand how previous tapestries unravelled.

The First Stage

Our story begins with the early arms control theory of the late 1950s and early 1960s. This theory explicitly excluded foreign policy considerations. The point of the theory was that even in a deeply antagonistic relationship, there could be substantial areas of mutual interest — most important, those pertaining to avoidance of nuclear war — and, hence, forms of co-operative behaviour.[5]

The main concern was with the military aspects of the cold war,[6] and therefore no provision was made for overcoming the basic antagonism. Furthermore, because the focus was on the bilateral superpower relationship, little provision was made for alliance considerations. Indeed, in the pure theory, there was no absolute requirement for any sort of diplomatic activity at all, even to identify and consolidate areas of common interest, although it was recognised that at times such activity was unavoidable. Tacit understandings and the careful structuring of forces could achieve as much if not more than set piece negotiations.[7]

In these terms, arms control was not so much a process as a state. If the strategic relationship was essentially stable, offering incentives neither to pre-empt nor to escalate the arms race, then the situation was under control. There was no image here of a world getting better — not even a promise that things would not get worse. Arms control offered not a long-term agenda for action, but a guide to the paradoxes of the nuclear age that statesmen would be wise to acknowledge. To the extent that they did, they might enjoy the benefits of nuclear stability rather than the terrors of a delicate balance. As Malcolm Hoag observed, the objective was to "institutionalise a less precarious balance of terror rather than to supplant it. The goal", he continued, "is stable mutual deterrence, which in practice amounts to playing for a stalemate rather than a win in the grimmest of games, should deterrence fail."[8]

This essentially managerial concept took the political context of the time largely for granted. Contrary to the contemporary image of the arms controller, the theory did not depend on the assumption that the Soviet Union was misunderstood or was turning itself into something more agreeable and trustworthy — only that it was run by moderately rational men who did not wish to preside over a smouldering ruin.

It was assumed neither that building on a sense of shared interest offered a way of eliminating the basic antagonism, nor that it rendered military action — including nuclear use — impossible should the antagonism turn into war. Even in these circumstances, the shared interest in avoiding the holocaust could still impose constraints. That did not preclude either side taking active and painful steps to signal displeasure and determination. The basic rule was that there should be no uninhibited fight to the finish for supreme victory. Any nuclear strikes were part of a bloody form of communication and bargaining, through which both sides would seek to define the limits to which they could be pushed before matters truly got out of hand. Presuming that a nuclear war could be kept within some bounds, such a war could come and go, leaving intact the basic political relationships that had led to the conflict in the first place!

As the theory was being developed, all sorts of weird and wonderful schemes were devised to make possible nuclear arms use that need not lead to complete devastation. However doubtful these schemes might appear now, they made it possible at the time to hold that there was no need for nuclear stability to undermine extended deterrence.[9] This meant that it was consistent to welcome a stable balance without worrying about the consequences for nuclear guarantees to allies. It was not necessary to withdraw from nuclear commitments, only to be prepared to adopt novel plans to meet these commitments.

Where did this theory fail? Not in its readiness to reinforce, and even to celebrate, the higher stalemate imposed by the balance of terror. Submarine platforms for nuclear missiles and the rejection of ballistic missile defences are testaments to the influence of the theory. It provided neat and simple guidelines for arms control. All that contributed to a second strike was good; anything that made possible a first strike, bad. If weapons developments and force planning naturally tended in the right direction, then nothing need be done. Corrective action was required only when plans tended in the wrong direction. Only if this tendency could not be combatted through some mutual understanding would it be necessary to enter into formal negotiations. Thus the great nuclear arms control effort that has recently ground to a halt was first set in motion in early 1967 when Secretary of Defence Robert McNamara realised that without a formal agreement the pressure on him to authorise deployment of a nationwide ballistic missile defence was likely to prove irresistible.[10]

As a first strike has now been ruled out for the rest of this century (even President Reagan's "Star Wars" speech of March 1983 did not envisage an early breakthrough in strategic defence), there ought to be no reason for those of this early arms control persuasion to view the current situation with dismay. Even highly accurate multiple warheads and other technological developments have not invalidated the original theory. For prospects such as "ICBM vulnerability" to be seen as truly destabilising required a doctrinal revisionism through which it could be claimed that propensities well short of a genuine first-strike capability could be a source of decisive strategic advantage.

The difficulty lay not in some misapprehension of the essential character of the strategic balance but in a failure to appreciate the implications of this balance for NATO. The early theory was seeking to reconcile persistent antagonism with a strategic stalemate. The objective was to ensure that the United States was never rushed into a war, or even just nuclear exchanges, by the pressures to pre-empt. But war itself was not ruled out. Where the theory failed to convince was in its efforts to develop an acceptable way of conducting a nuclear war without the benefit of a first-strike capability. The theories were too novel and subtle — "too clever by half" — to be convincing. They were full of half-baked notions of demonstration and resolve, and had only a limited appeal.

This problem might have been manageable had NATO not depended on the threat to use nuclear weapons first. The democratic administrations of the 1960s recognised the contradiction between this dependence (which to be credible required US nuclear superiority) and the reality of a stable balance. They therefore sought to persuade the Europeans that the situation required a greater reliance on conventional deterrence.[11] In this they failed. A move to "no-first-use" was rendered virtually impossible as a result of the exposed position of Berlin, whereas the logic of conventional deterrence was both economically and politically unacceptable in Europe.[12] Even if the logic had been adopted, formidable problems of extended deterrence would have remained in protecting the United States' allies from Soviet nuclear attacks. Nevertheless, these problems might have proved more manageable if they had not been compounded by the even greater difficulties resulting from the excessive dependence on the US nuclear arsenal to deter a conventional invasion of Western Europe.

The Second Stage

During the first stage, it had been hoped that the integrity of the theory would make it possible to cope with East-West antagonism at any level of intensity without either a re-appraisal of Alliance commitments or a risk of an inadvertent slide into all-out nuclear war. The second stage began as it was realised that neither the underlying assumptions nor the resultant prescriptions of this approach had political appeal. The position could be maintained only by revising the assumption of perpetual East-West antagonism.

The doctrinal amendments necessary to maintain a semblance of extended deterrence were instituted with the adoption of flexible response in 1967. Inevitably this involved drawing on some of the least satisfactory of the concepts devised by nuclear strategists — for example, the idea of a "demonstration shot" for initial nuclear use as a means of communicating resolve.[13] Extended deterrence was now to depend not so much on a confident nuclear threat but on the possibility that in extreme and desperate circumstances one nuclear firebreak after another would be crossed. The formal consultative procedures still envisaged deliberate and controlled use, but the only purposes clearly to be achieved by use would be to signal a situation rapidly getting out of control. Hence, "uncertainty" now became a virtue, and comfort was taken from the likely impact of even the smallest probabilities of nuclear exchanges on Soviet calculations. This offered few guidelines for force planning (for who can be certain about what produces uncertainty?) and even fewer for arms control. If anything, arms control made things more predictable and certain — which went against the grain of flexible response. This point was fully illustrated in the confusion over the entry of battlefield nuclear weapons into the Mutual and Balanced Force Reductions talks in Vienna and in the awkwardness surrounding intermediate forces in nuclear arms control. [14]

As the 1960s progressed, it became increasingly difficult to explain to those responsible why, let alone how, they should prepare to engage in a war that they could not, in any traditional sense, win. If war has become unwinnable, then the intuitive response is not to fight. Much ingenuity has been expended in devising ways to indulge in nuclear warfare in useful ways, even without obtaining a recognisable victory. But counter-intuitive policies rarely attract large constituencies. The lack of a convincing answer to the question of what to do if deterrence fails created a determination to ensure that the question never arose. Deterrence was spoken of increasingly as a special and wholly benign strategic objective, quite distinct from, and even opposed to, actual preparations for war. Despite the fact that any strategy of deterrence must involve at least the pretence of preparing for war, "deterrence" and "war-fighting" came to be counterposed as two alternative and exclusive defence policies.

If deterrence was not to be allowed to fail, then action had to be taken in the political sphere. First, the inevitably large question-mark against the US nuclear guarantee could not be allowed to become any more divisive than it had already proved to be. Forces had to be deployed with the effects on Allied confidence as much as those on Soviet wilfulness in mind. US nuclear weapons in Europe, for example, came to be taken as a symbol of the nuclear guarantee to NATO even though the nature of their role — should the guarantee need to be implemented — was never made clear.

The second requirement was to control the East-West political relationship so that the shaky military arrangements were never put to the test. This was made possible by the steady move away from the earlier assumption of ever-lasting antagonism. The prospect of decades of hostility without hope of resolution, possibly punctuated by periods of intense and vicious fighting and controlled at best by the manipulation of threats of devastation, was strikingly unappealing. In the 1960s this prospect also appeared unduly pessimistic. Despite all the world's travails, it was possible to forecast the end of the cold war and a super-power relationship in which elements of mutual under-standing went far beyond a recognition of the danger of nuclear war.[15] Some even pointed to a domestic convergence by which the West would become more socia-listic in its economic management and welfare policies while the East would become more liberal in its internal politics.[16] Others, on somewhat firmer foundations, pointed to the evidence of emerging ''conventions of crisis management'' that made it likely that most crises could be controlled well before they neared war.[17]

If NATO's military plans and the US guarantee were unlikely to be put to the test, then it seemed pointless to expend energy and political capital worrying about them. As the post war organisation of Europe began to congeal, there seemed to be no compelling reason why deterrence should fail. The diplomatic activity of the late 1960s and early 1970s was bound up with acknowledging the rigidity of the European security system and developing rules for managing relations in the more turbulent areas of the Third World.

This situation was reflected in arms control. In the initiatives that led to the Conference on Security and Co-operation in Europe and the Mutual and Balanced Force Reduction (MBFR) talks, the consolidation of the European status quo, including the maintenance of the two alliances, had very much come to the fore. Much arms control activity helped to define the limits to antagonism — on the seabed, in outer space, transferring nuclear technology to allies and clients. More significant still, arms control became organised to emphasise the extent to which neither superpower sought, let alone could attain, military superiority.

Initially this situation was achieved in the Anti-Ballistic Missile Treaty, which was taken as an endorsement of the concept of mutual assured destruction. It was thus in accord with purist notions of strategic stability. However, what was being celebrated was not simply the consolidation of a military stalemate. Henry Kissinger described to Congress how the 1972 SALT agreements reflected ''a certain commonality of outlook, a sort of interdependence for survival between the two of us''.[18]

As the preoccupation in SALT moved from defensive to offensive arms, the concept of parity rushed to the fore. This concept was soon adopted in the MBFR talks and by the mid-1970s was generally accepted as the ideal state for all aspects of the East-West military relationship. As Chancellor Schmidt of West Germany put it in his 1977 Alastair Buchan Memorial Lecture: ''No one can deny that the principle of parity is a sensible one. However, its fulfilment must be the aim of all arms-limitation and arms-control negotiations and it must apply to all categories of weapons''.[19]

It mattered not that strategists complained of the irrelevance of visible parity, the dangerous tendencies it created toward mindless force matching and the artificiality of the categories used for its measurement. With such an excess of military power around, there was plenty to spare to help make a political point without impinging on any fundamental military requirements.

It was not so easy to identify the spare military capacity. The generally fudged nature of NATO doctrine meant that there was no self-evident means of identifying which military capabilities were and were not dispensable. Moreover, it was difficult to keep control of the political points being made through the exercise. For a start, certain forces had already taken on a higher political symbolism — for example, in helping to ''couple'' the two halves of the Alliance. This symbolism might be undermined in an apparently innocent attempt to reconcile the forces of the superpowers.

The new symbolism that was being created through arms control could be ambiguous. Once one accepted the dubious proposition that simple comparisons of crude military power said something profound about the state of super-power relations, then something rather serious was implied if the particular measure employed displayed disparity. As no creditable doctrine could offer guidance on how best to measure the military balance, there were great opportunities for mischief-making in attempts to influence the choice of measure.

As the negotiations moved into more and more difficult areas, it became apparent that the force structures of the two sides did not lend themselves to close comparisons. The very act of negotiating turned trivial questions into matters of great moment, occupying the time of political leaders. The surplus capacity was transformed into tangible political assets that, it was soon argued, ought not to be squandered in a supine diplomacy. Arms control did not so much push the military factor to one side as propel it to the fore, threatening to overwhelm the awkward political relation-ship in a mass of technical detail. The original political point underlying parity thus proved itself to be extraordinarily difficult to make.

The question of the validity of this point had been begged. The Soviet Union was anxious to be recognised as equal to the United States in real political terms. In every index of power other than the military, the Soviet Union lagged behind the United States. In most areas of the world it had far less at stake, and what it did have was as often as not bound up with the particular region's most irritating local power. The United States could not have managed its inter-national diplomacy through accommodation to Soviet policy, even if it had wanted to, and the converse was also true. On the Soviet side, this situation led to a disillusion-ment with the apparent refusal to give the USSR an inter-national role commensurate with its superpower status. On the US side, the situation created increasing doubt as to whether acknowledgment of parity and, some argued,

concession of areas of Soviet superiority, had not emboldened the Kremlin rather than made it more responsible.

With these doubts, the negotiating exercise became
progressively more difficult. The disposition to compromise
declined and agreement required steering clear of obvious
controversy. As things turned out, there were sufficient
areas of non-obvious controversy to undermine even those
deals agreed between governments. Three US-Soviet agreements signed by both governments over the past decade —
on Peaceful Nuclear Explosions, a Threshold Nuclear Test
Ban, and SALT II — have not been ratified by the US Senate.

Thus an arms control process set in motion to encourage
and consolidate a positive movement in East-West affairs
eventually came to magnify an opposing tendency. As the
optimism of the early 1970s was dashed, the doctrinal
confusion that this optimism had served to obscure returned
to the fore. If détente could fail, might not deterrence as
well? And if deterrence should fail, then what do we do?

The Third Stage

The unfinished business of the third stage was doctrinal
confusion; that of the second stage was foreign policy
uncertainty. At the start of the 1970s, a solution to doctrinal
confusion was sought not through the adoption of some
new formula (unless one elevates the use of the term
sufficiency[20] to such a level) but through the proliferation of
options. This approach emerged first in a rhetorical question
in President Nixon's state of the world address in 1970 and
then more tangibly in the concepts of selective targeting
outlined by Secretary of Defence Schlesinger in 1974.
Schlesinger explained that "to be credible, and hence
effective over the range of possible contingencies,
deterrence must rest on many options and on a spectrum of
capabilities ... to support these options".[21] He did not
believe that this desire for options need be at all controversial. Schlesinger observed that "when you get down to
the hard rock of selectivity and flexibility in targeting plans,
there really is very little criticism of that".[22] Certainly

President Carter's Defence Secretary Harold Brown saw the main initiative with which he was associated — Presidential Directive 59 — as following directly from the 1974 innovation. He describes the essence of PD-59 as making ''flexibility in targeting options a factor in systems acquisition''.[23] The Reagan administration claimed, with some justice, a substantial degree of continuity between its nuclear weapons policy and that of the previous administration.[24]

The accumulation of options is generally considered to be above reproach.[25] Yet this approach constitutes a failure of doctrine, a preference for avoiding choice by means of the accumulation of instruments. The hope is that future decision-makers will be able to cobble together a suitable strategy for a future contingency out of the raw material bequeathed to them or that, in the competition for global influence, others may be impressed by aspects of military strength that might not actually look so impressive to those responsible for turning them to advantage. An approach that defers choice and panders to subjectivism provides no guide to force planners. Anything might be needed, so everything ought to be provided. Who knows what really impresses adversary or allied leaders now, let alone what will impress their twenty-first century successors? The natural result is to let procurement rip, constrained only by what the economy can afford and guided only by the advocacy of those with the greatest stakes in the process.

Arms control has not been used to prevent the proliferation of options. The lack of agreed doctrine means that there is no obvious way of distinguishing the stabilising from the destablising and the luxurious from the vital. Even when strong views are held concerning a particular set of capabilities, this is the case as often as not only because it has been identified in the force structure of the other side. Given the record of arms control, when some disturbing development is identified on the other side, the inclination is to develop an equivalent capability of one's own just in case it fails to be stopped by arms control.

If arms control is to succeed, freedom of choice and a clear sense of priorities are required, so that the dispensable and the indispensable can be identified. An absence of doctrine makes the art of choosing awkward and unwelcome. The process of choosing comes to be handled by the vagaries of bureaucratic, congressional, and budgetary processes. In these circumstances, arms control's most useful role often appears to be to help avoid choice. Hence the frequent deployment of the bargaining chip argument: when all other rationales are exhausted and the cost is starting to worry legislators, it is argued that a particular programme should not be abandoned unilaterally, but instead should be traded for some great concession by the other side.[26] In practice, this argument is more often invoked to ward off pressures for unilateral cuts than to prepare the ground for a bilateral deal. This presumed bargaining logic turns out to be yet another way to avoid judgements based on the sort of theory of requirements that ought to be provided by a strategic doctrine.

The logical consequence of this tendency is "dual-trackism", whereby the bargaining chip argument is brought in at the start. The effect of this can be seen in the history of the most famous "dual-track" of them all — NATO's December 1979 decision to pursue in tandem the modernisation of what were then called long-range theatre nuclear forces (now known as intermediate nuclear forces) and negotiations with the Soviet Union to limit these weapons. Initially, at least in Britain and the United States, the intention had been to keep well clear of arms control on the grounds that the problem had to be viewed in the context of the doctrine of flexible response and the need to deny the Soviet Union the prospect of maintaining its territory as a sanctuary, even while conducting nuclear operations in Europe. There was little respect for crude force-matching rationales. Chancellor Schmidt had always seen the issue in terms of arms control, and at the Guadaloupe summit in the first days of 1979 it was agreed that close links with arms control were necessary. Nevertheless, great care was taken to avoid force-matching arguments in the final communiqué.

The communiqué nodded in the direction of the culture of parity without endorsing the principle as a guide to force planning.[27] It was always unrealistic to expect that politicans would resist justifying NATO's modernisation programme by reference to that of the Soviet Union. Soon the SS-20 and cruise and Pershing missiles were inextricably linked in the public, and indeed much of the official, mind. The inevitable conclusion was the announcement of the ''zero option'' by President Reagan in November 1981.[28] Forgotten was the idea that the aforementioned weapons represented a unique NATO requirement essential to the coupling of the United States with its European allies. The Reagan administration had come into office promising to be true to an overall and coherent security policy, even in the area of arms control. But it turned out to be as susceptible to the temptations of political opportunism in this area as any that had gone before. The ''zero option'' was chosen for its short-term benefits in calming European opinion rather than as part of a long-term security policy, and when these short-term factors changed, it was jettisoned.[29]

This saga and the ease with which arms control is still spoken of as an alternative to an arms race demonstrate the extent to which the simplest notions of the potential and function of arms control have taken root. Arms control has been encouraged by decades of ''threat assessments'' appearing as the essential hors d'oeuvre of any statement on defence planning, as if every move was no more than a regrettable but necessary response to the defence statements made by the other side. This has been the case despite the evidence of weapons procurement on both sides responding to distinctive national traditions, pressures, skills, resources, and needs. In practice, arms control is the only place at which the forces of the two sides can be brought together in such a way as to facilitate close comparisons, and it is the fact that these comparisons bear no relation to the actual processes of force development that makes the exercise so fraught.

The net result of the attempt to construct strict equality through the medium of arms control has been to encourage force matching but not controls — imitation rather than limitation. The current appeal of arms control is political. It reflects not a sense of past accomplishment, certainly, but the widespread belief, a legacy of the 1970s, that arms control is the most appropriate instrument for restoring a modicum of comity to East-West relations. To abandon the exercise completely would involve a political statement of such profound pessimism that no government dares to make it. When the Soviet Union appeared to be on the brink of making such a statement in December 1983, following the Bundestag vote approving the introduction of Pershing missiles into West Germany, the Kremlin drew back from the full implications of its pique. At the time, Western governments were at one in urging the Soviets to carry on talking without much reference to the content of the talks. The form had become more important than the substance.

Outside the negotiations there are no obvious means for improving East-West relations, short of the occasional visit to a Soviet leader's funeral. There are no secular trends to be encouraged. There are no other outstanding issues ready to be resolved. The notion that if there is to be an improvement in East-West relations it must be negotiated is now deeply ingrained. No gestures. No tacit understandings dependent on good faith.

To make improvements in relations dependent on arms control would be an enormous gamble. Of course, agreement on the most dangerous and divisive area of relations would bode well and comfort the public. In addition, the need to appear reasonable in the negotiations can actually force reasonableness out of an unwilling bureaucracy. Most of all, the military position, especially in the higher nuclear area, allows great scope for a deal if people could become more relaxed in their assessments of the state of the military balance.

All that being said, the process in which the West Europeans in particular had invested so many hopes eventually collapsed and can be revived only with great difficulty following an improvement in East-West relations achieved by other means. Even when and if this process is revived it will still face enormous problems. In a less harsh political climate, it was driving itself into the ground by trying to create a contrived strategic relationship. It is likely that these kinds of deals would make marginal differences to force levels. More attractive deals normally depend on unequal concessions to a degree that has not been the practice in the past.

If we become obsessed with the picture of East-West relations as consisting of nothing more than tough bargaining, then the obvious prescription is to accumulate bargaining chips, no matter what there inherent worth or opportunity costs, so as to strengthen our hand. There is an influential view that the West's inherent strengths make it more able to cope with such determined competition. This view both underestimates the Soviet Union and overestimates the ability of Western governments, including that of the United States, to see through such a contest.

The Fourth Stage

The fourth stage is the one in which we begin to clear up the mess! That optimistic statement is based on no more than the belief that the existence of a mess is widely recognised. It has to be qualified by noting that there remain profound disagreements as to the nature and cause of the mess, as well as what to do about it, though there are many proposals on the table.

Much of the current thinking is bound up, not surprisingly, with the prospects for the various negotiations. Ideas such as "freeze"[30] or "build-down"[31] are presented as novel organising principles that might not only break the current impasse but would also make the effort more productive. These ideas, and even some of those of the administration such as the "zero option", often seem to gain influence because of their domestic political resonance. Although they do offer an image of a preferred strategic relationship, this is achieved only by keeping them one step removed from negotiating reality. Once the attempt is made to bring them closer, the new straightforward concepts become as complicated as the old discredited concepts.[32]

Another more promising line has turned out to be a certain amount of doctrinal revisionism. Some of this has also been enforced by domestic political requirements as in the case of the Scowcroft Commission, which began the work of burying the great bogey of the 1970s — ICBM vulnerability.[33] This is also true of the work set in motion by NATO's High-Level Group, which has begun the overdue job of reducing the Alliance's stock of nuclear warheads.[34] The revival of ideas for bans on first use of nuclear weapons reflects a similar desire to respond to wide concern over NATO's overdependence on nuclear weapons.[35] Other reformist ideas are stimulated by the prospect of exciting technological innovations.[36]

Out of all of this is starting to come a sort of consensus — a consensus more disposed to conventional deterrence, preferring long-range to short-range European-based forces, and full of second thoughts on MIRVing. It would be premature to suggest that this consensus is well-represented in the Reagan administration, although its spokesmen now find themselves paying at least lip-service to some part of the consensus, but it is quite strong in Congress and in NATO generally. The shift in German thinking on conventional deterrence, for example, is probably as significant as any shift in American thinking.

There is certainly a need for some sort of consensus to be forged before any new role can be designed for arms control. It would be best if this consensus were not only internally consistent but also capable of overcoming practical and political obstacles. The judgement of history on the strategic concepts of the Reagan administration may well be that they reflected a clear, if debatable, view of the desirable backed up by an inadequate sense of the feasible. This can be seen with the climb-down on MX; the criticisms of the inability of command, control, and communications to manage the sort of protracted nuclear conflicts that the administration has envisaged; and the far-fetched nature of the schemes for strategic defence. It will be a shame if the next stage in strategic thinking begins on the basis of equally unreal assumptions, concerning, for example, the ability of some of the new technologies to perform as specified or of Western democracies to raise their defence spending much further.

What is interesting about much of the new thinking, even from the ''doves'', is how small a part formal arms control plays in the scheme of things. There is a greater willingness now to argue the case on the strategic worth of the capabilities in question than to claim only that they will foul up delicate negotiations or be hard to verify. One might add that those wishing to put breaks on the new programmes are more likely to rely on economic factors than on negotiations. Inflation and the deficit remain the great arms controllers.

It is in fact arguable that the main lessons to be learned from the West's sorry experience with arms control are more relevant to foreign policy and diplomacy than to weapons procurement and doctrine. First, the West should have learned that action on research and development and production (either more of it or less) is not the key to East-West relations. Far better to meet the political difficulties head on. Doing so would require recognition of the fact that a degree of civil and correct contact signifies not enduring trust and friendship, but merely a means of avoiding stepping on each other's toes, drifting into unnecessary crises, or doing silly things out of petulance and spitefulness. The importance of military muscle in crisis management must never be forgotten, but recent history suggests that no amount of muscle can compensate for a fundamental misapprehension of the political context.

Second, the West needs to recognise that rhetoric is not a free good in international affairs. If it is used for domestic effect or political histrionics, with nods and winks that it should not be taken too seriously and with sudden changes of tone for no obvious reason, then national pronouncements become devalued. This devaluation happened with pronouncements by the Soviet Union. If every misdemeanor brings forth a spate of abuse, then what does one say, or indeed what sanctions does one impose, after the real transgression? If the rhetoric is to be taken seriously as a sincere representation of existing views, then it should not be surprising if it has consequences that are difficult to contain in the neat compartment reserved for the trading of insults.

Third, it must be recognised that to the extent that hard negotiations are a part of the relationship, then these will be concluded only as a result of at least some attempt to meet the concerns of the other side. Negotiations that were once supposed to be demonstrating that East-West relations need not be viewed as a zero-sum game seem to have turned into a zero-sum game themselves, in which it is all too easily assumed that if those on the other side want something, then there must be a very good reason for not giving it to them, even if the reason is not self-evident at the time.

Thus we come to the fourth proposition—that such deals can probably be arranged only behind closed doors. This is an uncomfortable proposition for someone like me who makes a living by commenting on the intricacies of negotiating positions, but the fact is that the hard bargaining necessary to conclude an agreement can probably be undertaken only by consenting adults in private. Once a negotiating position has been laid out in the open, any departure is going to be seen as a major concession and be fought over, and the job of opponents will be made that much easier. Serious damage has already been done to the general diplomatic credibility of the United States by the ease with which agreements can be overthrown by a well-organised Senate lobby. Furthermore, positions adopted with great publicity tend to be viewed with great suspicion as being designed for domestic effect.

If the political climate improves, then arms control might prosper. There are currently so many half-completed agreements or advanced negotiations around that, with a bit of a push, the famine could turn into a feast. More likely, the two sides may just regain their taste for being seen to negotiate, and great excitement will be generated by the mere spectacle of talking without much regard for the content. It is therefore important to have clear objectives for the revival of the activity so that the West does not reproduce the recent cycle of illusion and disillusion.

The major objective must be to bring the grand negotiations to an honourable close. Whatever a future arms control agreement may look like, and we all have our favoured designs, it is most important that it should be definitive and indefinite. No treaties of only five years duration, no protocols, no declarations of principles for START II, no awkward issues deferred until a more suitable time, no new initiatives designed to take in weapons types that have up to now escaped arms control's warm embrace, such as battlefield nuclear systems. A firm line should be drawn, preferably at a point below the current force levels, and the negotiating teams should then be released for more productive activities. If a "build-down" proposal were adopted, then the requisite impression of continual activity should be possible as opposed to the need to reconvene a conference to ensure further progress.

The West does need an impression of the best available strategic relationship — one that will not impose its own timetable on events if crises do occur, that offers hope of containing the violence should war occur, and that allows for some diversion of resources away from the military. It will also be one that supports rather than undermines stable alliances.

Such an impression should form an integral part of doctrine and be constructed through the force-planning process, thus possibly requiring one to ask questions different from those normally asked about weapons effectiveness and so on. A worthy thought was captured by the Arms Control Impact Statements, but their experience indicated that impact cannot be measured without clear standards against which programmes should be judged. These standards should not be those of a "distinct" arms control interest (*ie*, "verifiability"); rather, they should be set with reference to the nation's overall security policy. This Essay began by noting the aspiration to integrate arms control to such an overall concept. What I am arguing is that the overall security concept itself must embody the sort of objectives normally associated with arms control. The achievement of these objectives may then involve a variety of means.

It is a requirement of foreign policy in general, and not just arms control, to worry how things look to the other side. It does no service to a proper security debate to have one group invariably arguing that all weapons are provocative and another group just as routinely arguing that they will enable negotiating from strength.

If there is a need for new institutions they would

probably, and most sensibly, take the form of joint crisis management centres or bodies similar to the Standing Consultative Commission for SALT. There is a case for a "talking shop" in which informed and authoritative representatives of both sides explain each other's plans and fears in private, free from the constraints of formal negotiating. Part of the agenda of such a group should be the sort of command and control issues recently high-lighted by Paul Bracken.[37] Indeed, while the concept of confidence-building measures is perhaps of a more limited validity than often suggested,[38] the trend toward discussing forces in terms of their strategic context rather than as units of account in some grand military audit is to be welcomed.

Such a group might identify areas in which formal agreements might be both useful and feasible, and even engage in preliminary inquiries. The cases most suitable for formal treatment remain those that are discreet as well as discrete, those whose technology is still at an early stage. For example, a number of ideas for dealing with the specific problems posed by chemical and anti-satellite weapons have circulated over the years.[39]

For those arms controllers who judge matters by the number and variety of subjects covered by distinct negotiations, this idea may seem to be an unexciting prospect. The rather non-interventionist approach outlined here argues for the substance rather than the form, and seeks to protect arms control from those who would over-burden it with unrealistic political demands. Arms control is a means not of regulating East-West relations but of creating a system that can cope with antagonism. It is a state to be attained rather than a process to be indulged.

Notes

1. Leslie Gelb, "A Glass Half Full"; Richard Burt, "A Glass Half Empty," **Foreign Policy** (Fall 1979). A revised version of Burt's essay appears as the first chapter in Richard Burt, ed., **Arms Control and Defense Postures in the 1980s** (Boulder, Colo.: Westview Press, 1982). Note also Benjamin Lambeth's chapter entitled "Arms Control and

Defence Planning in Soviet Strategic Policy,'' in which he criticises the US strategic community (in contrast to that of the Soviet Union) as being "either oblivious or indifferent to the proposition that arms control ought to be a subordinate instrument of overall national security planning" (p. 61).

2. Eugene Rostow, "US Arms Control Objectives" (speech to the Council on Foreign Relations, 20 October, 1981).

3. Robin Ranger, **Arms and Politics, 1958–1978: Arms Control in a Changing Political Context** (Toronto: Macmillan of Canada, 1979).

4. Secretary of State Alexander Haig described the Reagan administration's strategic force modernisation programme as "an essential ingredient for accomplishing our foreign policy and arms control objectives." He went on to note that the United States could no longer, as in the past, "afford the illusion that defence policy and foreign policy were unrelated—that military power was applicable only after diplomacy had failed" (prepared testimony to Senate Foreign Relations Committee, 4 November, 1981).

5. For example, Thomas Schelling and Morton Halperin, in **Strategy and Arms Control** (New York: Twentieth Century Fund, 1961), saw arms control as including "all the forms of military co-operation between potential enemies in the interest of reducing the likelihood of war, its scope and violence should it occur, and the political and economic costs of being prepared for it" (p. 2). A similar understanding of the concept, including its wide-ranging scope, is found in Donald Brennan's introductory chapter to Donald Brennan, ed., **Arms Control, Disarmament and National Security** (New York: George Braziller, 1961). For an interesting memoir concerning the background to both of these seminal works, see Morton Halperin, "Arms Control: A Twenty-Five Year Perspective," F.A.S. Public Interest Report, **Journal of the Federation of American Scientists** 36, no. 6 (June 1983).

6. "An important premise underlying the point of view of this study is that a main determinant of the likelihood of war is the nature of the present military technology and present military expectations" (Schelling and Halperin, **Strategy and Arms Control**, p. 3).

7. "Arms control expressed in a treaty we should regard as a special case, a readily perceptible and particularly prominent example, of something more deep-rooted in international experience." See Hedley Bull, **The Control of the Arms Race** (New York: Praeger Publishers, 1961), p. x.

8. Malcolm Hoag, "On Stability in Deterrent Races," **World Politics** 13, no. 4 (July 1961), p. 522.

9. See, for example, Herman Kahn's proposal for a "European Strategic Defense Community (ESDC) based on a tactical doctrine that could be called "proportionate nuclear reprisal" in Herman Kahn, **On Escalation** (London: Pall Mall Press, 1965), p. 266.

10. See Morton Halperin, "Arms Control: A Twenty-Five-Year Perspective," p. 5 (n. 1). As Halperin notes, in the terms in which it was originally conceived this effort was spectacularly successful.

11. Alain C. Enthoven and Wayne Smith, "How Much is Enough?"

Shaping the Defence Program 1961–1969 (New York: Harper & Row, 1971). A number of those involved in the attempt have been deploying similar arguments in the 1980s to those first advanced in the 1960s. See McGeorge Bundy et al., "Nuclear Weapons and the Atlantic Alliance," **Foreign Affairs** 60 (Spring 1982).

12. See David N. Schwartz, "A Historical Perspective," in John Steinbruner and Leon Sigal, eds., **Alliance Security: NATO and the No-First-Use Question** (Washington, D.C.: Brookings Institution, 1983).

13. J. Michael Legge, **Theatre Nuclear Weapons and the NATO Strategy of Flexible Response** (Santa Monica, Calif.: RAND, 1983).

14. Uwe Nerlich, **The Alliance and Europe: Part V, Nuclear Weapons and East-West Negotiations,** Adelphi Paper 120 (London: IISS 1975); Lawrence Freedman, "Negotiations on Nuclear Forces in Europe, 1969–83," in Hans-Henrik Holm and Nikolaj Petersen, eds., **The European Missile Crisis: Nuclear Weapons and Security Policy** (London: Francis Pinter, 1983).

15. See, for example, Marshall B. Shulman, **Beyond the Cold War** (New Haven, Conn.: Yale University Press, 1966).

16. Alfred G. Meyer, "Theories of Convergence," in Chalmers Johnson, ed., **Change in Communist Systems** (Stanford, Calif.: Stanford University Press, 1970).

17. Coral Bell, **The Conventions of Crisis: A Study in Diplomatic Management** (London: Oxford University Press, 1971). Bell reports McNamara's remark following the Cuban Missile Crisis: "There is no longer any such thing as strategy, only crisis management" p. 2.

18. Senate Foreign Relations Committee, Strategic Arms Limitation Talks (Washington, D.C.: Government Printing Office, 1972), pp. 394–395.

19. Helmut Schmidt, "The 1977 Alastair Buchan Memorial Lecture," **Survival** (January/February 1978), p. 4.

20. As deputy secretary of defence, David Packard observed the following when asked the meaning of "sufficiency" in this context: "It means that it's a good word to use in a speech. Beyond that it doesn't mean a god-damned thing". Quoted in Desmond Ball, **Déjà Vu: The Return to Counterforce in the Nixon Administration** (Santa Monica: California Seminar on Arms Control and Foreign Policy, 1974), p. 8.

21. James R. Schlesinger, Annual Defence Department Report, FY1975 (Washington, D.C.: Department of Defence, March 4, 1974).

22. Testimony of Secretary of Defence Schlesinger, US-USSR Strategic Policies: Hearings Before the Subcommittee on Arms Control, International Law and Organisation of the Committee on Foreign Relations (US Senate, March 4, 1974), p. 10.

23. Harold Brown, **Thinking About National Security** (Boulder, Colo.: Westview Press, 1983), p. 82. He distinguished PD-59 from the 1974 National Security Memorandum 242 in that the latter was calling only for "targeting plans, including options to threaten Soviet military targets based on available weapons systems".

24. See Jeffrey Richelson, "PD-59, NSDD-12 and the Reagan Strategic Modernisation Program," **Journal of Strategic Studies** 6, no. 2 (June 1983).

25. For two sceptical views from opposed positions, however, see William R. Van Cleave and Roger W. Barnett, "Strategic Adaptability," **Orbis** 18, no. 3 (Fall, 1974), and Bernard Brodie, "The Development of Nuclear Strategy," **International Security** 2, no. 4 (Spring 1978).

26. For the history of the bargaining chip argument in nuclear arms control, see Robert J. Bresler and Robert C. Gray, "The Bargaining Chip and SALT," **Political Science Quarterly** 92, no. 1 (Spring 1977). The point about a bargaining chip is that it must be deemed both dispensable yet worrisome to the other side. This is a rare combination. Also, if the negotiations are to be viewed as a test of bargaining skill, then it makes sense to boast of one's own assets and to belittle those of the opponent. This has not been the tendency in the past.

27. "Any agreed limitations on these systems must be consistent with the principle of equality between the sides. Therefore, the limitations should take the form of de jure equality between the two sides." See NATO Communiqué, Special Meeting of Foreign and Defence Ministers (Brussels: NATO, 12 December, 1979).

28. President Reagan, Speech to the National Press Club (Washington, D.C.: State Department, 18 November, 1981).

29. For some background, see "Limited War, Unlimited Protest: The Anti-Nuclear Weapons Movement in Europe," in Paul Cole and William J. Taylor, eds., **The Nuclear Freeze Debate: Arms Control Issues for the 1980s** (Boulder, Colo.: Westview Press, 1983).

30. Edward F. Kennedy and Mark O. Hatfield, **Freeze! How You Can Help Prevent Nuclear War** (New York: Bantam Books, 1982).

31. Alton Frye, "Strategic Build-Down," **Foreign Affairs** (Winter 1983–1984).

32. "Negotiating a Build-Down," **Time** (17 October, 1983).

33. Report of the President's Commission on Strategic Forces, known as the Scowcroft Commission (Washington, D.C.: Department of Defence, April 1983). See Blair Stewart, "The Scowcroft Commission and the 'Window of Coercion,'" **Strategic Review** (Summer 1983).

34. Annex ("The Montebello Decision") to NATO Nuclear Planning Group Communiqué (Montebello, Quebec, Canada: NATO, 23 October, 1983).

35. McGeorge Bundy et al., "Nuclear Weapons and the Atlantic Alliance," **Foreign Affairs** (Spring 1982). For an earlier discussion, see Richard Ullman, "No-First-Use of Nuclear Weapons," **Foreign Affairs** (July 1972).

36. Report of the European Security Study, **Strengthening Conventional Deterrence in Europe: Proposals for the 1980s** (London: Macmillan Publishers, 1983).

37. Paul Bracken, **Command and Control of Nuclear Forces** (New Haven, Conn.: Yale University Press, 1983).

38. See Lawrence Freedman, **Arms Control in Europe** (London: Royal Institute of International Affairs, 1981), Ch. 6.

39. Mathew Meselson and Julian Perry Robinson, "Chemical Warfare

and Chemical Disarmament,'' **Scientific American** (April 1980); Donald Hafner, ''Outer Space Arms Control: Unverified Practices, Unnatural Acts,'' **Survival** (November/December 1983).

(First published in **NATO: The Next Generation,** ed. Robert Hunter, 1984 Washington, Westview).

9 Europe and the Anti-Ballistic Missile Revival

Written prior to President Reagan's "Star Wars" speech in March 1983, this prediction of the likely European reaction to any such development was reasonably accurate; although there was no anticipation of the ambition of the Reagan Initiative.

West European members of NATO have a number of possible interests in the revival of activity in the field of anti-ballistic missiles (ABMs). These interests can be divided into two: those which might conceivably flow from the maximum possible objectives behind the current research effort being realised, and those likely to flow from the superpowers simply making the effort.

In the first category it is necessary to consider the consequences for Europe of the general upheaval in all strategic assumptions that would follow from a successful breakthrough in ABMs by either the United States, or the Soviet Union, or both together. In a sense, ABMs represent the last best hope of a real strategic superiority. It is a measure of the desperation of those seeking such a superiority that they are still attempting to revive an option that requires enormous economic and scientific investment, that is severely restricted by international treaty and that has always suffered in practice from the inherent advantages accruing to the offence in nuclear warfare.

A number of American strategists are now arguing that the only way to save the US nuclear guarantee to Europe would be to neutralise Soviet offensive strength by an effective defence. Alternatively a Soviet success, it is argued, would completely undermine the guarantee because the US would be left so vulnerable. If the two superpowers are successful more-or-less simultaneously, then the result will be to re-order the strategic balance on a basis that is somewhat less terrifying but possibly more uncertain than that involved in mutual assured destruction.

European attitudes towards all these possibilities are likely to be shaped first by whether they will be found in front of or behind the defensive barrier to be constructed by the United States. If Europe were to be protected as much as the United States then that would be a cause for general satisfaction. Despite some limited research on anti-tactical ballistic missiles (ATBM) Europe cannot confidently expect such protection and so its position would be extremely uncomfortable for it would now offer the most available set of Western targets for the Soviet Union, and could thus find itself as a sort of hostage.

When we turn to the second category of issues, this very possibility of Europe being left alone exposed, between the trenches as it were, could well have an impact on views in Europe as to its long-term strategic position and the value of the relationship with the United States. Even as an indication of a US aspiration to superiority, a visible and determined ABM development effort in the US could unsettle opinion in Europe and lead to questions as to the wisdom of associating with a superpower which was intent on such a high-risk strategy. Questions of this sort are also likely to result from any abrogation or even just amendment of the 1972 ABM Treaty in order to pave the way for the full-scale exploitation of the new defensive technology. As this would be taken to undermine the cause of arms control such a move would be regretted in Europe, given the general disposition in favour of this cause. Even if the hypothetical gains of effective defence were accepted, an immediate cost of unravelling the whole arms control process, which is politically extremely important, would not be considered worth paying. Lastly, in this category, there are the special fears of the British and French that their efforts to preserve national strategic nuclear forces would be put under severe strain by the development of a defence network surrounding the Soviet Union.

By definition, the second set of European interests come

into play as soon as there is any evidence that the super-powers are embarking upon an ABM race, while the first only become relevant when, if ever, there are signs of one side reaching the finishing post or even of a pending dead-heat. Moreover, the gap between embarkation on an ABM programme and its yielding results is likely to be lengthy. This gap will ensure that European attitudes will be governed for many years by their immediate reactions; probably that the whole ABM effort is unsettling and there-fore undesirable. It will take time before Europeans will seriously consider the consequences of such a decisive shift in the strategic balance. Even then, their reactions are still likely to be unfavourable.

This negative assessment will be a great disappointment to those in the US defence community who believe that a successful ABM programme would inject new credibility into the US strategic position. However, this disappoint-ment is unlikely to influence US decisions. A reading of the current American interest in ABMs suggests it is driven by the search for some technical fix to the problem of inter-continental ballistic missile (ICBM) vulnerability rather than as a political fix to the problem of general European vulnerability. This search to solve the problem of ICBM vulnerability has been a constant feature of US strategic debate since 1969 and is now getting somewhat desperate, with the intrusion of political and financial reality into the consideration of basing modes of the MX missile.

There are no signs that European views are believed to be at all relevant on this matter. For example, the report of a conference held in Washington in Spring 1981 on the ABM issue finds not one contributor even starting to put the issue in an Alliance context. The only mention of a possible European interest is a reminder by Jack Ruina that ''US nuclear allies are not going to be very enthusiastic about ABM deployment, given their uneasiness about the adequacy of their own nuclear deterrent''. There is not a mention of the political impression that such a deployment might create in Europe. [1]

The risk is therefore that such a vital decision could be taken in the belief that it is a matter of prudent technical adjustment, concerned solely with ensuring the survivability of US retaliatory forces, while ignoring the effect on a European public opinion that is already in quite a state on nuclear issues. To illustrate the risk it will be useful to examine the first great ABM debate of 1966-1972.

Europe and the First ABM Debate

Anti-ballistic missiles have not traditionally been taken as an Alliance issue. Symptomatic of this was the American announcement of September 1967 that a "thin" defence, known as the Sentinel system, was to be deployed against some eventual Chinese ICBM threat. This was made before a meeting of NATO's Nuclear Planning Group. There was no consultation on the matter, and European views appear to have had no relevance to the decision-making in Washington.[2]

The West European governments' reaction to the Sentinel decision was negative. If taken at face value it reflected another example of America's obsession with China, with an exaggerated view of China's nuclear potential. If, as many suspected, it was a ruse to ease the US into the deployment of ABMs which would soon be re-oriented against the USSR, then this could prove to be politically and militarily unsettling. There was little expectation at the time that Europe could eventually prove to be a beneficiary of a ballistic missile defence. There was some suggestion that the crude SS-4 and SS-5 intermediate range ballistic missiles (IRBMs) facing West Europe might not be as difficult to intercept as the ICBMs facing the US, but the short flight-time of the IRBMs argued against such optimism, as did awareness of the vast array of other nuclear devices that could be used against West Europe. Attacking West Germany from the East by some nuclear means or other is not one of the most demanding tasks ever to confront a military planner. Nor was there much of an inclination to commit large sums of money to a programme surrounded by so many technical doubts. Estimates at the time suggested that the deployment of a US-developed system to protect West Europe could cost as much as $12 billion.[3]

This background of a decision-making process in the United States that considered ABMs by reference to some very distinctive interests and prejudices, a formal lack of Alliance consultation and an awareness that West Europe was likely to be left out of this latest stage in the strategic arms race, did not encourage an intense or particularly well-informed public debate. Such debate as did take place only really got underway in 1967. This followed the announcement by Secretary of Defence Robert McNamara in late 1966 that the USSR was constructing its own ABM system and the consequent arguments in the United States over whether to follow suit. Because the American debate was so divided, Europeans were not faced with the problem of attempting to assess a prevailing American view but were able to choose between alternative positions.

By and large those Europeans who took an interest opted for the liberal position in this debate — that ABMs were a snare and a delusion, unable to offer real safety from attack while possibly triggering a new, unnecessary and costly stage in the arms race. There was concern that such a development would abort an embryonic East-West détente. An opportunity to put strategic relations onto a more sensible and stable footing would be lost.[4] It was thus possible for Theodore Sorenson, reporting West European views for the main "anti" contribution to the great ABM debate of 1969, to describe, probably correctly, European reactions to the Nixon administration's ABM programme as if they were by and large the same as those of American liberals.[5]

There were two other features of European attitudes along with this general anti-ABM disposition. The first was a lack of interest in the sort of distinctions common in the American debate. It was hard for Europeans to take seriously the American anxiety over China, so there was little respect for distinctions between anti-Soviet and anti-China systems. Outside the technical community (which in Europe at the time did not extend far beyond official circles) there was little appreciation of the difference between hard-point (*ie* specific military installation) and area defence. The assumption was that the issue under discussion was an area defence against Soviet attack, even though this was the least likely, in practical terms, of the American options.[6]

Instead, the debate was viewed through the filter of European strategic fears. Ian Smart observed of the 1967-9 debate:

> One persistent element in West Europe was a type of anxious irritation — not with reference to America's predicament but with reference to America's preoccupation. Outside technically sophisticated government circles, the military arguments for and against ABM deployment fell on deaf ears. What was generally recognised was the implication, justified or otherwise, that the United States might be about to insulate itself from its European allies, practically and emotionally, by deploying a new defence of its own homeland.[7]

This concern with the spectre of a "Fortress America" features prominently in all contemporary accounts.[8]

The sort of transformed strategic relationship that might be brought about by an effective anti-Soviet ABM system could appear promising as well as dangerous. The prospect of successful area defence was "interpreted contradictorily as either a step toward withdrawal to Fortress America from the hazards of nuclear diplomacy or as a measure to increase the credibility of US deterrence on behalf of Europe by attempting to re-establish the pre-Sputnik era of diplomacy".[9]

As Johan Holst observed, the view adopted was likely to depend on "the existing images in Europe of the nature and development of the Atlantic Alliance".[10] Basic prejudice would determine the assessment. An ABM would alter the whole balance of risks within the Alliance: the risk to America in nuclear crises would decline while that of its allies would remain the same. The inequalities in NATO would be accentuated. Anything which made it easier for the US to issue deterrent threats ought to work to the benefit of the Alliance, but only presuming that Washington's new freedom of manoeuvre would be used to general advantage. If the United States adopted a high-risk foreign policy as a direct result of ABM protection, then Europe might be picked upon by a frustrated Soviet leadership unable to get at its main adversary. A further transformation of the strategic relationship, by which both superpowers achieved effective defence, would not ease the latter fear but would undermine, once more, the credibility of US deterrent threats.

However, as Holst also pointed out, such dramatic and far-reaching strategic relationships were hardly on the cards. "Marginal trends" rather than "major shifts in the international system" were all that was at stake. Absolute invulnerability was simply not an option, and therefore the systems under consideration would not lead to the sort of profound changes feared (or desired). The sort of ballistic missile defences under consideration would "not constitute a sufficient or even a necessary prerequisite for the development of a superpower condominium".[11]

What this analysis suggests is that the importance for Europeans of US policy on ABMs, and indeed any significant departures in the development of nuclear weapons, had less to do with the direct impact on the US military position and much more do with what was taken to be revealed about underlying US interests and motives.

Europe and the next ABM Debate

If this analysis of the 1960s experience is at all valid then it has important implications for the European reaction to any revival of interest in ABMs in the 1980s. Once again it is likely to take time for the issue to attract much notice in Europe and, if it does, there will be the same disinclination to make distinctions between different types of ABMs. The cognoscenti believe that there is no comparison between a dedicated hard-point defence and area coverage, and so will become exasperated at the general assumption that such distinctions are unduly subtle and largely irrelevant. Even many who recognise the distinctions will argue that a hard-point defence is the "thin edge of the wedge" and that demand for an area defence will inevitably follow.

The evidence that the Soviet Union is close to a

"breakthrough" in ballistic missile defence is circumstantial and not highly regarded in West Europe.[12] Progress in those futuristic concepts is not expected for many years, while there are few signs that the USSR has an equivalent interest at the moment to that of the US in hard-point defence. If the USSR did take the initiative to break out of the constraints of the 1972 Treaty then it would suffer the opprobrium and a US response would be accepted. However, it is more likely that the initiative will come from the US.

Partly but not only because of this Treaty the reactions in Europe to such a US initiative may well be much stronger than in the 1960s. The reason for this is the current large-scale agitation in Europe concerning alleged US plans for "limited nuclear war". The claim is that US nuclear forces are being based in Europe so as to confine any future war to the continent. The East-West conflict, it is argued, will be fought out over European soil even if the immediate cause of hostilities has nothing to do with the allies and results from American actions that they oppose.[13]

This set of fears is based on the divergence in US and West European perceptions of each other's interests and behaviour. It also derives from a misinterpretation of past practice, existing and planned capabilities and trends in US strategic doctrine. A move to ABMs would exacerbate both these factors.

In terms of the analysis of US strategic doctrine it would tend to support a perception of Washington's underlying indifference to the fate of Europe. It can be argued against the protestors that cruise missiles are quite inappropriate as instruments of limited nuclear war. As American missiles that are prepared for attacks against Soviet territory, their use would be less likely to keep a nuclear war limited than to ensure that it engulfed both superpowers. But if the possibility existed of a Soviet retaliation being caught by US defences, all the worst suspicions would be confirmed. It would hardly be of comfort to Europe to host US offensive missiles so complicating to the Soviet defensive task, while Americans rested securely behind an effective defensive barrier. The Europeans would feel terribly exposed.[14] As in the 1960s, the likelihood of the worst fears being realised is very slight. An expressed US interest in hard-point defence would not justify the spectre of "Fortress America"; but, as was argued earlier, new departures in nuclear weapons tend to be understood, in the context of existing prejudices, as revelations about the basic character of the responsible power.

A move to ABMs which meant the end of the 1972 Treaty would have a direct impact on European attitudes. The anxiety over the nuclear arms race has encouraged a firm commitment to arms control in Europe. European political leaders put a lot of effort into persuading the Reagan administration of the vital importance of being seen to be exploring diplomatic alternatives to an arms race. On 30 November 1981, US and Soviet negotiators began discussions on Intermediate Nuclear Forces, a category which includes the cruise and SS-20 missiles that have generated the greatest alarm in Europe. These talks are described as taking place "within the SALT context" and depend on substantial parallel movement taking place at the intercontinental level. These core strategic arms talks became stalled with the US Senate's unwillingness to ratify SALT II. New negotiations are now under way with START, ostensibly designed to produce real reductions at the strategic level. It would be fair to say that the Reagan administration has yet to convince European opinion that there is any real flexibility in its negotiating position or that it is at all serious in the pursuit of arms control.

American protestations of interest in an arms control route to security would therefore be unlikely to survive any abrogation of the ABM Treaty, particularly given the non-ratification of the SALT II Treaty. If the only substantial achievement of arms control were removed the whole enterprise could collapse. If this risk was taken in order to make possible a series of marginal adjustments to the US force posture it would simply not be understood in Europe except in the most sinister terms. At the very least it would be taken to symbolise the high priority attached by the Reagan administration to purely military considerations as against the broader needs of foreign policy. Unless this image of American priorities is corrected, there will be increasing questioning in Europe of the wisdom of too close a connection with the United States.

Britain and France — Special Cases

While the rest of Europe may assess a new "ABM race" in these broad political terms, Britain and France must consider its effects on their own military planning. The problem is not new, for the Soviet deployments of ABMs in the 1960s raised severe doubts about the British and French ability to remain viable nuclear powers. Their position was complicated by the apparent feasibility of a thin ABM protection against small nuclear powers.

The two countries were unimpressed by American claims in the 1960s that ABMs could constitute an important anti-proliferation measure, as this measure could well cut them out of the business along with more reckless would-be nuclear powers. American policy at the time was still hostile to the development of extra nuclear capabilities in NATO, and this had been a major cause of the friction with France (Britain, as a long-established nuclear power, received more favourable treatment).

The fact that the Soviet ABM system might negate the European nuclear forces was one of the few things that might have commended it to Washington. McNamara's concern was with the bad impression a US anti-Soviet ABM might make on Moscow. He seemed to have been less aware of the adverse impression in Europe made by the anti-China Sentinel system, which was seen as a symptom of excessive Sinophobia and, in being directed against a small nuclear power, as an unfortunate precedent.

The possibility that an effective Soviet ABM system would force Britain and France out of the nuclear business was widely recognised at the time. In Britain, for example, the irony of such a strong Soviet counter-move taking place just as the first Polaris missiles were being prepared for initial operational deployment was pointed out.[15] However there is some evidence that officials in both British and French governments were more sanguine about the actual problems likely to be caused by Soviet ABMs.[16]

The British response to the Soviet "Galosh" system surrounding Moscow is now reasonably well documented. The announcement by Secretary of Defence McNamara in late 1966 that the US intelligence community was now convinced that "Galosh" was for the purposes of ballistic missile defence[17] served as the cue for Britain's small nuclear élite to consider the implications. Britain could have opted for the same response as the United States — a move to MIRVing with the Poseidon SLBM. Politically this was not really an option for a Labour Government that had been able to persevere with Polaris only because the costs had not proved to be excessive and because there had been no need to draw attention to the nuclear force. Those officials who would have liked to stay in step with the United States recognised that there was no immediate need for Poseidon.[18]

However, the division of the Poseidon front-end into numerous separate warheads was designed to accomplish two functions, only one of which was of interest to Britain. The early separation of the warheads, coupled with other penetration aids, served to complicate enormously the defender's task. The ability to aim the individual warheads independently served to increase the potential target structure. As Britain had only reasonably simple targeting requirements, her prime interest was in the first of these features.

In 1967 British nuclear scientists began a research protect geared to designing a warhead which concentrated on penetrating ABMs, even if this emphasis came at the expense of the number and variety of individual targets that could be attacked. The research programme, initially drawing on US concepts developed under the Antelope project of the early 1960s, looked particularly at warhead hardening to protect against the effects of exoatmospheric nuclear explosions from Soviet ABMs, and decoys to confuse Soviet defenders.

In 1972 the Conservative Government considered whether to push forward with this indigenous project or to purchase Poseidon from the US. It decided against Poseidon, largely on the grounds that while an anti-ABM system might be required, a full MIRV system would not be appropriate for Britain. By the early 1970s MIRVing had started to acquire the same bad name in Europe as had ABMs a few years before. Politically life would be easier without having to justify acquiring MIRVs in another highly public deal with the US. Persevering with a secret national progamme, with a much less controversial objective in mind, would be easier. It was recognised, probably correctly, that a future Labour Government would be unable to endorse Poseidon. This general political judgement was supported by technical and cost estimates, which favoured the British programme. These later turned out to have been extremely optimistic.

The British programme, which became known as Chevaline, was supported by successive Labour and Conservative governments. Although technically it was a success, in providing a manoeuvering, hardened, decoy-based front-end for Polaris, this success came at greater cost (£1,000 million) than expected and its introduction was delayed. It was not scheduled for introduction into UK forces until 1982.[19] By this time, and partly because of the experience with Chevaline, the British Government had decided to a adopt MIRV technology along with the US Trident missiles for the replacement of Polaris in the early 1990s.

For the purposes of this Essay it is important to note that the decision to proceed with Chevaline was taken *after* the 1972 ABM Treaty, when the USSR became restricted to 200 launchers. There were only 64 launchers in the "Galosh" system at the time, and by 1974 it should have been clear that there were unlikely to be many additions.[20] The rationale for Chevaline was that if Britain was to have a credible deterrent then it was necessary to be able to threaten Moscow.[21] Chevaline was designed to meet the specific problem posed by the "Galosh" system. Under the 1972 Treaty the quantity of ABMs if not the quality was restricted, and this made it a manageable problem. If, as currently planned, Britain introduces the Trident system in the early 1990s (either in the C-4 or D-5 variant) then it is likely to be in a position to penetrate any conceivable defences, at least for the rest of this century.

France, too, has designed its forces so as to be able to operate in the post-1972 ABM environment, though the issue has not been as fully discussed as in Britain. It was reported that in the 1975 series of tests, the hardening of the warheads was a major concern.[22] The M-4 warhead under development for introduction in 1985 with the submarine-based force, is to be used in a six-warheads MRV system. Although this is not a MIRV system, so the warheads are not independently targeted, it may well be that they separate early enough to pose major problems for the defending forces.

It is commonly believed that both the British and French forces are vulnerable to any future enhancement of ABM capabilities, either in an expansion of defensive systems following abrogation of the 1972 Treaty or in the development of some of the more exotic new systems, such as those based on directed-energy. One critic of the British government's choice of Trident argues that the pending arrival of laser or particle-beam defences is likely to undermine deterrent based or ballistic missiles.[23] This view has naturally enough been rejected by the Government.[24] Leading British defence scientists are privately quite sceptical about the likelihood of any breakthrough in the field of directed-energy weapons being translated into a viable defensive system until well into the next century if at all. Nevertheless, even if this more exotic threat is discounted, the British and French governments have made no secret of their anxiety that the 1972 ABM Treaty should not collapse.

Yet even here the risk to the viability of the European deterrents may not be as great as is often supposed. If the United States does decide that some form of hard-point defence is absolutely essential to the survivability of at least a portion of its ICBM force, and that the allowance under the 1972 Treaty (as amended in 1974) of 100 launchers is insufficient, then it is most likely to approach the USSR to amend the Treaty to make possible hard-point defence but to continue to exclude area defence. It is unlikely that the Soviet Union would agree to such amendment, but it is also unlikely that if American pressure led to the collapse of the

Treaty by other means, the USSR would move to a massive new investment in area defence, given the advantages that still accrue to the offence.

Even if the USSR were only interested in defending itself against Britain, France and China that would still require a major investment. It would not be enough to spread large numbers of ABMs around Soviet territory. On any given line of attack, many of these ABMs would be useless. As the mobility of the British and French submarine allows for attacks to be launched from a great variety of points, there would be many lines of attack to be covered. To accomplish this, a massive network would be required. It might well be possible for the USSR to protect Moscow effectively by enhancing substantially existing capabilities but it would be difficult to deny the smaller nuclear powers access to all economic and political centres.

So as a practical matter, the end of the ABM Treaty need not mean the end of the British and French deterrents. But as a political matter enormous public doubts about the viability of the national strike forces would almost certainly be raised. Officials would find it difficult to insist that little had changed and that no counter-measures were necessary. And if counter-measures were deemed necessary then that would raise the whole question of cost. Particularly in Britain, where there is already a widely-held view that even a minimum deterrent is an unwarranted burden on the public purse, any development which made it difficult to be confident in existing or planned force levels could prove to be decisive in the continuing argument over the value of retaining a national nuclear force.

Conclusion

This analysis has stressed the importance of prejudice and perceptions in shaping European attitudes to anti-ballistic missiles. Given the current state of West European public opinion on the nuclear issue, with the widespread anxiety that the nuclear arms race is once more getting out of control, and in such a way as to create novel dangers for

Europe, a stress on defensive technologies would just add to the prevailing sense of danger and anxiety.

Whatever the ultimate potential of the new defensive technologies, Europe would take some convincing that the opportunity to re-order the strategic relationship based on something other than mutual superpower vulnerability could be of benefit to them. If the superpowers could defend themselves effectively then the European vulnerabilities would be accentuated, for not only could West Europe not be protected but also the British and French nuclear forces would appear ineffectual.[25] Even if none of these dramatic developments ever came about, the very act of making an effort to promote the relevant systems would prompt suspicions in Europe.

Alternatively it might be claimed that the US intention was to achieve no more than an added degree of survivability for the land-based ICBM force, and that though it might entail altering the ABM Treaty this would add to, not detract from, the stability of the strategic balance. Even if the Europeans could be convinced that US objectives would stay so modest, they would be unlikely to understand why it was worth jeopardising the whole arms control process for such a minor improvement. Either way the severity of the political reactions to a new ABM race would probably far outweigh the actual shifts in military relationships that could eventually be achieved.

Notes

1. Conference on "ABM Revisited" **The Washington Quarterly,** VI:4 (Autumn 1981). The Ruina quote is from p. 65. Consideration to the alliance dimension is given by Albert Carnesale, "Reviving the ABM Debate". **Arms Control Today,** II:4 (April 1981). He is certain of the negative allied reaction to Soviet BMD deployment but less sure of the reaction to US deployment.
2. As negative evidence one can note the total absence of any mention of alliance considerations in Morton Halperin. "The Decision to Deploy the ABM". **World Politics,** XXV (October 1972).
3. **Economist,** 3 Dec., 1966.
4. These impressions can be gleaned from the two most informed analyses of West European views: Laurence Martin, "Ballistic Missile Defence and Europe", in Eugene Rabinowitch and Ruth Adams

(eds.), **Debate the Antiballistic Missile** (Chicago: Bulletin of the Atomic Scientists, 1967); Johan Holst, "Missile Defense: Implications for Europe", in Johan Holst and William Schneider Jr. (eds.). **Why ABM? Policy Issues in the Missile Defense Controversy** (New York: Pergamon, 1969).

5. Theodore C. Sorenson, "The ABM and Western Europe" in Abram Chayes and Jerome B. Wiesner (eds.), **ABM: An Evaluation of the Decision to Deploy an Antiballistic Missile System** (New York: New American Library, 1969).

6. The Sentinel programme was for area defence against Chinese attack; the Safeguard programme (of the Nixon Administration in 1969) was to protect ICBM silos against Soviet attack.

7. Ian Smart, "Perspectives from Europe", in Mason Willrich and John B. Rhinelander (eds.), **SALT: The Moscow Agreements and Beyond** (London: Collier Macmillan, 1974), p.187.

8. Thus Sorensen suggested that whatever the declared role of the Safeguard system in protecting ICBMs, it would be seen in a more sinister light. "Many if not most West Europeans will believe instead that the United States is increasing its capacity to ignore some future Soviet nuclear threat which European nations cannot escape." Op. cit., p. 179.

9. Martin. op. cit., p. 125.

10. Holst, op. cit., p. 196.

11. Ibid., p. 190.

12. One author that does accept claims of Soviet progress in directed-energy technologies is Dr. David Baker, **The Shape of Wars to Come** (London: Patrick Stephens Ltd., 1981). This book opens with a "scenario" for 1995 in which the USSR introduces a "ground-based particle beam device designed to screen Soviet territory from incoming warheads", while the US is rushing to get in place Star Raker, a space-based anti-missile beam weapon. The result is "stalemate: nobody can strike the other with the holocaust of armageddon" (pp.8-9). Unfortunately for this scenario, the position of Western Europe as Soviet hostages in such circumstances is not discussed. See also Air-Vice Marshal Stewart Menaul. **Countdown Britain's Strategic Nuclear Forces** (London: Robert Hale, 1980).

13. For a discussion of the arguments behind the current movements see pp 81–101. "Limited War and Unlimited Protest".

14. At a conference in Washington just after the 1980 Presidential election, I was witness to a prominent Reagan supporter (an academic who later was appointed to a job on the National Security Council staff) doing his best to promote such fears. After stressing the importance of NATO's long-range theatre nuclear force modernisation programme being implemented, he then mused aloud about how the US had fallen so hopelessly behind in the ICBM race that it might be sensible to concentrate on defensive technology.

15. For example the **Economist**: "On the assumption the anti-missile technology is now really getting under way, the only safe estimate is that by the mid-1970s Britain's Polaris missiles will be capable of inflicting only marginal damage on the Russians" (28 Oct., 1967).

16. This seems to be the message of Martin, op. cit., p.126.
17. There was also intense debate over whether a series of installations known as the "Tallin Line" were also for ABM purposes. It later transpired that they were for air defence purposes. For the background to the US intelligence debate see Lawrence Freedman, **US Intelligence and the Soviet Strategic Threat** (London: Macmillan, 1977), Chapter Five.
18. Much of this section is based on the relevant chapters in Lawrence Freedman, **Britain and Nuclear Weapons** (London: Macmillan, 1980).
19. **The Times**, 30 Jan., 1982.
20. A 1974 Amendment brought the permitted numbers down to 100. In 1980 the USSR cut the number of launchers in the "Galosh" complex from 64 to 32, probably in order to bring in a replacement. The possibility was, however, raised that Chevaline might now be a battering ram for an open door.
21. Whether or not this makes much sense as strategic theory is not relevant to this article. For a documentation of the theory see Freedman, **Britain and Nuclear Weapons.** Chapter Five.
22. **The Times**, 10 June, 1975.
23. See Menaul, op. cit., and Letter to **The Times,** 5 July, 1981. Curiously Menaul appears to believe that cruise missiles will still be able to survive the breakthroughs in defensive technology, though most analysts would argue that cruise missiles are already vulnerable to known means of defence.
24. Defence Secretary John Nott when asked about Menaul's letter (see note 23) said that there were no grounds for believing that a system would be developed to knock out ballistic missiles in the next decade. **The Times**, 9 July, 1981.
25. For an interesting discussion of the possibilities of damage-limiting anti-tactical ballistic (or cruise) missiles for Europe see David Yost. "Ballistic Missile Defense and the Atlantic Alliance". **International Security**, Fall 1982 (Vol. 7, No. 2). Despite his own sympathy for such a project the author is unable to find much evidence to suggest that this sympathy would be widely shared in Europe.

(First published in **Anti-Ballistic Missile Defence in the 1980s** ed. Ian Bellany & Coit D. Blacker, 1984 London, Frank Cass & Co Ltd.)

10 The Strategic Defence Initiative — ''Star Wars''

Few Presidential announcements on strategic policy have caused such controversy as President Reagan's proposal of the Strategic Defence Initiative (SDI) which would replace the current dependence on Mutual Assured Destruction (MAD) with something more akin to Mutual Assured Survival. The following somewhat sceptical discussion of the SDI began as a conference paper for the International Institute for Strategic Studies; it has been revised and brought up to date for inclusion in this volume.

> I call upon the scientific community in our country, those who gave us nuclear weapons, to turn their talents now to the cause of mankind and world peace, to give us the means of rendering these nuclear weapons impotent and obsolete.[1]

If these words are to be taken seriously then President Reagan's speech of 23 March 1983 will be seen as setting in motion a revolution in contemporary strategic affairs. He committed his government to the overthrow of the entrenched and domineering offence that has reigned supreme in nuclear matters since 1945 and has exercised an overbearing influence on international affairs. It was the dawning of the age of the defence.

For such a revolutionary declaration the President's speech was something of a curiosity. It was not the result of any major analytical effort within government nor the subject of consultations with allies. The origins appear to lie with lobbies as exotic as the technologies they promote. When the bureaucracy was tasked to bring about the new strategic order it did so in such a slow and confused manner that the initiative was soon robbed of much of its revolutionary credentials, although the President and his most senior officials persist in surrounding it in revolutionary rhetoric.

There was certainly a revolution in method. We have become used to the idea that in the modern world technology leads doctrine. Here strategic requirements were put to the fore and the scientists and engineers were charged to meet them, even though the necessary technology was well beyond the current state of the art and the weight of scientific opinion appeared to be that the President's utopian goal would remain far out of reach. Even if all went according to plan the new strategic order was unlikely to arrive until well into the next century.

Most successful revolutions are better prepared and run more clearly with the tide of history. The full implications of the Strategic Defence Initiative do not appear to have been particularly well thought out in advance. Given the lack of enthusiasm in Congress and in the bureaucracy it may peter out of its own accord. However, it also has a substantial measure of popular support, a large number of research contracts have been awarded and the effort has now got some central direction from within the Pentagon.

The notion that it would be both more moral and prudent to concentrate on defence rather than on a destructive offence has been around from the earliest days of the nuclear age and can be expected to retain some popularity and influence even if the current Initiative lapses. The fact that the concept of strategic defence has managed to reach centre stage at least provides us with an opportunity to discuss its merits and failings.

In what follows I will talk about the Strategic Defence Initiative rather than ''Star Wars''. SDI is not only the official term but is also more descriptive. President Reagan did not actually refer to space-based systems in his speech — they were mentioned in the associated White House briefing. It was inevitable that anything in this area would attract such a label — indeed it had already been applied to discussions of anti-satellite weapons and the two are still confused. In the same way similar projects two decades ago attracted the ''Buck Rogers'' label.

It is impossible to discuss this subject without being drawn into a number of technical debates. I will touch on these debates without exploring the various systems being proposed. The preoccupation with the efficacy or otherwise of high-technology systems detracts attention from the more basic questions concerning the objectives of strategic defence and their desirability, should they prove to be feasible.

In the past the idea that a nation should do its best to protect itself against all forms of attack would not have been considered revolutionary; indeed, to suggest anything to the contrary would have seemed bizarre, even treacherous.

What has persuaded policy-makers of the limited value of defences against nuclear attack is the high cost of even the smallest failure and the continuing success of the offence in coming up with new measures to trump any attempts to establish an effective defence.

As the United States began to consider its vulnerability to attack from the Soviet Union there was a natural inclination to explore the possibilities for defence. In 1952 President Truman created a special sub-committee of the National Security Council (NSC) to consider the Soviet ability to injure the United States. Its conclusions, reported in May 1953 to the new Eisenhower administration, were rather gloomy. The lack of an ability to protect the United States from a nuclear attack was deemed by the NSC to constitute an ''unacceptable risk to our nation's survival''. Complete unvulnerability was recognised to be impossible but ''a reasonably effective defence system can and must obtained''.[2] By 1960 some $20 billion had been spent on the development of an air defence system that was to be rendered virtually obsolete by ICBMs.

This experience did not deter advocates of an anti-ballistic missile defence but it made the US Government more wary of committing large sums of money to measures to defend cities from an all-out Soviet attack. At best ABMs were seen to be useful in protecting high-value military targets or in acting against small-scale attacks such as might be posed from China. During the 1960s the United States came to the conclusion that the best method of deterring a nuclear attack on the United States was the threat of retaliation in kind. This view appeared to have been accepted by the Soviet Union when it joined the United States in signing the 1972 ABM Treaty. The prevailing view was summed up by Secretary of Defence James Schlesinger in 1974 when arguing in favour of cutting air defences:

> Since we cannot defend our cities against strategic missiles, there is nothing to be gained by trying to defend them against a relatively small force of strategic bombers. I am sure the Soviet leaders understand that an attack on our cities, whether by bombers or missiles, would inevitably result in the destruction of their cities. [3]

There were always objections in the strategic studies community to this view. During the 1970s the critics grew in strength. Their main target, however, was not the view that nothing could be done to protect populations from nuclear attack but that the only option available to the West in initiating nuclear exchanges would be all-out attacks on cities. If there was criticism of the restrictions on anti-ballistic missiles it was in the denial of one option for protecting land-based missiles.

The Reagan administration came to power less than well-disposed towards the 1972 ABM Treaty. There were dark hints that abrogation might be necessary when the Treaty came up for review in 1982. In the debate over the basing of the MX (Peacekeeper) ICBM, anti-ballistic missiles were canvassed as potentially valuable complements to some of the proposed schemes. However the administration could not bring itself to propose abrogating the Treaty to save MX. Indeed, even when announcing the Densepack basing mode for MX in November 1982 the President clearly dissociated this system from a ballistic missile defence despite the widespread view that such a defence was needed to make it work.

Because ABM technology was discussed largely in the context of the survival of US land-based ICBMs, it did not appear central to the administration's attempts to wrest US strategy away from the grip of assured destruction, which were largely based on changes to targeting plans and developments of more sophisticated offensive systems. This is not the place to review the administration's efforts in the area of strategic doctrine. Suffice it to say that the efforts to build on the Carter administration's countervailing strategy and plan for "prolonged" nuclear wars have failed to convince. The main result was to stimulate adverse reaction at home and abroad, and some substantial critiques by analysts concerned with both the inner logic of the doctrine and the practicality of conducting a nuclear war along the lines envisaged.

Assured destruction was criticised as a strategic doctrine for failing to provide the United States with options other than the mass destruction of civilians in the event of nuclear hostilities (a crime of which it was not actually guilty). To the critics, the failure was compounded by the unwillingness of the Soviet Union to limit its plans in this manner. The resultant debate revolved around what the US might wish to inflict on the Soviet Union rather than what the Soviet Union might do to the US and the West in general. This was quite reasonable, given that it is the West that is presumed to be the most dependent on a credible nuclear strategy. The difficulty was that whatever offensive tactics might be developed for the West, the problem of the character of the Soviet retaliation and the form taken by later nuclear exchanges — leading to Mutual Assured Destruction — remained.

In the end, if the administration was serious about its commitment to escape from the grim logic of Mutual Assured Destruction it had to get round its critics' fundamental argument — that MAD was not just a policy choice but was a fact of life in the modern world. If only the Soviet second-strike capability could be undermined then US nuclear strategy would gain a formidable credibility. In this sense the President's speech represented the logical conclusion of the search for a credible nuclear strategy that has occupied US policy-makers since Robert McNamara's days as Secretary of Defence.

Two Steps Forward

There were no hints that a revolution was being prepared in the White House in the early months of 1983. In the discussions within the Scowcroft Commission, attempting to forge a bipartisan policy on strategic forces, the potential benefits of ballistic missile defence were not seen to extend much beyond the protection of land-based missiles. The Commission's Report (released after the President's 23 March speech) concluded:

> Applications of current technology offer no real promise of being able to defend the United States against massive nuclear attack in this century...
> At this time... the Commission believes that no ABM technologies appear to combine practicality, survivability, low cost, and technical effectiveness sufficiently to justify proceeding beyond the stage of technology development. [4]

A continued research programme was deemed necessary just in case there was a need to respond to a Soviet "breakout" from the constraints of the ABM Treaty.

This sense that any collapse of the ABM Treaty would be at the instigation of the Soviet Union and not the United States seemed to be in line with administration thinking. Less and less was heard about the review of the ABM Treaty. Official policy, as outlined in a Presidential statement of November 1982 declared that the United States

> did not wish to embark on any course of action that could endanger the current ABM treaty so long as it is observed by the Soviet Union.

There were no plans to deploy any ballistic missile defence system, even that permitted under the 1972 Treaty, but research would continue on the relevant technology. The objectives of this research effort were:

> stability for our ICBMs in the 1990s, a hedge against Soviet breakout of the ABM treaty, and the technical competence to evaluate Soviet ABM developments. [5]

These objectives were broadly similar to those of the Carter administration. [6] The positive interest was confined to protection of ICBM silos; otherwise the only requirement was to be ready to respond to any initiative taken by the Soviet Union.

The new policy announced by the President in his speech of 23 March was elaborated further in background briefings and in supporting statements, speeches and interviews by the President and his senior officials, particularly Secretary of Defence Caspar Weinberger and Science Advisor Dr George Keyworth. Its key features were as follows:

1. It was self-consciously revolutionary and visionary. In his speech the President described an "ultimate goal" of eliminating the threat posed by nuclear weapons. A few days later he spoke of his initiative as offering an alternative to one in which

   > the great nations of the world will sit here like people facing themselves across a table each with a cocked gun, and no one knowing whether someone might tighten the finger on the trigger. [7]

   Assured destruction would be turned on its head: people and not weapons have to be protected; weapons and not people were to be threatened. The objectives went well beyond guarding against Soviet first strikes or protecting offensive missiles. The system would provide total and not just partial protection. As Casper Weinberger put it:

   > The defensive systems the President is talking about are not designed to be partial. What we want to try to get is a system which will develop a defence that is thoroughly reliable and total ... I don't see any reason why that can't be done. [8]

2. It was specifically concerned with "strategic ballistic missiles" (the only weapons mentioned in the original speech). This aspect appears to rest uneasily with the requirement for total protection. However the argument was that ballistic missiles posed the most critical test to any defence and if they could be stopped then slower-moving forces would pose far less of a challenge.

3. The protection would be extended to Allies. The President's "vision" was to "intercept and destroy strategic ballistic missiles before they reached our own soil or that of our Allies". This statement implies a wider (if not wholly inappropriate) definition of a strategic missile than is normally

adopted by the United States. Unfortunately elsewhere in the same speech the President referred specifically to ''intermediate nuclear force,'' confirming the impression that the inclusion of Allies was something of an after-thought.

4. At least for the time being the 1972 ABM Treaty would be respected. The Treaty permitted research, and deployment decisions were years away.

5. The objective was ''neither military superiority nor political advantage''. Indeed, in a later Press conference, the President suggested that when the defensive system was developed one option would be to pass the technology on to the Soviet Union. Secretary Weinberger stated that:

> I would hope and assume that the Soviet with all the work they have done and are doing in this field, would develop a similar defence, which would have the effect of totally and completely removing these missiles from the face of the earth.[9]

One Step Back

Since the Spring of 1983 the policy has been revised substantially and is in a number of respects now reverting to the sort of rationales adopted prior to March 1983. Instead of being presented as a self-conscious piece of doctrinal revisionism the SDI is increasingly being described as a prudent response to an initiative already undertaken by the Soviet Union. Even more significantly, although the objective of a population defence has not been disavowed, especially at the highest political level, scientists and officials at the working level have reverted to the protection of US military capabilities against a Soviet first strike. There is now little pretence that it will prove possible to eliminate offensive weapons as a result of this initiative — at least until the ultimate goal is within reach.

The revisionism may even have moved a stage further. Lt-General James Abrahamson, directing the SDI, told reporters in May 1984 that:

> My specific charge is to ensure that possibility of early deployments in case there is a breakout of the Anti-Ballistic Missile Treaty on the part of the Russians.[10]

Some proponents of strategic defence now find it very hard to imagine that the President ever even considered the idea of defending civilians, although clearly he did. [11]

This more modest tendency has been reflected in the actual development of the SDI. National Security Study Directive 6-83 required an examination of the technology that could eliminate the threat posed by nuclear ballistic missiles to the security of the United States and its allies. A Defensive Technologies Study, headed by Dr James C Fletcher, and a Future Security Strategy Study, headed by Fred Hoffman, reported in October 1983. The essential conclusion of the Fletcher Panel was that ''a robust, multi-tiered ballistic missile defence system can eventually be made to work''. The stress, however, was on ''eventually''. This was a matter for long-term research.

This approach angered a number of the more enthusiastic advocates of strategic defence. In his National Security Decision Directive of 6 January 1984 the President supported the more cautious approach and called for

> initiation of a focused programme to demonstrate the technical feasibility of enhancing deterrence and thereby reducing the risk of nuclear war through greater reliance on defensive technology.

Key officials stressed the long-term and speculative nature of the programme. [12] In late March, General Abrahamson was appointed to direct the Strategic Defence Initiative. With a certain amount of bureaucratic friction, Abrahamson's office began to pull together a number of disparate BMD-related programmes from around the Department of Defence.

As things stand the Strategic Defence Initiative now takes the following form: (a) it is concerned with long-term research rather than medium-term deployment. The proposals of those in lobbies such as ''high frontier'', for a move to early deployment based on available technology, have been rejected on the familiar grounds of over-estimated performance and under-estimated cost. Known but unfashionable technologies such as nuclear ABMs are being discarded and while a short-term capacity to respond to a Soviet break-out from the ABM Treaty is being maintained it is not being taken much further. In long-term research the easier technologies are being kept for later while priority is given to the most challenging problems, especially laser technology and the computational capabilities necessary to manage large-scale defences. The assumption is that a layered defence, that is threatening the offence at the boost, post-boost, mid-course and terminal phases, will be necessary to ensure against leakage at any one layer. The effort remains directed towards ballistic missiles. While a system capable of dealing with intercontinental ballistic missiles can also deal with intermediate range systems (although not necessarily using multiple layers) the problems of dealing with bombers and cruise missiles are quite different.

There appears to be some debate within the administration as to the need for or the desirability of combining an effort to deal with the "air-breathing threat" with one to deal with strategic missiles. According to one school of thought it is by no means clear that in the future, as in the past, bombers and cruise missiles will pose far simpler defensive problems. They do not leave rocket flares at boost stage to allow them to be detected at launch nor enter the atmosphere. Although their speed is slower than missiles they are difficult to detect by radar and with "stealth" technology this will pose greater problems in the future. Some proponents of SDI have argued that "air-breathers" are more stable than missiles because of their slower speed. William Furniss of the Pentagon has been quoted as suggesting, rather curiously, that if the strategic competition were pushed back towards bombers it "would get us back to the relatively stable period of the 1950s". However, it is hard to see how ballistic missile defences could remain credible with an unrestricted bomber and cruise missile threat. One obvious problem is that ground-based components of the defence would be vulnerable to a pre-emptive cruise missile attack. As Major-General John A Shard of the USAF put it: "If you're going to fix the roof, you don't want to leave the doors and windows open".[13]

The current plan is for the research phase to be completed

in the early 1990s when decisions will have to be taken on whether or not to move on to systems development, when prototypes are designed, built and tested. This will be followed by a transition stage during which there will be ''incremental, sequential deployment of defensive systems'' and a final phase of deployments of highly-effective, multi-phased defensive systems. It may be another 30 years before this final phase is completed.

The eventual cost remains a matter of conjecture. Current spending is quite modest although it is projected to rise significantly over the next four years. Richard DeLauer, US Under-Secretary of Defence for Research and Engineering, has warned that costs would be ''staggering'', and suggested that over 10 years of deployment they would be equivalent to present expenditure on offensive arms — some 14 per cent of the total budget each year. At current prices this would be some $400–450 billion and after already substantial development costs.

More seriously, it does not include the costs of introducing parallel defences against bombers and cruise missiles. Furthermore, there can be no expectation of compensating savings in offensive arms. Indeed, it is not inconceivable that there will be increased expenditures on offensive arms to meet the challenges posed by the introduction of Soviet defences. So clearly a substantial amount of new money is going to have to be found if these schemes are to come to fruition. There are signs that those responsible for other aspects of US defences are already worried that their programmes will be crowded out by SDI.

Protect or Avenge

The most important development has been the shift away from the protection of civilians as the prime objective of the programme. After the President's speech, Congressional supporters tabled a People Protection Act to

> implement the call of the President for a national strategy seeking to protect people from nuclear war and to render nuclear weapons obsolete.

They must now feel as if they had succumbed to a life insurance salesman only to discover that the policy only covered the car.

There is as yet no clearly formulated strategic defence doctrine: only a variety of arguments used to support the Initiative. For those concerned to put the best face on the programme the difficulty lies in President Reagan's original ''vision'' (as it is now officially described). This has not been disavowed, as illustrated by the regular recourse to the theme ''It is better to protect lives than to avenge them''. [14]

Such a statement constitutes no challenge to the conventional strategic wisdom. It has always been deemed better to protect than avenge. According to the traditional theory of deterrence, protection was a result of a clear readiness to avenge. If the President is now saying something new there are two possible interpretations. The first, is that it is now possible physically to protect people so that there is no need to prepare to avenge them. This is certainly what most people read into his original speech. For this to be true it is necessary to develop a watertight protective umbrella over the United States and its Allies so that none will come to any harm from a Soviet attack.

The alternative meaning is that our capacity to avenge may no longer be sufficient and this undermines the capacity to protect through the mechanisms of deterrence. It is this second interpretation which has been seized on by officials in the administration. According to this argument the deterrence relationship might well break down if the Soviet Union can develop nuclear attack options that will undermine the American capacity to avenge. It can be restored if the Soviet Union can no longer be sure that it will achieve military objectives in its attack. In this sense there is no requirement for the defences to be watertight. [15]

In the first case, the SDI truly represents a strategic revolution. The problem to be addressed — vulnerability to nuclear attack — is simple to understand but immensely difficult to solve. If the second case, the SDI does no more than shore up the status quo. The problem to be addressed — denying the Soviet Union targets of strategic significance — can be hard to define and not easily shown to deserve all this effort but it might be in the realm of technological feasibility.

In principle these two approaches diverge in their rationales and requirements. They can be reconciled only by asserting that the more modest approach is truly "intermediate" in nature, in that it will provide opportunities to prove technologies essential to the more ambitious schemes and that it will be possible to move to a complete defence through the addition of extra layers. The various intermediate objectives identified by supporters of the programme have long been associated with ballistic missile defence:

(a) **Hard-Point Defence**: Protection of land-based missiles and command and control centres against a Soviet first strike. This has always been a favoured rationale for ABMs.
(b) **Strategy-Denial**: A more sophisticated variant of (a) assuming the concentration in Soviet strategy on a variety of forms of counterforce targeting in the conduct of campaigns against Western Europe as well as the United States. By denying the Soviet Union preferred strategic options it will be deterred from engaging in any nuclear operations.
(c) **Protection against small attacks**: Even if the system cannot deal with a massive assault it should be able to deal with accidental launches of missiles or smaller nuclear forces.
(d) **Damage Limitation**: By reducing the total number of warheads detonated the damage to civilian life and property can be reduced though it would still be very high. It has even been suggested that strategic defences offer one way of staving off the "nuclear winter" by keeping the number of warheads detonated beneath the threshold that might trigger a climatic catastrophe.

The United States has insisted that the fundamental purpose is to enhance deterrence, and this is particularly clear with regard to objectives (a) and (b). With regard to (c) it is only China that could conceivably pose a ballistic missile threat to the United States. It would be somewhat ironic if the anti-China rationale, which was deemed to be rather feeble when adopted by McNamara in 1967, was resurrected now. For the moment, it is the Soviet Union which will find this rationale most appealing. As for objective (d) the administration is sensitive to the suggestion that it is preparing for war and has tended to play this down.

There are, in addition, three subsidiary objectives that might justify continuing with a substantial research effort even if it did not achieve any major goals:

(e) **Response to Breakout**: Maintaining the capability to respond to a Soviet breakout from the constraints imposed by the ABM Treaty. This objective tends to be supported even by those who object to the SDI.

(f) **Bargaining Chip**: The prospect of a successful US deployment of an effective defence will encourage the Soviet Union to take arms control more seriously.

(g) **Diversion of Resources**: In order to deal with developing US defensive capabilities the Soviet Union will be forced to divert resources into improving its offensive counter-measures.

It should be noted that these subsidiary benefits still depend on there being a reasonable possibility that the primary objectives can be obtained. For example, the bargaining chip argument is normally taken to suggest that reductions on offensive arms will be easier to obtain as the Soviet Union recognises the futility of persevering with offensive arms in the face of ever more impressive US defences. However, if US defences fail to impress then no negotiating leverage is provided at all, except possibly in encouraging further restrictions on the defence.

Nor would there be much point in responding to a breakout from Treaty constraints with a comparable defensive build-up if the resultant defences were likely to be ineffective. The Soviet Union has been more energetic in the past with both air defences and ABMs; the US response has been to strengthen the offence.

The President's vision of nuclear weapons being rendered "impotent and obsolete" was vulnerable to the standard criticisms made against comparable visions in the past. The first side to achieve an effective defence would put the other at a considerable disadvantage. But the latter would have advance notice of this shift in the strategic balance and might be tempted to pre-empt before the shift had become absolute. So the transition period would be one of immense strain, and indeed the problem of transition will be stressful if any serious change in the existing strategic order is contemplated. Once the new defences were in place the favoured side might be tempted to exploit its advantage during a crisis by launching a nuclear strike in the expectation (which might turn out to be disastrously mistaken) that it would receive nothing in return.

Given the more modest objectives of protecting high-value military assets rather than civilians, these somewhat grand strategic problems are now rather pushed into the background. The SDI will achieve less than originally envisaged and so, by the same token, is less potentially destabilising than its detractors have suggested. Most important of all the "intermediate" objectives do not take us out of the condition of Mutually Assured Destruction. An opponent determined to inflict unacceptable damage could still do so. In principle these objectives are perfectly consistent with 1960s-vintage strategic doctrine.

Indeed their most likely effect is to reinforce a concentration on city-targeting. As any defence would have some damage limiting capacity the Soviet Union might feel obliged to compensate by improving its area-attack capabilities to guard against any diminution in its "ultimate" threat. Furthermore, to the extent that the United States succeeded in denying to Soviet planners lucrative military targets the planners would have little choice but to stress "soft" targets such as cities. There seems to be some attempt by supporters of the SDI to suggest that this does not matter because of a lack of Soviet interest in counter-city targeting. This argument is hard to take seriously. It is particularly difficult to imagine any President taking it seriously during a crisis or in the early stages of war. A historical precedent warns against over-reliance on this judgement. In the early 1960s when the United States adopted a "cities-avoidance" targeting policy and backed this up with a surge in missile production, the Soviet Union, which lacked a comparable doctrine or productive capacity, was forced to stress the more terroristic aspects of its arsenal. (One means of doing this was the test of a 56 megaton device!) It is anyway a bit much for the President's supporters to claim a major strategic breakthrough in our protection when at the end of the day all they are saying is that the Soviet Union will not undertake an attack which it is agreed that the United States would be unable to block completely because they would be fearful of US retaliation. This comes down to the policy the President has derided of "avenging" rather than "protecting".

It is certainly true that Soviet doctrine puts a lot of stress on counterforce targeting but the conviction with which this is done can easily be exaggerated. Furthermore, this approach is most relevant to the European theatre where the problems of protecting military assets are much greater. It is important to deny the Soviet Union a first-strike capability, but they are nowhere near achieving such a capability at the moment. The problems of land-based missile survivability are acute but that is not the case with sea-based systems and strategic defence is irrelevant to the problems of anti-submarine warfare. Moreover there are known forms of defence for ICBM silos, if that is what the President really wanted, without having to embark on a massive research programme.

It has to be asked how much expense and bother it is worth to deny the Soviet Union a series of options for its nuclear strike plans that already look implausible and reckless. As strategic problems they may not be as urgent as suggested by those proposing the SDI as a solution. Any major deployment of strategic defences will add to Soviet uncertainties about what they can get away with and so to some extent reinforce deterrence. However, it is doubtful whether the increment of deterrence will have been worth the price, especially if other elements of the force structure have declined as a result of the diversion of resources to SDI.

A definition of the objectives of the SDI which could be considered neutral might be: "the progressive elimination of offensive nuclear options through the application of defensive technologies". This definition raises the question of which side is likely to benefit most from the denial of targeting options. In the past it has been the West rather than the East that is believed to have been most in need of a credible nuclear strategy.

Unless the advocates presume that the Soviet Union will not be able to follow a US breakout, which would require a considerable act of faith and contradict their own statements on the advanced stage of Soviet research and development, then it must be expected that Western options will also be reduced. Contrary to the received wisdom, the presumption behind much of the advocacy of the SDI appears to be that the Soviet Union is in the greatest need of nuclear options. We find George Keyworth suggesting that the great advantage of the SDI in the long-term will be "to enforce retaliation as the sole rationale for nuclear delivery systems".[16]

This is by no means an unreasonable objective, but it contradicts NATO's current position that it is most in need of a threat of nuclear escalation to deter aggression. The response by the US administration, and other Western governments, to proposals to remove nuclear weapons from strategic calculations in Europe through no-first-use declarations has been that this would make Europe "safe for conventional warfare". Presumably this objection also applies to achieving the same effect through the neutralisation of both sides' offensive nuclear weapons. The introduction of effective defences therefore could reduce the risks surrounding conventional operations — the very area where the Warsaw Pact is believed to enjoy its most significant advantages. Even if the result of both sides protecting vital military assets was to reduce the opportunities for sophisticated nuclear operations according to the conventional wisdom in NATO, the Alliance has most to lose from such a development. It may well be that we would be better off if neither side had the ability to mount such operations at any nuclear level. The point is that the SDI only appears to be improving the position if it presumes that NATO's fundamental problem — the incredibility of the threat to use nuclear weapons first — has already been dealt with by other measures. To stabilise strategic relations on this new basis, the SDI would have to be accompanied by a major improvement in conventional defences.

The only alternative argument would be if the proposed breakthrough in defences were a one-sided development that could regain for NATO the lost superiority that once served as a credible basis for its nuclear threats. However not only do United States spokesmen cast doubt on the likelihood of moving alone to strategic defences but even if the US did gain superiority in this area that superiority would be inadequate unless it was absolute and part of a true first-strike capability. The doubts on the US nuclear guarantee stem from the vulnerability of American cities to retaliation. Unless this can be removed there would be no protection for the American people against a Soviet attempt to avenge the US initiation of nuclear hostilities.

Perceptions in Europe

This brings us to the whole question of the impact of all this on the Alliance. The Allies were not consulted about President Reagan's speech and their response has been muted to say the least. The initial reaction was simply to hope that it was an aberration and that there would be no significant follow-through. This is still the hope but no longer the expectation.

In addition to sending round briefing teams to NATO capitals, Defence Secretary Caspar Weinberger gave an exposition to ministers at the Nuclear Planning Group meeting in Turkey in early April 1984. This seems to have had a negative reception and was followed by the Germans expressing their doubts publicly. The French, after initially toying with the idea of developing their own defensive systems (in line with the established practice of asserting that France can follow any new technological line should she so desire) became quite hostile and even tabled a proposal at the Geneva Committee on Disarmament that would prohibit space-based defences. The French have been particularly concerned at the possible impact on the viability of their own national deterrent. The British also have doubts on this score but have felt it was too parochial a basis for a broad critique of the SDI. [17]

European concern has been not so much with the wisdom of pursuing advanced research into defensive technologies (it is accepted that this may be prudent for all sorts of reasons) but more with the rhetoric that surrounds the pro-gramme, especially the stress on its revolutionary nature and the need for an alternative system to Mutual Assured Destruction. Governments, which have spent much of the 1980s trying to reassure their voters that nuclear deterrence not only worked effectively in preserving the peace but could endure for many decades, have been irritated to find the President echoing the claims of the anti-nuclear move-ment that nuclear deterrence is immoral and unstable. While in the United States an answer to the threat of nuclear attack removes the most direct threat to national security, in Europe the conventional threat still looms large. To the West European governments the President's rhetoric could be viewed as an indication of a desire to release the United States from the risks attendant on its nuclear commitments. If the "technical fix" of the SDI failed, was not the logical next step to withdraw from the commitments?

The European governments suspected that if the SDI was taken too far they would suffer the consequences. In the short term progress would be incompatible with a serious arms control effort, or even the preservation of the existing arms control régime. If the West were deemed responsible for a failure in this area then it would become more difficult to hold together pro-NATO coalitions. While supporters of the SDI argue that an effective defence would render the US nuclear guarantee to Europe much more credible, the Euro-pean concern has been that the overall effect would be "de-coupling". Either the Europeans would remain extremely vulnerable and so be kept as hostages by the Soviet Union or else the United States, now safe behind its protective shield, would withdraw from its international commitments. If, as was more likely, the whole effort was going to fail why denigrate a perfectly acceptable status quo before it had proved possible to demonstrate the value and practicality of an alternative?

On the other hand, the European governments saw the risks of playing into the hands of their opponents and undermining Atlantic relations. They therefore sought a compromise. The concern was to ensure that no irrevocable decisions were taken before the research programme was concluded and evaluated according to rigorous and pragmatic criteria; that the research was conducted within the terms of the 1972 ABM Treaty; and that rationales were sought in hedging against a Soviet breakout from this Treaty rather than a preparation for an American breakout. As in many ways the most irritating feature of the programme had nothing to do with the technology but stemmed from the President's persistent reiteration of his "vision" it would have been preferable if the President could have kept his dreams to himself.

The British Prime Minister, Margaret Thatcher, made some progress in this direction in December 1984 when she visited the President at Camp David and secured agreement on four points along these lines. In return for this (and in her own careful terms) she endorsed the Initiative.[18] When the administration cashed in the British endorsement while appearing to forget the agreed four points, the British Foreign Secretary, Sir Geoffrey Howe, weighed in with a speech clearly outlining his misgivings.[19]

For its part the United States sought to gain European support by addressing two particular concerns relating to the programme itself. The first was that the massive research effort on strategic defences would provide a boost for US high technology that would take it well beyond European capabilities; the second, that in the end the Americans might be defended while the Europeans would be left vulnerable.

The United States offered to let suitably qualified Europeans participate in the SDI research. The Europeans became greedy at the thought of lots of US defence dollars crossing the Atlantic boosting high technology research and so were prepared to be bribed in this way. Unfortunately the problems raised by the limited funds available (taking into account all those in the United States anxious for a piece of the action) and by the restrictive US provisions on technology transfer meant that the high expectations created by the original American offer were likely to be dashed. As a

precaution the Europeans sought to organise their own
boost to high technology in the form of the "Eureka"
project.

The United States sought to ease the second concern by
insisting that the protective shield would indeed extend to
Western Europe. Having already promised to do one impossible thing why not promise another? There is every
indication that the promise was made lightly. There has
been no discussion of how, if at all, the Allies would contribute to either the construction or the costs of such a
system. It is true that the ability to intercept during the boost
phase would provide some defence against medium and
intermediate range missiles and that terminal defences may
be facilitated by the slower speed of the re-entry vehicles.
However, the shorter flight time would limit what might be
achieved by multiple layers and the sheer diversity of
threats faced by Western Europe (especially those Allies
bordering Warsaw Pact countries) would threaten to overwhelm all defences.

The European debate has by and large not taken into
account the more modest objectives actually being pursued
by those responsible, as distinct from those described by the
President's vision: that is, the protection of military assets
rather than people. Yet less dramatic objectives for the SDI
change the debate. The problems faced by Britain and
France remain and one can expect their anxiety levels to
grow the more it looks as if the ABM Treaty is close to
collapse. Otherwise, the fact that real invulnerability for the
United States is unlikely means that there is less need to
worry about "Fortress America". It does not of course,
follow that the Europeans will stop worrying. The most
significant result of the shift to the more limited objectives is
that it puts the promise of extending strategic defence to
Europe in a completely different light.

There are a large number of military targets of interest to
the Soviet Union in Europe. Protection against air attack is
already considered necessary for many, so protection
against missile attack could be seen as a natural complement. Furthermore, anti-tactical-ballistic missiles (ATBMs)
are not directly prohibited by the ABM Treaty and their

deployment would therefore have fewer international repercussions than strategic defences. Furthermore, there is already a candidate for an ATBM in the Patriot missile which is being readied for deployment in an air defence role. [29] It would be ironic if an initiative that began stressing the defence of the American people against strategic ballistic missiles ended up providing extra protection for military installations in Europe!

Patriot reveals more about the problems than the possibilities of strategic defence. The current bill to introduce it to perform its primary air defence role is $11 billion. Testing has been disappointing and the current expectation is that deployment may not be complete until the 1990s. Furthermore, as one proponent of ATBMs has warned:

> I don't think we can afford the numbers required. . . . One response by the Soviet Union would be to MIRV the front-end of their heavy tactical missile systems, which would stress any ATBM system. [21]

The Offence-Defence Duel

This brings us to the whole question of the feasibility of the attempt to introduce effective defences. The SDI controversy has been a gift to disputatious scientists and therefore rather forbidding to the non-scientist. But it is also true that the scientific debate is highly speculative since no specific systems have as yet been adopted. General Abrahamson has complained that many of the critics of the SDI are "creating an Edsel and then going back and shooting it down". [22] They have, of course, nothing else to aim at for the moment. The variety of concepts still being pursued by the SDI Office indicates that, despite the promise of technological breakthroughs, no single approach has yet been identified as so compelling that it can be pursued to the exclusion of others. Each defensive concept has its own adherents and the United States risks losing powerful scientific supporters if it abandons a particular concept. One might suspect that this is one reason why the X-ray laser, supported by Dr Edward Teller, continues to receive support. At some point if the administration wishes to sustain the claim that it is on to something it will have to start to be more specific in the technologies that it backs.

The President's original speech was not made on the basis of any new technological assessments, and we have seen the initial lack of enthusiasm of the responsible figures in the Pentagon. The Fletcher Report's endorsement of the SDI was cautious, certainly too cautious for many of its more enthusiastic proponents. More positively, America's past great technological triumphs have been cited — especially the *Apollo* project that put the first man on the moon. Unfortunately the analogy is not apt. The moon was not attempting to repel boarders by shifting its position and shooting at the approaching astronauts. The need to anticipate counter measures puts this sort of challenge on to quite a different plane.

In this context the criteria used to evalute the Initiative's progress are very important. Those of a more cautious disposition have therefore welcomed the adoption of two criteria — survivability and cost-effectiveness at the margins — which have been given their fullest elaboration by Ambassador Paul Nitze:

> ... they must be cheap enough to add additional defensive capability so that the other side has no incentive to add additional offensive capability to overcome the defence. [23]

It is generally agreed that the fundamental question behind the technical arguments is whether or not a trend is underway to shift the advantage from the offence to the defence in the long-standing duel between the two. It is also generally agreed that there is as yet no firm evidence that such a shift is underway. However one proponent of the SDI, Robert Jastrow, has argued that the shift has already been developed for protection of specific military installations. It will, he argues, cost twice as much to counter the defence as to build it. [24]

This argument needs to be examined very carefully. The equation for the offence-defence duel does not just involve weighing the cost of protecting an individual target against the cost of penetrating that defence. It is also necessary to put into the equation the value of the target being protected. As hard-point defence is designed to protect high-value military assets its failure might be decisive — in which case this is what is going to matter much more to the enemy than the cost of the offence or the defence.

Second, the defence costs include protecting assets that may be important but which the enemy has no intention of attacking. The more complete the defence the more there will be a wasted effort. If, on the other hand, it is desired to protect only a few critical installations then the offence-defence duel may only be a small part of the total battle and so the relative costs will be comparatively unimportant and outweighed by the value of the installations themselves.

Third, because of the problems of lead times the defence has to anticipate possible changes in the offence; yet these might not be the changes the offence actually chooses to make. It is being suggested that this position may now be reversed, in that the offence will need to prepare counter-measures before it can be sure that any particular defensive problem will actually materialise. By following a number of defensive possibilities in research, the Soviet Union will be forced to hedge against a wide range of possible develop-ments. The Pentagon has argued:

> If, for example, the Soviets persisted in attempts to expand their massive offensive forces, a flexible research and development programme would force Soviet planners to adopt counter-measures, increasing the costs of their offensive build-up and reducing their flexibility in designing new forces in a manner that they would prefer.[25]

So, in addition to arguing that the past cost advantages favouring the offence are to be relinquished, it is claimed that the lead time advantage is also to pass to the defence. This is not yet self-evident. It would be surprising if the Soviet Union was so far doing much more than tentative research in response to the SDI, and given the enormous length of time needed even to deploy the sort of systems envisaged, there seems no reason why the Russians should not bide their time until American plans become clear.

This leads us to a more general proposition that only holds if things can be truly shown to be moving the way of the defence. It has been asserted that the development of an impressive defence will force the USSR to stop investing in offensive missiles and thus serve the cause of stability. In the "transition phase", as outlined by General Abrahamson in May 1984, it is envisaged that:

> as the US and Soviet Union deploy defences against bal-
> listic missiles that progressively reduce the value of such
> missiles, significant reductions in nuclear ballistic missiles
> would be negotiated and implemented. [26]

Elsewhere he has made it clear that he envisages a down-grading of Soviet offences as a natural response to the progress of the SDI. [27] But if, in practice, it is nuclear ballistic missiles that are still reducing the value of strategic defences, and there has yet to be anything beyond an assertion that the reverse is likely to be true, what does that mean for the new Initiative?

There seems no reason to believe that the Soviet Union will not continue to invest in offensive arms. It has shown itself in the past, perhaps foolishly, willing to resist technological trends. When the offence was clearly in the ascendant it still invested heavily in defences. It would be surprising if in the face of the SDI it meekly bowed to US technological supremacy and provided the US with a strategic walkover. The Soviet Union has stated at the highest level that its natural response to SDI will be to increase the number of its offensive warheads. [28]

The SDI only looks promising so long as the offensive problem is not allowed to get out of hand. Two judgements are worth quoting on this issue. The first is that of James Thomson of Rand Corporation on the basis of an extensive project conducted on strategic defences with full access to classified information. In testimony to Congress he considered whether the offence or the defence would have the economic advantage in an arms race:

> We concluded that the offence would have the advantage.
> This advantage became overwhelming if we were attempt-

ing to protect populations to a very high level of effectiveness, or what might be called near leakproof defences. At lower levels of protection, the offence still had an advantage, but not so pronounced.[29]

The second observation is that of the Fletcher Commission:

> The ultimate utility, effectiveness, cost, complexity and degree of technical risk in this system will depend not only on the technology itself, but also on the extent to which the Soviet Union either agrees to mutual defence arrangements or offensive limitations.[39]

Consequencies for Arms Control

The Strategic Defence Initiative may well be dependent on a prior agreement limiting offensive arms. The continued lack of progress in the Strategic Arms Reduction Talks (START) poses the problem of an unconstrained offence. But if the SDI cannot succeed without the sort of arms control that we currently lack, it cannot prosper with the sort of arms control we currently have.

It cannot move beyond the research stage without abrogation of the 1972 ABM Treaty. Those wishing to stop the SDI need take no exceptional arms control measures. Their task is only to ensure compliance with the current provisions. This, of course, is easier said than done; it is difficult to draw the line between research and development and between ABMs and the related anti-aircraft and anti-satellite technologies. If both sides step up their strategic defence activities then the Treaty is going to be put under severe strain even if there is no formal abrogation. Furthermore, the question of unambiguous violation may arise soon rather than later as a result of the need to test critical components. A "demonstration test" would be a highly risky venture if it could only be undertaken after rejection of the Treaty but without confidence that it would lead to a successful system.

The only possible area where deployment might be permitted would be with ATBMs and here there would be problems if it were designed to deal with systems of any significant range because it would also be able to deal with SLBMs. It may also be that the development of anti-satellite weapons (ASAT) provides opportunites to develop components of ABMs without doing so directly, although these tests may be sufficiently direct to lead to charges that the ABM Treaty is being violated. Equally, recent developments in mid-course interception systems are of value in the development of ASATs. It is therefore likely that an ASAT Treaty would impede the SDI.

This to some extent would depend on the nature of the systems banned under an ASAT Treaty. Current thinking in the US administration appears to be that low altitude systems cannot be verified and therefore should be excluded. If only high-altitude systems were banned, though this might interfere with development in the short and medium term, in the long-term it could help the SDI because it would alleviate a critical vulnerability of any system dependent on space-based components.

For the very same reasons that the administration might prefer an arms control régime that allowed unconstrained defensive deployments and a highly restricted offence, the Soviet Union is unlikely to provide them with such a régime. The linkage between offensive and defensive arms control is well established, and has always been stressed by the United States. At the time of the 1972 Treaty the US issued a unilateral statement to the effect that it would reconsider its support for the Treaty if there were no subsequent treaty on offensive arms. This position was apparently reiterated in the run-up to the 1982 review conference (although it was hardly the Soviet Union that was responsible then for the lack of a treaty on offensive arms). The linkage is now likely to be played back at the United States. Any treaty on offensive arms will depend on continued adherence to the ABM Treaty. The same is likely with an ASAT Treaty. Soviet, and for that matter French, proposals against the militarisation of space are designed to get at both the SDI and ASAT. Those promoting the SDI are clearly anxious that any early agreement in this area could abort the Initiative before it had a chance to prove itself.

When US-Soviet talks resumed in 1985 one of the three

areas of negotiation was concerned with space and defensive weapons (the other two were about strategic and intermediate offensive forces). The Americans gave the impression that the main value in talking about the SDI in this context was to begin the process of educating the Soviet Union in the virtues of the new defence-based strategic order: it was certainly not to negotiate an end to the programme. For its part, the Soviet Union insisted that there was little point to the negotiations if the SDI were allowed to continue. Even to many critics of the Initiative it was not altogether clear why the Soviet Union was taking such an uncompromising view. A complete ban on research would be impossible to verify and was anyway unnecessary if the provisions in the ABM Treaty relating to allowance for research and provisions for withdrawal could be clarified and tightened. This led to some suspicions that the main Soviet objective was to exploit divisions within the Alliance.

It is unlikely that the United States will ever agree to abandon the SDI but it might be persuaded to accept further restrictions on its progress. In return it would want severe restrictions on offensive arms. The difficulty is that the Soviet Union has its own objectives in the offensive arms area and so the extent to which the SDI is a bargaining chip may have been exaggerated. Perhaps more important, the Soviet Union is unlikely to feel able to accept any restrictions on the numbers of its offensive warheads so long as it feels that it may need to saturate some new American defences.

Yet if this means that no limitations on offensive arms can be reached the United States may be reduced to arguing, as the Nixon administration was forced to do when promoting the Safeguard ABM system 15 years ago, that the Soviet Union will maintain sufficient offensive forces to warrant making the effort but would not build them up to a level that would overwhelm the defence.

The offence-defence duel is not about to swing in favour of the defence and the effectiveness of strategic defences in the future will depend as much on offensive constraints as on technological innovations. This leads to the proposition that the primary objectives of the SDI might be more readily achieved by negotiated offensive limitations. Disarmament is certainly cheaper than strategic defence: it could begin right away and the margins of error with regard to verification might well be far less than the potential leakage in a high-technology defensive system. It would also be under human control and not depend on a highly complex system to perform exactly to specification at its first serious test in the moments after a Soviet missile launch (or what might be suspected to be a Soviet missile launch) and while the President is still being alerted to the fact that something may be up.

Consider the consequences of a failure of a multi-layered defence to perform as advertised. If, as a result of its deployment, the enemy had increased its offensive capabilities to deal with expected performance levels which were, in fact, not reached at the critical moment, the result would be far more warheads landing on the homeland, and the system would have been utterly counterproductive.

If the President really wants to eliminate offensive nuclear weapons from the face of the earth why not propose just that to the Soviet Union? If it is desired to reduce the targets available to the nuclear offensive then reduce the flexibility by cutting its numbers. If it is desired to limit the damage to the United States should deterrence fail and reduce the risk of the nuclear winter, then at the very least propose reductions to small stockpiles.

There are of course objections to all these proposals but the issues of principle raised are no different from those connected with the SDI, and the practical difficulties, while significant, are nothing as compared with the introduction of effective strategic defences.

Conclusion

One major difference between disarmament and the SDI is that whereas the former requires early and active co-operation between the United States and the Soviet Union, with the latter there is only a presumption that the two will follow a similar path because of similar calculations as to their security interests. This may lead some to hope that if only the United States can identify its interests more clearly, inherent economic and technical strengths will carry it to a decisive strategic breakthrough.

There is an ambiguity running through the whole Strategic Defence Initiative. Is this designed to restructure the superpower relationship on a different but still essentially equal basis or is it a unilateral strategic move by the United States to achieve an advantage over the Soviet Union?

In the more recent promotion of the SDI considerable stress has been put on the risk of the Soviet Union winning this new stategic race. Thus General Abrahamson has stated:

> Were they [the Russians] to deploy the fruits of their programmes unilaterally, the consequences to our national security would be grave.[31]

Why would it be grave? Possibly for the same reasons that the Soviet Union might believe it to be grave if the United States got there first. Whatever the protestations of peaceful intent and in the absence of negotiated constraints, a strategic defence is likely to be most effective only if the other side's offence has already been depleted through a first strike — the logical first layer of a multi-layered defence. In his original speech the President remarked:

> I clearly recognise that defensive systems have limitations and raise certain problems and ambiguities. If paired with offensive systems, they can be viewed as fostering an aggressive policy and no one wants that.

It is now clear that, with the revision of the SDI away from the President's original utopianism, defensive and offensive systems are likely to be paired. What seems at times to be envisaged is not so much a tidy substitution of the defence for the offence but a continuing competition in offensive and defensive systems, with strategists on both sides exploring areas of comparative advantage. It appears to be part of the continuing effort to develop plans for a nuclear strategy that is similar to conventional strategy in its flexibility and control.

The problems that have already been identified in conducting a controlled nuclear war in today's relatively straightforward strategic environment would be nothing compared with the more confused enviroment now envisaged. A President is even less likely to confronted with a credible war plan in this environment. Meanwhile the problems of crisis management would intensify. There would be doubts as to whether the defences were functioning properly, combined with fears that those of the other side were totally reliable, and uncertainties over what sort of interference with them would be sufficiently provocative to trigger war. And still there, at the back of everybody's mind would be the sure knowledge that if things got out of hand, and who could say that they would not, the end result could be mutual destruction.

President Reagan's speech of March 1983 may have launched a thousand research projects but it did not launch a strategic revolution. He was offering a false prospect of invulnerability, an illusion that he had some bold escape plan from the harsh realities of the nuclear age. This would have quickly been dismissed as the ramblings of a sentimental idealist had he not been President of the United States and had he not backed up his vision with the promise of a technical fix that was soon found to be wanting.

As a practical matter this dream did not last long — about six months. The idea of release from the perils of nuclear vulnerability is one that is bound to recur. It would be surprising if it did not. Nevertheless, whatever has been set in motion by the President's speech, it is no historic project to provide us with such release. The Initiative is still imbued with a contrived sense of scientific adventure and masquerades as a strategic revolution. So far the resources devoted to this enterprise have not been large but they could become substantial. Other costs will be incurred. This episode did little for the President's reputation as a responsible leader, put additional strain on arms control and inserted another controversy into the Alliance. Most seriously of all it has served as yet another distraction for those unwilling to face up to the real dilemmas that confront us.

Footnotes

1. President Ronald Reagan, Speech on Defence Spending and Defensive Technology, 23 March 1983.

2. David Alan Rosenberg, "The Origins of Overkill: Nuclear Weapons and American Strategy, 1945-1960", **International Security** (Spring 1983), p. 32

3. Secretary of Defence James Schlesinger, **Annual Defence Department Report, 1975** (4 March 1974), p. 67.

4. Report of the President's Commission on Strategic Forces (Washington DC: April 1983), pp. 9,12.

5. President's Statement, 22 November 1982, **Current Policy**, No. 435 (Washington DC: Department of State, November 1982). This was the statement that announced the MX Densepack basing mode.

6. "We continue treaty-permitted R&D on Ballistic Missile Defence (BMD) as a hedge against Soviet breakthroughs or breakouts that could threaten our retaliatory capability, and as a possible point defense option to enhance the survivability of our ICBM force", Secretary of Defence Harold Brown, **Department of Defence Annual Report.** 1982 (19 January 1981). p. 116.

7. Press Conference, quoted in **New York Times** 26 March 1983.

8. **NBC,** Meet the Press 27 March 1983 (Quoted in **Baltimore Sun** 28 March 1983). See also report of news conference of 24 March (**New York Times,** 25 March 1983).

9. Reagan Press Conference, 29 March 1983; Weinberger, "Meet the Press" 27 March 1983.

10. **New York Times** (10 May 1984).

11. For example Robert Jastrow: "Reagan vs. the Scientists: Why the President is Right about Missile Defence", **Commentary** (January 1984) "Critics of President Reagan's plan spoke as if he were proposing a defense of entire cities and their populations, but he made no such suggestion of that kind in his speech".

12. For example Charles Mohr in **New York Times** 23 March 1984 quotes Richard DeLauer, Under Secretary of Defence for Research and Engineering informing Congress that "Our state of knowledge of the relevant technologies is inadequate" and that an informed decision on whether to go ahead with a system could not be taken until the early 1990s, and Robert S. Cooper, Director of the Defence Advance Research Projects Agency admitting that the researchers had no "gold, silver or platinum bullet" in sight against missiles. See also **Washington Post** 24 March 1984.

13. **Washington Post** 25 August 1984.

14. President Reagan radio broadcast, quoted in **New York Times,** 14 July 1985.

15. Thus a carefully constructed White House presentation makes it clear that no absolute protection is on offer: "To achieve the benefits which advanced defensive technologies could offer, they must, at a minimum be able to destroy a sufficient portion of an aggressor's attacking forces to deny him confidence in the outcome of an attack or deny an aggressor the ability to destroy a militarily significant portion

of the target base he wishes to attack.'' The President's Strategic Defence Initiative (US Government Printing Office, January 1985).

16. Speech delivered at University of Virginia, reproduced in **Science and Government Report** 15 July 1984.

17. For a discussion of the stakes of the British and Frerch in the ABM Treaty see Lawrence Freedman, ''The Small Nuclear Powers'', in Ashton Carter and David Schwarz (ed), **Ballistic Missile Defence** Washington DC: Brookings Institution, 1984).

18. The four points are:
    i) The US and Western aim is not achieve superiority but to maintain balance, taking account of Soviet developments.
    ii) SDI-related development would, in view of Treaty obligations, have to be a matter for negotiation.
    iii) The overall aim is to enhance, not to undermine deterrence.
    iv) East-West negotiations should aim to achieve security with reduced levels of offensive systems on both sides.
    Washington Post 23 December 1984.

19. Rt Hon Sir Geoffrey Howe, Speech to the Royal United Services Institute, London. 15 March 1985.

20. Richard DeLauer told a Congressional Committee that: ''Included in the programme are technologies for defence against the shorter range nuclear ballistic missiles ... which may not have trajectories high enough to permit their attack with exoatmospheric systems, and which have short times-of-flight. Such technologies are important for defence of our allies''. Statement before the Subcommittee on Research and Development of the Committee on Armed Services, House of Representatives (1 March 1984). On Patriot as a ATBM see **Aviation Week and Space Technology** 9 April 1984; **International Herald Tribune** 5 April 1984. The Hawk is being considered as an anti-cruise missile.

21. **Aerospace Daily** 18 November 1983.

22. Quoted in **Washington Times** 19 June 1984. The two most substantial critical studies are the report prepared by the Union of Concerned Scientists, **Space-Based Missile Defence,** (Cambridge, Mass.; March 1983) and Ashton B. Carter, **Directed Energy Missile Defence in Space** (Congress of the United States: Office of Technology Assessment, April 1984).

23. Paul Nitze, Speech before the World Affairs Council of Philadelphia, 20 February 1985, **New York Times** 21 February 1985.

24. Jastrow, op. cit., p. 29. Jastrow develops this argument further in a recent book, asserting his point with figures apparently plucked out of thin air. Robert Jastrow, **How to Make Nuclear Weapons Obsolete** (London: Sidgwick & Jackson, 1985), pp. 123-130.

25. DOD Report (March 1964).

26. Lt-General James Abrahamson, Testimony to the Defence Subcommittee of the House Appropriations Committee (11 March 1984).

27. ''When they see that we have embarked on a long-term effort to achieve an extremely effective defense, supported by a strong national will, they will give up on the development of more offensive

missiles and move in the same direction''. **Science**, 10 August 1984.

28. According to Soviet scientist E. P. Velikhov, ''Our country — relying on its powerful scientific, technological and economic potential — is quite capable of responding as appropriate. But we will take our own road. **Washington Post** 24 June 1984. For an extremely useful discussion of the Soviet response see Sidney D. Drell, Philip J. Farley, and David Holloway, **The Reagan Strategic Defence Initiative: A Technical, Political, and Arms Control Assessment,** A Special report of the Centre for International Security and Arms Control, Stanford University (July 1984).

29. James A. Thomson, **Strategic Defence and Deterrence**, Statement before the Defence Appropriations Subcommittee of the House Appropriations Committee (9 May 1984).

30. Dr James Fletcher, Statement before the Subcommittee on Research and Development of the Committee on Armed Services, House of Representatives (1 March 1984).

31. **Aviation Week and Space Technology** 21 May 1984. There is little doubt that the Soviet Union has been engaged in active research in the relevant areas. According to Richard DeLauer, the two sides are equal in laser technology, the Soviet Union is ahead in large rockets able to lift heavy loads in space and the United States is ahead in data processing. What is interesting is that heavy boosters is one of those areas where the Fletcher Commission recommended putting off research because it would be relatively easy to catch up if progress was made in the more difficult areas. On the other hand, data processing has been acknowledged to be the most critical area for the success of any SDI.

(First published by the **International Institute for Strategic Studies** London, 1985, as Adelphi Paper No. 199).

11 Nuclear Weapons and Strategy

In some ways this concluding Essay might seem optimistic in its confidence in the robustness of the East-West nuclear balance. This confidence does not argue for complacency: only for attending to the factors making for conflict in the political relationship rather than allowing ourselves to become transfixed by the detail of the nuclear relationship.

For the last 40 years something called "nuclear strategy" has been discussed extensively in official circles and beyond, and in a variety of languages. Nuclear strategy ostensibly covers the ways and means by which nuclear weapons can be used to achieve the ends of policy. The nature and extent of the literature surrounding this issue suggests something that is infinitely rich and complex: the product of an interaction between a dynamic technology and a changing political order; and the analysis of circumstances that are by definition dramatically different from those that obtain at the moment.

Yet it can be argued that much of what passes for nuclear strategy is in a fundamental sense completely beside the point. The carefully constructed scenarios designed to show how a nuclear war might start are artificial, and thus provide us with few clues as to the political context in which the really hard decisions concerning nuclear threats, or even employments, would have to be taken. The discussions of what might happen after the first nuclear volleys are even more fanciful. It is hard to avoid the conclusion that whatever the nuclear strategists may propose in terms of deliberate moves up a well-defined escalation ladder, the manifold uncertainties connected with this sort of high-intensity warfare renders its course almost impossible to

predict and any attempts at intellectual or even organisational preparation even harder.

One school of strategy has fought hard against such nega-
tivism, arguing that despite the uncertainties and the
complexities it is possible to anticipate at least some of the
critical factors that will determine the outcome of a future
war, and that the attempt must be made because if we fail to
come up with any intelligent ideas as to what to do should
deterrence fail, the whole basis of the West's policy of
deterrence is revealed to be the most gigantic bluff, with the
revelation itself making it even more likely that the bluff will
be called.

Others, while less convinced that serious strategies can be
divined for actually fighting a nuclear war, are less despon-
dent about the implications of this limitation for deterrence.
Deterrence, it can be argued, does not depend on anybody's
deliberate strategy at all: just on the recognition that in the
fraught and chaotic circumstances that would accompany
the collapse of the current international order somebody,
somewhere, in a position of authority will think that there is
a strategy that would be worth a try.

This line of argument suggests that nuclear strategy as it is
practised under current conditions, can involve little more
than drawing the attention of the world's statesmen to
something that by and large they seem able to work out for
themselves: that the existence of large stockpiles of nuclear
weapons argues for great caution in the event of any major
international crisis.

In the 1940s and 1950s, as the two great alliances of the
post-war world took shape and adjusted to the new logic of
the nuclear age, it did at times appear as if fear of nuclear
war was not sufficient to prevent a fight and that the arms
race was one that might be won with some sort of decisive
advantage. With the growth of the nuclear stockpiles, and
the Berlin and Cuban crises of the early 1960s, the two sides
cured themselves of any illusions about the nature of power
politics in the nuclear age. For the last two decades there
have been plenty of harsh words, the occasional pointed
reference to nuclear capabilities and even one low-level

nuclear alert but the two superpowers have never come close to blows. Whatever is to be decided between East and West, neither side has shown itself inclined to decide it by force of nuclear arms.

Though most strategic analysts prefer not to notice, the actual conduct of international affairs bears no relation to their models which tend to magnify the importance of every nuance or asymmetry in the strategic balance. Because nuclear weapons play such an overbearing role in international relations it is assumed that the details of the nuclear arsenals must be important. Much doctrinal debate and arms control activity proceeds on this assumption. It is arguable that the opposing proposition is closer to the truth: nuclear weapons are so overbearing that they have the same political effects within remarkably wide quantitative and qualitative limits.

Nuclear strategy would therefore only come into its own at the point when the situation was in the process of, or close to, breakdown. What then might nuclear strategy have to offer? There are three possibilities. First, it might be possible to prevent such a breakdown by helping to construct a strategic balance with features irrelevant to the current relatively relaxed conditions but vital when it comes to withstanding the stresses and strains of a major crisis. Secondly, they might be able to propose strategies of crisis management that do more than simply avoid war but are also able to exploit the situation to secure a more satisfactory political position; thirdly, and much more ambitious, it might be possible to develop operational strategies for the employment of nuclear weapons to ensure that any nuclear hostilities that did break out could be terminated on tolerably favourable terms.

The disposition among professional strategists (rather than academic dabblers) is to assume that the third requirement is the key. Should a convincing operational strategy be devised by the United States then the Soviet Union will be less tempted to challenge Western interests, would back off in a major crisis and would not be able to prevail should war occur. A failure to develop such a strategy will make the first two tasks all the more difficult. Against this, it is argued that

that few things are likely to undermine a stable strategic balance more than just the appearance — never mind the reality — of a successful operational strategy (usually described pejoratively as "war-fighting"). Either way, the first question to be asked is whether there can be a nuclear strategy in the active sense, an employment of nuclear weapons to gain a military victory through which political objectives would be secured.

First Strike, Second Strike

The most familiar concepts of nuclear strategy revolve around the terms first and second strike. It is generally agreed that the minimum objective of a nuclear arsenal is to deter a nuclear attack. Some would argue that this is the only realistic and tolerable objective and might then, in a resigned manner, admit that such deterrence will be a continuing strategic task since neither nuclear weapons nor international antagonism can be wholly eliminated. President Reagan has raised the possibility of an alternative involving the application of the most futuristic defence technologies, but this thought need not detain us for long as even his advisers have found it prudent to describe this concept as a "vision" and have admitted that there is no practical way by which the United States, never mind its allies, could render itself invulnerable to a nuclear attack.

For the foreseeable future this task of minimum deterrence will be handled by ensuring that any nuclear aggression will trigger a response in kind. Both sides have worked to protect their means of retaliation from a first strike by the adversary and to the extent that they have succeeded we can talk of a *condition* of Mutual Assured Destruction. This is to be distinguished from a *strategy* of Assured Destruction which implies (though it was never actually adopted in this form) that the most appropriate nuclear employment will in all cases be the utter destruction of the enemy's society, economy and political structure.

One of the reasons why it seemed appropriate in the past to stress the potential for Mutual Assured Destruction was that, whatever the assumptions about less horrific outcomes with which a belligerent might enter nuclear hostilities, this would be the most likely result. Another reason was that the only sort of nuclear employment that might make sense would be a first strike that could remove the enemy's means of retaliation, and that prospect might alarm the enemy into doing something rash and pre-emptive while the weapons were still available. Any employment which could not disarm the enemy would be inviting retaliation and so would be quite foolish.

The conclusion that second-strike capabilities are likely to remain the most impressive features of nuclear arsenals for some time to come encourages confidence that these weapons can continue to meet their basic strategic objective of deterring each other. But it also throws into relief the problem that has in practice been the source of the great dilemmas of strategic thought in the nuclear age: the more profound the disincentives to going on to the nuclear offensive the weaker, at least in theory, extended deterrence appears.

The nuclear guarantee to Europe depended initially on an imbalance of power which made it plausible that the United States, if faced with Soviet aggression against Western Europe even at the conventional level, would set in motion nuclear attacks. This undertaking has now become institutionalised and embodied in the security policies of many nations and the orthodoxy of a supranational organisation — NATO.

If such a guarantee were suggested now, under conditions far less favourable than those of NATO's early days, the very idea would no doubt be deemed preposterous. As the Soviet Union developed its retaliatory capability, the US nuclear guarantee suffered a loss of credibility that it has never been able to recover despite the sterling efforts of at least two generations of nuclear strategists. To restore this lost credibility some way has been sought to create either a cast of mind or a physical condition that would make it conceivable that an American President would authorise a nuclear strike of one kind or another. He might believe that the use of short-range weapons tucked away on a German hillside would be less inflammatory than the use of longer-range weapons on submarines lurking under the Atlantic Ocean; or that an attack on military targets might induce comparable restraint and so spare cities; or that releasing just a few kilotons would be seen at worst as a stern warning.

The difficulty with all these options is that their success depends on their being received in the right way by the other side so that the response is at worst comparably mild and at best surrender. The difficulty for the strategists is that they cannot show with any certainty or confidence why this should be so. It would only be if the other side could be physically prevented from mounting an effective form of retaliation that a nuclear offensive would make any sense. This explains the continual hankering after a first-strike capability or at least some technical fix to the problem of controlling the consequences of first nuclear use. Hence the continuing sense that secure second-strike capabilities are both welcomed for the constraints they impose on the adversary and resented for the resulting limitations on the West's freedom of manouevre and the doubts cast over the credibility, and thus the durability, of the US nuclear guarantee.

The Political Dimension

Until there is some breakthrough in anti-submarine warfare capabilities that would render ballistic and cruise missile-carrying submarines vulnerable to a co-ordinated and decisive attack (rather than just steady attrition) a genuine first-strike capability can be ruled out. Even if such a breakthrough were achieved, a successful first-strike would involve a quality of target acquisition, weapon reliability and performance, timing and tactics that has in the past eluded generals attempting much more modest military operations. It seems implausible with untried weapons in unique circumstances. It is inconceivable that a serious military planner in the coming decades will be able confidently to inform his political masters that an available mix of offensive and defensive systems and tactics can remove the possibility of a devasting nuclear retaliation to either zero or as near as makes no difference (and that would have to be very near).

A variety of schemes have been suggested for strategic nuclear exchanges in which the relevant weapons are directed against each other or at least substantial military targets, rather than civil targets. The main difficulty here is that a large number of the relevant military targets are found within or close to populated areas. Another approach, also assuming that one can render nuclear strategy more moral by attacking weapons rather than people, is President Reagan's Strategic Defence Initiative. This is often discussed, in its less ambitious guise, as a means of denying the enemy access to certain high-value military targets (but not the country as a whole) by attacking offensive weapons en route to these targets. However the point remains that unless success in either counterforce or strategic defensive operations is total, or that the war has been terminated while they are underway, once the non-assured destruction strategies are exhausted the condition of and potential for Mutual Assured Destruction remains.

Arguments in favour of partial first strikes depend very largely on a political judgement concerning the likely reactions of the enemy leaders to a strike directed against military targets but which has also destroyed some 10 per cent or more of the population and left large areas devastated. Will they be paralysed with fear and recognise that a response against the enemy will only make things worse or be so furious that they unleash a devastating riposte? The fact that the question can be posed indicates that there might be such a thing as a successful partial first-strike. However, the fact that the enemy is left with such a choice indicates the enormous risks incurred in launching such a strike. Nuclear strategy in peacetime and in war therfore appears to be essentially political in nature — with success in the end determined by the effects on the perceptions and attitudes as much as the capabilities of the adversary.

Precision Weapon Potential

This point is reinforced when considering an alternative approach to nuclear strategy, based on using these weapons almost as if they were conventional weapons so as to turn the tide of a land war in Europe. If nuclear weapons are to conform to the dictates of traditional strategy then it can be argued that the features they share with traditional weapons must be accentuated while those features which are distinctly nuclear — such as radiation and massive destructive effects — need to be correspondingly reduced. To some extent this has been made more possible with steady improvements in warhead technology (allowing for some effects to be enhanced at the expense of others) and weapon accuracy which mean that the destruction of a given target requires far lower explosive yields and the risk of collateral damage is thus reduced. In principle this process could develop to the point where nuclear weapons were little more than a higher form of artillery and all connection with instruments of mass destruction was lost. In this case there would be nothing special about nuclear strategy; it would just be another branch of conventional strategy.

There are limits on this sort of development. The basic difficulty is that not all nuclear weapons can be expected to take this form. So long as those that are essentially instruments of mass destruction are still deployed in large numbers, it is they, rather than the less awesome types, that will set the tone of nuclear strategy. Strategies based on integrating battlefield nuclear munitions with general purpose forces depend on the possibility of nuclear use being contained at this level and not escalating to something more generally destructive and less controllable. This in turn depends on the relevant weapons being accepted as more akin to conventional weapons than the longer-range and more powerful nuclear weapons which are still understood as instruments of mass destruction.

The proposition that any nuclear employment could be restricted to these new precision, low yield, low collateral types has been challenged on a number of grounds. At the most mundane level, enemy efforts at the passive and active protection of targets, or the need to attack a variety of dispersed and mobile targets, may push up the requirements for the numbers of weapons to be employed to a point where the cumulative effect approaches the most fearful consequences of older generations of weapons. Another problem is that the enemy may respond to an attack involving limited numbers of precise and "clean" nuclear weapons selectively used with an undiscriminating attack involving large numbers of crude and "dirty" bombs. If restrictions are to be sustained then both sides must honour them and in conditions where use was being contemplated that would be unlikely.

Whether or not such a strategy would be possible, NATO has shied away from adopting it. In its statements and procedures it has made it clear that it recognises that nuclear weapons are quite different from other types of weapons and that any use would be the result of the most careful and considered political decision. In fact the procedures that have been established for this decision ensure that the most opportune moment for use would have passed by the time authorisation for nuclear release had been obtained by the military commanders. If nuclear weapons are to be employed as if they were conventional weapons they need to be available along with conventional weapons from the start, when the enemy is making the initial thrust and may be providing just the sort of concentrated targets for which super-artillery might be deemed especially appropriate. The longer the wait before authorisation, the more likely that nuclear use will simply be an act of desperation.

The connection with mass destruction ensures that release would only be imaginable in the most extreme circumstances. Nuclear use only as a last resort is in fact the message NATO seeks to convey to the Soviet Union. The strategy does not revolve so much around the actual employment of the weapons but the creation of circumstances sufficiently extreme for employment even to be considered. Nuclear weapons are still seen in this concept to have their greatest strategic effect by scaring the enemy into restraint or hesitation. Again they cannot enforce such restraints or hesitations or even withdrawals on the other side by straightforward force majeure. Whatever positive strategic effects they produce depend on the perceptions and responses of enemy decision-makers who will still retain a substantial freedom of manoeuvre.

So both nuclear deterrence and nuclear war-fighting depend on the quality of the political assessments used to support them. A judgement has to be formed on, for example, the likely responses to nuclear threats, or indeed nuclear strikes, as well as lesser threats and inducements; the ability of one's own society and political structure to cope with such challenges; and of the likely cohesion of alliances in such stressful circumstances. Relevant to such judgements will be the actual issues which prompted the confrontation in the first place. It will not be enough to assess the matter in terms of the crude categories of will and resolve, let alone the personalities of the national leaders involved (tough, soft, unpredictable, cautious, robust, impetuous, etc). It cannot therefore, be said that a moderately non-Pyrrhic nuclear victory is an impossibility; but it could only be achieved through an enormous and desperate gamble that is likely to appear reckless and suicidal when proposed.

Political Stability and Military Balance

This leads to the proposition that there can be no peacetime calculation that could offer high confidence — far less certainty — of prevailing in a nuclear war, even though it cannot be wholly ruled out that one side might actually prevail. Thus a strategy which depends on a threat of nuclear first use to deter an attack with conventional forces must be inherently suspect. It is doubtful that any further bursts of ingenuity in strategic studies can remove these risks (and with the Reagan administration this particular bolt has now probably been shot). But this argument represents no sudden revelation or insight. The limitations of a first-use strategy have been acknowledged since the problem of a strategic stalemate first arose. So the real question is why has not extended deterrence already failed?

Part of the answer has already been mentioned. The propensities among national leaders to take enormous risks are not as high as strategists often assume. The circumstances in which the relevant decisions on nuclear use would be taken would hardly be conducive to rational (or, for that matter, moral) decision-making and so all sorts of terrible things might well happen even if they could not be forecast beforehand. The leaders of East and West have been wary of getting involved in any military confrontation, even at the lowest rings of the escalation ladder, which does not suggest enormous confidence in the promise of escalation dominance.

The second point is that the respect for the consequences of any confrontation has encouraged the two sides to consolidate the political status quo (at least in Europe) rather than maintain the option of mounting a serious challenge at some point. Extended deterrence is now easier than it ought to be because the state of the nuclear balance does not, on its own, shape all other basic international relationships.

Here it is, I think, worth considering the conventional view that there is a close and positive relationship between a military balance and political stability. In the first place political instability can have many causes other than self-evidently destabilising military developments. Political change is a constant. As individuals, peoples and nations act on their grievances and aspirations they come into conflict with others. This provides the dynamic to international life.

Political relationships can break down and lead to war even when the military relationship is stable and the high commands on all sides lack confidence. This was more-or-less what happened in 1939. In the nuclear age we tend to assume, and hope, that the point at which a severe breakdown could lead to war has been pushed back further because the risks of war are so drastic and obvious. However, the point remains that even an ultra-stable military relationship might still be overcome by a ferocious political dynamic. Stability in the nuclear age, as in previous ages, still requires attention to political as well as military dynamics.

Nor are the effects of military instability on political stability self-evident. A military imbalance need not in itself create political instability. Nations can live perfectly amicably beside one another despite great disparities in military capabilities without threatening violence. It did not need the nuclear age to turn war into a matter of last resort. Nor does it become attractive just because of a favourable balance of forces. Even the exercise of superior force involves blood and treasure and military commanders are aware that things can go wrong.

Seeking Crisis Stability

At most, military instability might exacerbate political instability rather than create it. The idea that a certain configuration of forces might force the pace of a crisis lies behind the concept of crisis stability, which has always figured strongly in arms control theory. According to this concept the tempo of diplomacy and the search for a political settlement should not be driven mercilessly by the tempo of military preparations and the fear of pre-emptive attack, as was assumed to be the case in August 1914. Instability in this sense is synonymous with any incentive to initiate hostilities or possibly to raise the profile of military preparations.

Crisis stability, therefore, concerns anything that might make it impossible to leave the military option as the last resort and force it into play before the diplomatic possibilities had been exhausted. It is not synonymous with equality or balance. A relationship in which one country is decisively superior to another will generate its own political logic (normally hegemony) and can so be extremely stable. Instability only becomes a problem when the identity of the victor is in doubt and is thus as likely to result from a true balance as any other type of relationship. This is despite the fact that the major powers often claim that they are assisting some tense region by helping to create a military balance.

Three forms of crisis instability might be identified:

(a) The transition from one military relationship to another, in which one side sees its position worsening. There is an incentive to act while the position is relatively favourable.

(b) A condition in which there is a clear premium attached to getting in the first blow. When the nation that takes the military initiative can alter its position decisively in its favour, both sides are nervous about waiting for diplomacy to take its course. There are two variants of this:

    (i) At any given time and whatever the stage of mobilisation, the first strike can make a significant or even decisive difference.

    (ii) The implementation of crisis- and war-plans imposes its own momentum. Once mobilisation begins it will take time to halt or reverse it. The build-up of front line forces increases the threat to the other side which is tempted to attack before the process is completed. Alternatively, plans are based on forward movement and once the motion had begun it is difficult to stop.

(c) The likely outcome of a war is sufficiently unclear for both sides to feel that they have a good chance of prevailing. Neither side therefore feels obliged to back-down or make concessions to facilitate diplomacy.

Of these only (a) is wholly dependent on a particular relationship of forces. It is argued, in connection with the reciprocal fear of surprise attack, that two sides with the same set of forces could find themselves nervous lest the other move first. At issue in (b) is the availability of, or dependence on, a particular strategic move which, if implemented, could put the other side at a disadvantage. Involved in (c) are judgements over technical skill, tactical prowess and physical adaptability as well as assessments of force levels.

It is also interesting that in these three areas the degree of instability depends on the perceptions of the belligerents. What political and military leaders believe to be the case can matter more than what an objective observer (should such a body exist) knows it to be. Unfortunately recognition of this factor has been overdone and has allowed too great a tolerance of subjectivism. If it is ''all in the mind'' anything can be disturbing and strategy becomes either impossible or an exercise in speculative psychology. It is suggested, out of respect for perceptions, that perhaps we ought to use weapons to engineer a particular view of the balance, by emphasising sheer size or numbers of warheads or some such. It is doubtful whether those truly obsessed are impressed by the evidence, or that even those who care moderately are influenced by much more than a broad sense of the other's power rather than the detail.

Furthermore, if nuclear arsenals come to be interpreted in a particularly distorted way the sources of distortion will as likely as not be in the manner of the interpretation (which might involve bureaucratic, cultural and political factors) as much as in their presentation. If nuclear strategy is about presentation then it must be said that both sides pay far more attention, though in quite different ways, to the impression created on their domestic audience than on the potential adversary. The concern about perceptions never seems to be backed up with much market research!

In fact, in the case of Europe there are fewer grounds for misperception than there might be with other potential trouble spots. It is one of the features of the East-West relationship that the military balance is a continual preoccupation, even an obsession. There would be no excuse for either of these two powerful alliances being shocked or surprised at the strength of the opposition at a time of crisis. This, one can argue, is a positive source of stability.

In practice the most profound source of crisis instability is likely to take the form of the disintegration and formation of alliances, which would appear to individual countries as questions of neutrality or commitment. If one is going to war it is a natural objective to limit the number of enemies to be faced, and if one wishes to deter war then it makes sense to put together as powerful as possible a coalition of states enjoying at least a temporary coincidence of interests.

All this leads to the conclusion that the cohesion of the alliance system in Europe is as vital for the stability of East-West relations as is the particular hardware at the disposal of each side. The greater the doubts about the willingness of individual states to follow a superpower leader, the greater the temptation for the aggressor to adopt a strong and adventurous approach in a crisis in order to sow divisions among its potential enemies. It is the very rigidity of the alliance system and the consequent lack of fluidity in the fundamental political arrangements that makes it so difficult (thankfully) to think of plausible scenarios for the outbreak of a war on the continent of Europe.

For the same reason much nuclear strategy has as its political objective not so much deterrence of the adversary as the cohesion of the alliance. Key questions of nuclear policy are as often as not about sustaining a set of understandings within the alliance as to each member's rights and duties. Opponents of US bases in Europe may feel that there is sufficient nuclear capability facing the USSR from the other side of the Atlantic. However, the real issues concern the political consequences of the link between the US nuclear arsenal and the defence of Europe becoming severely attenuated: the effect on European policy of the US being seen as a pushy, unpredictable and high-risk protector or the effect on American policy of the Europeans appearing unwilling to share the risks of the nuclear guarantee generously proffered by the United States.

As a result an objective of NATO policy has been described as "coupling" the two halves of the Alliance together. Unfortunately there are few precise guidelines on exactly what serves to couple. According to one school of thought the more nuclear weapons there are in US bases in Europe, the greater the commitment to its defence that has been demonstrated. Others argue that these bases serve to endorse — and even create — doubts as to the credibility of the US guarantee. The point is that nuclear policy in the end is not so much an independent variable in Alliance relations as itself shaped by broad economic and political factors. If Alliance cohesion is a function of much more than a military relationship then it should be more resilient in a crisis. This still leaves nuclear strategy as being less important than the nuclear strategists would like to think.

This paper has reflected the view of those who suspect that the current nuclear relationship is extraordinarily stable and can therefore accommodate all manner of variations in current plans and armaments — upwards, downwards and sideways — without it making a great deal of difference to the calculations of military risk in a crisis. The fundamental features of the nuclear age is the unavoidable risk of horrific devastation. Unless a way can be found of removing that risk, wars will remain an unacceptable option. The basic questions that need continual attention are the sources of tension between East and West and within the two alliances. Nuclear policy is as often as not directed towards these tensions, so that the weapons themselves serve as political symbols either in arms control negotiations or in affirmations of the US nuclear guarantee. The real challenge for nuclear strategy will come when this relationship between nuclear policies and political relationships is more immediate and urgent and less routine than it is at the moment. The Great East-West Crisis serves as the focal point for all nuclear strategy, but often only in the sense that the character of the nuclear relationship will determine the basic outcome. The challenge in such a crisis, however, would be to match any military, including nuclear, moves to a developing political situation. Nuclear strategists' pre-occupations with the detail of force structure and highly stylised nuclear exchanges have left their political leaders ill-equipped for such a task.

(This paper was prepared for the **Nobel Symposium***, June 1985)*

Index